Meaning in Children's Art

PRENTICE-HALL, INC., ENGLEWOOD CLIFFS, NEW JERSEY 07632

MEANING IN CHILDREN'S ART

Projects for Teachers

EDWARD L. MATTIL / BETTY MARZAN

North Texas State University

Library of Congress Cataloging in Publication Data

MATTIL, EDWARD L
    Meaning in children's art.

    Bibliography: p.
    Includes index.
        1. Art—Study and teaching (Elementary)
2. Children as artists.   3. Project method in
teaching.   I. Marzan, Betty, joint author.   II. Title.
N350.M34   372.5′044   80-23915
ISBN   0-13-567115-9
ISBN   0-13-567107-8 (pbk.)

MEANING IN CHILDREN'S ART: Projects for Teachers
Edward L. Mattil and Betty Marzan

10 9 8 7 6 5 4 3 2 1

Editorial/production supervision and interior
design by Hilda Tauber
Page layout by Gail Cocker
Cover design by Linda Conway
Manufacturing buyer: Harry P. Baisley

PRENTICE-HALL INTERNATIONAL, INC., *London*
PRENTICE-HALL OF AUSTRALIA PTY. LIMITED, *Sydney*
PRENTICE-HALL OF CANADA, LTD., *Toronto*
PRENTICE-HALL OF INDIA PRIVATE LIMITED, *New Delhi*
PRENTICE-HALL OF JAPAN, INC., *Tokyo*
PRENTICE-HALL OF SOUTHEAST ASIA PTE. LTD., *Singapore*
WHITEHALL BOOKS LIMITED, *Wellington, New Zealand*

CONTENTS

7 Printmaking

8 Masks and Papier-Mâché

9 Ceramics

10 Folk Art and Miscellany

PREFACE

In preparing the materials for MEANING IN CHILDREN'S ART, we have been aware of the changing conditions of our elementary schools. Where a decade ago many schools had the assistance of trained specialists in the arts, a more recent trend, brought on largely through economic pressures, has greatly reduced that form of educational support. To a large extent, today's elementary school teacher has to "go it alone." With that in mind, we have prepared a text that supports the educational philosophy of most art educators yet is in a form that the typical in-service teacher can use effectively.

We begin with several assumptions with which the majority of good and dedicated classroom teachers will agree. In spite of the persistent cry for "back to basics," education must include the arts—art, music, poetry, drama—as fundamental to the wholeness of learning, experiencing, and enjoying. School captures only a small part of each child's life, and in that brief period it must lay the groundwork for all the productive years that lie ahead. If school fails to open up the avenues of knowledge, skills, and appreciation, there are few other chances for our young people to fully develop the potential that they have.

Classroom teachers without specialized art training can do a good job of teaching art. Many have been doing so for years. It requires a positive attitude, being unafraid to try new things, finding joy in the creativeness of children, and seeing their work as an art form that has its own validity.

The projects in this book are grouped into eight areas: drawing and painting, modeling and sculpture, textiles, puppets and marionettes, printmaking, masks and papier-mâché, ceramics, and folk art. An introduction to each section provides useful background information and specific pedagogical pointers. For each project we suggest a few suitable topics or subjects, offer some objectives to strive for, give assistance in the selection of materials, and provide procedural steps to help with management. These all represent starting points, recognizing that every classroom situation is different. Some schools are well equipped and well supplied; others are not. Some classrooms have flexible arrangements; others are inflexible. Some teachers enjoy great freedom in scheduling activities, while others are on stricter schedules. But most teachers, like children, are flexible and imaginative, otherwise they would not survive as teachers. In every project there is ample opportunity to use ingenuity, to modify the lesson to fit the needs of a particular situation, or to do it *your* way. And every lesson includes references to other books for supplementary ideas, materials, and directions.

In addition to the projects, the text includes (in Chapter 1) a series of examples illustrating how a typical child's visual concepts change through the school years, and a visual alphabet (see Appendix) to stimulate ideas for subject matter. Underlying all of the discussions about the art processes is an emphasis upon the *meaning* of art.

One of the exciting things about teaching art is that art not only lends itself to understanding children, but it also can be an extraordinary means of helping children learn about themselves and others. Wherever possible we relate the project to the art experiences of other peoples whose cultures and life styles differ from our own. Art is the ideal subject to develop understanding and give meaning to so many of the objects people have made since the beginning of life on earth. Many of the things that children do can be given meaning by relating them to the activities of others, past or present. Art is indeed a timeless and universal language.

A valuable visual resource for many lessons is the *National Geographic*. This magazine provides a wealth of interesting and authentic information about many different cultures and art forms. It is an excellent source of photographs of nature and of man-made objects. With the help of parents and friends, begin to accumulate a good collection of past issues.

As the teacher begins to work with this book, some classroom practices will become routine, such as keeping a supply of newspapers to cover work tables as a means of saving clean-up time. Parents and others often are only too glad to cooperate when called upon to do a special task. It allows them to feel included and important to your work. You might, for example, ask some mothers to make smocks for smaller children out of men's old shirts; or ask a father with a home shop to supply wood blocks cut to size when needed. Some projects create dust, some require a well-ventilated area or might have to be done outside. Remember to stress caution when using sharp tools and electric powered devices; only students mature enough and who have demonstrated that they are responsible should be allowed to handle potentially dangerous items. Some materials such as wallpaper paste should be prepared in advance by the teacher or a helper. Some materials may be distributed before a lesson; others which might distract from the discussion should not be distributed until it is time for their use.

Although we have suggested levels in the elementary school for each of the projects, almost all of them can be adapted for higher levels of education. Some of the more complex projects require a longer working and attention span than is typically found in the lower grades.

Have confidence in yourself and in the children—the rest will come easily. Don't worry about mistakes; they are one of the most effective ways to learn. Art classes can be the most enjoyable and the most rewarding experiences in your teaching career. As you watch children learning to express their ideas openly in a visually delightful way, you will find yourself sharing in their successes and sense of fulfillment. And you will know the added satisfaction of having contributed meaningfully to their individual development and growth.

Meaning in Children's Art

TEACHING ART
TO CHILDREN

Teachers open the door. You enter by yourself.

CHINESE PROVERB

Understanding Children and Their Art

To successfully teach art to children and to capture the meaning and the significance of their art products requires considerable understanding and appreciation of young people and a friendly feeling for art. As teachers, most of us seem reasonably secure in our understanding of children, but we are a lot less confident about our knowledge of art and our ability to use art experiences as one of the principal bases for learning. But even with limited knowledge or experience in art, all of us can teach art successfully; we can learn and grow along with the children while "on the job."

For those of us who really want to know, there is a substantial literature describing the ways children grow and develop through the arts. A number of specific theories have been put forth dealing with the typical developmental patterns of children at various age levels and how this development shows itself in the children's art products. Without going into the details of those studies, we can safely make five general assumptions with which most art educators would agree.

Assumption 1. Art is an important part of every person's life; without art life would be drab and colorless and the world a dull, unpleasant place in which to exist. Imagine a world without attractive buildings, clothes, cars, furniture, and gardens. Blank walls would stare at us, devoid of paintings, decorations, drawings, posters, and prints. Without art there would be no visual records of our culture or of past cultures. In such a world life itself would cease to have meaning. Even the primitive peoples who inhabited the earth twenty or thirty thousand years ago recognized intuitively the importance of art. They covered the walls of their caves with magnificent drawings, and carved exquisite fertility figures and animals from pieces of bone or antlers. They related art to magic and through their art tried to control the forces of nature.

Assumption 2. Among life's greatest joys and rewards is the pleasure and gratification that accompanies the successful completion of a task— whether that task is baking an apple pie, making a needlepoint chair seat, or rebuilding a classic car. It makes us feel good when we create something tangible, doing it ourselves. A bonus gratification comes when other people like what we have made.

Children are creative and productive when given the opportunity.

Assumption 3. Children have the capacity to think, to feel, to respond, and to create—in other words, to use their senses fully. All of us who have taught, believing in children and being aware of their enormous potential, have been rewarded by the children's response and their production. Children are creative and productive whenever we give them the opportunity.

Assumption 4. Every teacher has the capacity to understand art and art teaching. Art is not an elusive, mystical thing that only a few can understand and enjoy. Each of us experiences art in some form every day, whether it is simply looking at newspaper advertisements and magazine photographs or selecting the day's wardrobe and accessories—choosing the right dress, suit, scarf, shoes, jewelry, etc. We make aesthetic decisions day after day, whether we are aware of it or not. Aesthetic decision making is as much a part of life as it is a part of art.

Assumption 5. As teachers we want to become the most effective leaders possible within the limits of our assignments. We want to understand more, enjoy more, and share more. To want to grow, learn, and broaden our interests are desires we share with our students. Indeed, learning and growing throughout a whole lifetime ought to be everyone's goal.

Art experiences ought to have a place in everyone's life, and most certainly they have an important part in the curriculums of the schools at all levels. Children of every age level need the kinds of opportunities that art offers in order to find a means of creative self-expression. Art offers the opportunity to learn about, understand, enjoy, and identify with cultures past or far away. Children ought to have the opportunity to learn the skills and processes with which man has created art in the past so they can create art now and in the future. There is no bond more common among people of all cultures than the common bond of art. All men are creatively equal.

Unfortunately, some school practices pretending to be art are very limited. Sometimes so-called art lessons tend to restrict the growth and enjoyment that is possible through more carefully considered approaches. Practices based upon direct tracing or copying, patterns, or coloring book approaches tend to result in stereotyped interpretations and cause children to develop a strong dependency upon mechanical assistance. This is the opposite of what good art education should strive for. It is more desirable for us as teachers to foster imaginative thinking, independent thinking, confidence in children's own ideas and means of expression, individuality, personal style, and persistence.

As teachers we need to be *believers*, and our first task is to believe in our own abilities as a teacher and person. *It is important for us to think well of ourselves.* Then, as teachers, we need to believe in the children's creative ability: that children's ideas are valid and need to be used and respected; that the art forms of children have their own aesthetic value and need not look adult. *It is important for us to think well of the children.* When we think well of ourselves *and* of the children, we will find the children better able to think well of themselves and of us as teachers. That is the condition we should strive for. Then growth will be clearly evident and quality will improve. When both the children and the teacher are motivated, when expectations are high, good things will happen in the classroom. As "believers" we will be amply rewarded.

Although vast amounts have been written on the subject of child art by art teachers, artists, psychologists, sociologists, philosophers, and others, many of us have neither the time nor the interest to search out and study much of this literature. Numerous writers, including Viktor Lowenfeld, Kenneth Lansing, Al Hurwitz, Frank Wachowiak, Earl Linderman, Barbara and Donald Herberholz, Elliott Eisner, Edmund Feldman, Laura Chapman, and Phil Rueschoff, have presented in their books sound, understandable, and compatible bases for good art teaching. The teachers who base their work upon any of these authors will be on safe ground and can expect to produce positive art programs.

A learning environment that is free and encouraging enables children to open up.

The Creative Development Stages

There is a fairly simple approach to understanding the various stages relating to creative development through which children pass. Most authors who have written on developmental stages tend to concur to a large extent, and they describe essentially the same phenomenons. However, there seems to be a professional reluctance about using the same terminology as used in another book by another author. Educators like to invent new terminology, and as a result the same phenomenon may take on different names. "Schematic" becomes "symbolic," or "scribbling" becomes "manipulative." This adds only a bit of confusion and not much new knowledge. The terminology is unimportant. Recognizing development is important. In very simple terms the various stages may be grouped as follows.

SCRIBBLING (MANIPULATIVE) STAGES

Children begin their drawing and modeling in a way that Lowenfeld and others label "scribbling." It is the period of exploration before the eyes and hands are fully coordinated, before the drawing represents a specific object or idea, before the drawing is named by the child, and before the subject of a drawing can be recognized or identified by teachers or parents. It is a time when muscular coordination is developing and when children are trying to coordinate hand and eye activities. This is an essential stage in creative development. Children need the time, materials, and the encouragement to scribble. Children would never learn to walk if we did not allow them to crawl first, or to talk if we did not allow them first to babble.

GENERALIZATIONS (PRE-SCHEMATIC, PRE-SYMBOLIC) STAGE

At this period of development, children draw or model objects or figures which can be recognized or identified by adults. Now, drawings or modeling represent people, animals, houses, or trees, but not specific people, animals, houses, or trees. There is a general quality to each figure or object. Each child's "man" looks about like every other "man" that she or he draws. Of course, each child develops a very personal style for "man" or "woman." In other words, Mary's man won't look like John's man, but all of Mary's men will be similar and all of John's men will be similar. This is a stage in which children are searching for a style (schema) or means to represent their ideas.

CHARACTERIZATION STAGE

Following the period of generalized people and objects, the child begins to develop special characteristics for each person or object. The drawing of a woman becomes "Mother" because this woman has curly red hair, is wearing eyeglasses, high-heeled shoes, a plaid dress, earrings, lipstick, etc. A drawing of a house becomes "my house" because this house is brick, two storied, has a chimney, a fenced yard, a pine tree, a swing, etc. The more creative and more observant children include numerous details with increasing accuracy, making it possible to identify and recognize specific people or objects. As more attention is focused on details, there may be a tendency toward "stiffness," or what appears to be a lessening of the earlier freedom of expression. And the children are becoming more consciously aware of their productions and much more critical of them.

VISUALIZATION STAGE

As children reach the upper elementary grades, some, but not all, begin to focus more upon the actual visual appearance of an object, paying greater attention to the visual contour, to shadows and highlighted areas, to how color changes if it is up close or in the distance. This stage is a move toward making the drawing "look like," in the photographic sense, the real object. Not all children have this special ability to see and record. Those who work this way should be encouraged but should not be singled out as the "talented" or serve as models for all others to follow.

Often at this point those children who do not work in a visual manner or who seem unlikely ever to achieve a high degree of visual ability become discouraged through comparisons. These youngsters lose confidence in their means of expression and may discontinue their creative efforts. The "I can't" syndrome takes over. Don't let that happen! This is the time for us to bring in examples of the works of a wide range of famous artists, some who were visually oriented and some who were nonvisual in their approaches. Go to the library and borrow books with examples of Renoir, Van Gogh, Gauguin, Toulouse-Lautrec, Henry Moore, Picasso, Matisse. Children will see that a photographic likeness is not that important in art. Don't let children feel that because their work isn't photographic it isn't good.

A Foundation for a Good Art Program

Recognizing the stages of creative development plus preparing topics or problems of interest to the children, with which they can identify, is the basis for a good program. There are, of course, many other factors which will add to the success of any program. Everyone works better in a supportive environment. Children are going to be more open, more responsive, in a situation where your praise is more prevalent than negative criticism, where enthusiasm replaces boredom, where a so-called "mistake" is a positive learning experience, where differences in creative approaches are recognized as a sign of good teaching and are encouraged, where variety exists and something new is always emerging, where children learn to describe and talk about their own work as well as the work of others, where value judgments are carefully considered so that children are not told what is "good art" or "bad art," and where there is time to be creative and a place for working. No one expects classroom teachers to be trained, practicing artists who are knowledgeable about every facet of art. Rather, as teachers we are expected to provide the kind of environment where things can happen, where learning and creating take place. We need to set the stage by stimulating thinking, challenging children to be more imaginative, encouraging observation, asking questions, giving suggestions or directions, helping to organize, occasionally prodding, and giving encouragement and sincere praise. All of this adds up to exciting teaching—expecting things to happen and enjoying them as they happen.

We can forget about success if our teaching consists of handing out dittoed patterns, or simply saying "draw what you want to draw." In either case the teacher who works that way has contributed little or nothing to the student. That type of teacher will get little or nothing in return for the little he or she has offered.

Teaching art takes on meaning when we plan and prepare. Take the time to read each lesson beforehand, review the chapter introduction, and consult library references. Then open your lesson with a short but authentic account of the relevant aspect of art, such as the meaning of masks in primitive cultures, or a similar topic as it relates to the selected project. This will enable you to impart cultural knowledge in addition to providing motivation for design ideas. It is amazing how a bit of authentic information can add to the understanding of an art form, and how this understanding will lead to greater appreciation. As teachers we are seldom conscious of the potential we have for planting the seeds of interest one by one, and how each of those tiny seeds may grow into larger and more important interests in different children in various ways.

Art is an outlet for the young mind's ideas and fantasies.

A RECORD OF ONE CHILD'S CREATIVE DEVELOPMENT

This series of drawings and paintings traces one child's development from pre-school (age 4) through the 8th grade (age 13). It points up, better than words can say, the dramatic changes in visual concepts as the child grows in awareness and understanding. These changes show the child's continuing search for a satisfying way to express ideas visually. Progress is not always a smooth, continuous, and gradual incline which starts at scribbling and ends with visual realism. Progress is more like stock market charts: there are many ups and downs but, when the economy is good, the finishing level is higher than the starting level.

This child, now a young adult, has found in art a wholesome outlet for the expression of many ideas about himself and about the world. In the process of creating he has learned about himself and his environment, become more aware of and sensitive to nature and design, and learned about artists of his and other cultures. He has also derived the satisfaction of being able to make personal visual statements unlike any others in the entire world—statements pleasing to him and to others.

*Age 3–4,
preschool*

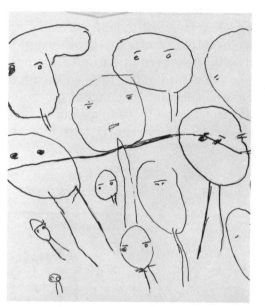

*Age 4–5,
kindergarten*

No two children have identical concepts or express identical ideas in identical styles. But every child experiences a similar *pattern* of growth, and this phenomenon is universal. It can be easily observed in the work of children shown at international exhibitions. Where unusual differences occur they can generally be attributed to strong cultural or educational influences. For example, the work of Japanese children often shows a high degree of patience, persistence, and attention to detail resulting from a more controlled and more highly disciplined home and school environment. However, when we examine the individual concepts of the children, we find many similarities with American children.

In any school environment vast differences can be expected. Some children develop more quickly; some are slower. Some children seem more aware and sensitive, and produce richer concepts than others. Some children have the ability to understand visual illusions while others never fully develop that ability and tend to work in other ways. But all children grow and can find an outlet for their ideas if the conditions for growth are present, and they all will end up richer for the experience that art provides.

Age 5–6, 1st grade

Age 6–7, 2nd grade

Age 7–8,
3rd grade

Age 8–9,
4th grade

Age 9–10,
5th grade

Age 10–11,
6th grade

Age 11–12,
7th grade

Age 12–13,
8th grade

11

A simple yet sound approach to art teaching can be based upon two things: (1) *production*, that is, the creating of art products; and (2) *art appreciation*, that is, providing interesting, accurate, authentic, and significantly related information about art by means of books, pictures, discussion, slides, narration, films, artists, or field trips. Through both the production phase and the appreciation phase children will learn to see, to touch, to respond, to arrange, to evaluate, and to describe. They will learn about other cultures, learn about the history of art, learn new art vocabulary, and gain knowledge and skill in the basic processes of art.

Because of a "hands off" teaching approach that began in the 1930s and still tends to persist, some teachers have been very reluctant to impose their own ideas or suggestions upon students in the fear that their ideas might inhibit or contaminate the children. Some teachers have often relied on letting the children decide everything for themselves. This has frequently led to disorganized, undirected, aimless programs in which there is little evidence of growth or satisfaction on the part of either the teacher or the children. Teachers have the major role in planning and preparing, and must always be involved in providing stimulation, direction, and suggestions. Good art teaching helps children move from where they are to higher levels of understanding, perception, skills, enjoyment, and sensitivity. That does not happen by chance or by some magical or automatic pattern of growth. It happens when we teach, using every resource available to provide the kind of richness that will stimulate awareness, growth, and understanding.

Success in art teaching depends to a large extent upon our willingness to be open and our acceptance of the variety of work of both children and contemporary artists. This does not mean that everything is acceptable and good. But only by having the opportunity to experiment, to innovate, to make mistakes, and to try new ideas can the individual develop judgment, sensitivity, and discrimination. Children become afraid to try only when they are made afraid to try because we apply adult standards or criticize harshly. The creativeness of children can flourish only in an environment that is accepting and free. This does not suggest that we avoid talking about the child's work. On the contrary, it is only through discussion, suggestion, encouragement, even prodding at times, that quality improves. We have everything to gain when we establish high goals and strive to achieve them. Without that kind of classroom attitude, mediocrity will result.

The school and the individual classroom teacher are two of the major factors for the development of children's potential. It is up to the school and to us as teachers to provide the conditions which foster growth and development. A main condition is opportunity—a situation where time, materials, and work space are provided so that children can use their abilities. A good program allows for regular opportunities to use one's abilities in a variety of activities, and to have a chance to repeat regularly those activities of special interest to the individual. Another necessary condition is the presence of a sincere, mature, and sensitive adult (that's us) who guides, directs, suggests, evaluates, and encourages the children. This kind of teacher grows as the children grow, enjoys along with them, *and cares*. Teachers create the learning

A good program allows students to repeat activities of special interest to them.

environment, whether it be rich or impoverished. It is our responsibility to surround the students with experiences that keep them feeding on the stuff of learning, growing, and living. Children, like turtles, will stay in their shells when the environment is threatening. But when we provide them with an environment that is encouraging, children will open up.

Children are curious by nature. They start going to school all perception—ready to touch, smell, taste, feel, look, listen, and ask about everything. That natural curiosity is precious. It needs to be encouraged and developed. But educational life has a way of progressively squelching the individual's drive and capabilities, and as a consequence by the time most people mature they have lost some of those fundamental abilities or else their interest has dried up.

Our role as a teacher is a most important one. The potential of many children depends on our sensitivity. It requires that we be critical in a constructive, positive way in order to avoid damaging the child's self-confidence. It requires being selective without being biased, giving direction without establishing all the final goals, being patient without being indifferent, and praising sincerely and openly without being indiscriminate.

In childhood, when imagination is unfettered, the arts serve as a useful outlet for the many ideas and fantasies that come into the young mind. Every new thing that has ever been created resulted from the imaginative ability of one individual whose vision went beyond the realities of the known world. Children need the chance to wonder, to ponder, to dream, and to have a positive, constructive outlet for their imaginations. A work of art is really the artist's visual report of the discoveries he has made about himself and his environment. All children possess a creative instinct. Sound art education provides the climate for the fullest development of this instinct. Art experiences will ultimately cause the child to grow into a more observant, discriminating, confident, and sensitive adult.

In the broadest sense the art of children is comparable to folk art, or the popular art of the people, as distinguished from the sophisticated, elite, or professional art that makes up the mainstream of our society. Folk art is not created for museums; rather it is made to be enjoyed, used, consumed, even thrown away after its function has been served. There is not even a great deal of concern for permanence except for household objects. Yet folk art is full of individuality and ingenuity, never hampered or inhibited by arbitrary aesthetic rules which can very easily prevent the discovery of new directions.

The folk artist, like the child, learns to use effectively the materials at hand—often ordinary materials such as straw, tin, or papier-mâché—which do not seem especially appropriate for the trained sophisticated artist. With the limited available material the folk artist develops original ideas in unique ways; in fact, the limitations often cause new approaches to be developed. Folk art is sometimes described as "childlike and fresh." As with children, there are few common styles that can be applied to everyone. The work may be free and spontaneous or it may be controlled and meticulous; it might be bright and cheerful or somber and serious. It might be literal and accurate, simplified, abstract, exaggerated, or distorted. And while the sophisticated art of our museums tends to focus on the esoteric and unusual, folk art and child art seem more closely allied to the everyday immediate human concerns. Children, like folk artists, depict the world which they experience and know.

Selected References

BANNON, LAURA. *Mind Your Child's Art.* New York: Pelligrini and Cudhay, 1952.

BLAND, JANE C. *Art of the Young Child.* New York: The Museum of Modern Art, 1958.

COLE, NATALIE ROBINSON. *The Arts in the Classroom.* New York: John Day Co., Inc., 1966.

FELDMAN, EDMUND BURKE. *Becoming Human Through Art: Aesthetic Experience in the School.* Englewood Cliffs, N.J.: Prentice-Hall, Inc., 1970.

GAITSKELL, CHARLES D., and HURWITZ, AL. *Children and Their Art: Methods for the Elementary School,* 2nd ed. New York: Harcourt Brace Jovanovich, 1970.

LANSING, KENNETH. *Art, Artists and Art Education.* New York: McGraw-Hill Book Company, 1969.

LINDERMAN, EARL W., and HERBERHOLZ, DONALD W. *Developing Artistic and Perceptual Awareness.* Dubuque, Iowa: Wm. C. Brown Company Publishers, 1969.

LINDSTROM, MIRIAM. *Children's Art.* Berkeley: University of California Press, 1960.

LOWENFELD, VIKTOR, and BRITTAIN, W. LAMBERT. *Creative and Mental Growth.* 6th ed. New York: The Macmillan Company, 1977.

RUESCHOFF, PHIL H., and SWARTZ, EVELYN. *Teaching Art in the Elementary School.* New York: The Ronald Press Co., 1969.

VIOLA, WILHELM. *Child Art.* London: University of London Press, 1952.

WACHOWIAK, FRANK, and RAMSAY, THEODORE. *Emphasis: Art,* 3rd ed. Scranton, Pa.: International Textbook Co., 1976.

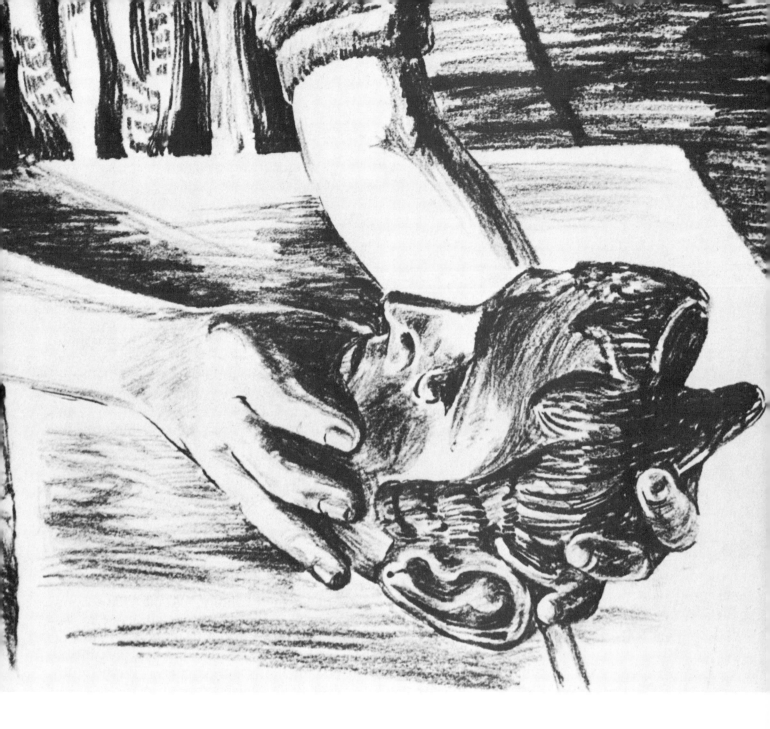

UNDERSTANDING ART

Every work of art means more to one
the more one knows about its
subject.

       BEN SHAHN

How Tastes Are Conditioned

The old cliché "We are down on what we are not up on" often applies in the arts. How many times have we heard people dismiss a whole category of art as "no good" simply because they did not understand it. Lack of understanding can make people feel uncomfortable, inadequate, even guilty.

Many of us may have had our first exposures to art conditioned by the remarks of adults, perhaps parents or teachers, who called something "pretty" or "ugly" or assessed it as "good" or "bad." Such remarks, usually left unexplained, set our value systems in motion early and without our being aware that it was happening. No one lives in a vacuum. People pick up the values and traditions of their culture. Enjoyments and approvals tend to conform to the cultural pattern in which we live. Often this may occur so automatically and quietly that we never realize that our tastes are being directed or controlled. We tend to carry into adulthood the same beliefs and values formed during childhood without ever questioning their validity. We may have rightfully assumed that if something was "pretty" it was attractive to the eye; or, if it was "ugly" it offended our sense of beauty. What most of us have not learned is that "pretty" in the sense of being pleasing to the eye is only one valid criteria for some aspects of art. "Pretty" does not deal with the many other qualities that have equal merit and that can occur in various forms of art. These qualities include mood, emotional impact, uniqueness, technical virtuosity, social meaning, inventiveness, etc. Some art forms such as drama, music, poetry, and dance evoke feelings of sadness, happiness, anger, shock, frustration, confusion, despair, elation, etc. The great range of different feelings and different qualities are, of course, characteristic of the arts. So it is necessary to learn to look far beyond "pretty" to determine if an art work has merit or has meaning to the viewer.

Artists sometimes shock viewers with works that seem offensive or confusing. Some may be trying to educate, others to persuade. Some artists record history, tell stories, or share with viewers the various feelings of mankind. Each artist uses her or his talents to make personal statements to share with others.

Some of the problems in appreciating art arise when we discover that the values we hold seem quite different from those of art critics, museum staffs, teachers, and scholars who have a recognized level of competence in art judgment. A newspaper review by an important art critic of the work of a particular artist might cause us to want to view the artist's work. The critic may have labeled the work as "important," "valuable," "significant,"—even "monumental." But when some of us view it we are shocked and offended by its appearance and want to dismiss it immediately as "junk," "ugly," or "bad art." Why? Our sense of what is good in art may have been built largely upon the idea of beauty in the traditional sense. This may be because our concept of beauty is related only to beauty as it appears in nature. Our own experiences and exposures may never have included art works that are dramatically different. The same thing happens to some people when they hear a concert of contemporary music. They can't pick out the melodies; they can't remember what they have heard; they hear sounds that they can't relate to past experience; they can't associate it with anything—so it seems natural to get angry at the composer and dismiss his work as "poor music."

When that happens the question arises why some of us can appreciate new works while others cannot. As good teachers we are aware that we must always maintain an openness to new things and always give ourselves as many opportunities as possible to broaden our own range of enjoyments. None of us needs to feel left out when we don't appreciate everything the "experts" praise. Even the most sophisticated art lover needs time to adjust to new and unfamiliar works of art.

As society changes, so does art. New methods, new purposes, new aims emerge. Art never repeats itself, and art doesn't stand still. When it does, it becomes stereotyped. But it isn't necessary for everyone to go overboard and do the faddish thing by pretending and praising everything simply because the "right" people say it's good. Learning to like art takes time. Slowly try to learn to appreciate what you observe based upon careful examination, trying also to understand what the artist is trying to convey.

If our range of enjoyments is small and shallow, and if there seem to be many more dislikes than likes, then it is time for us to find ways to increase and deepen the range of enjoyments and, at the same time, decrease the range of dislikes. Pleasure is certainly more desirable than pain, and it follows that enjoyment is more desirable than disapproval. Then in teaching, the opportunity exists for us to enrich the experiences of children through works of art by helping them to respond more fully through greater understanding and appreciation. After all, in the simplest sense appreciation is nothing more than having an enjoyable experience by responding to something man-made or something from nature.

In John Dewey's view, the artist creates an art object which has the potential to develop interaction between the object and the viewer. Thus, as viewers, we interact creatively and imaginatively with the art object. When this happens, we have a work of art. In Dewey's words (*Art as Experience*, 1934): "The work takes place when a human being

Whatever the teacher does to help children increase their visual perception and understanding will lead to appreciation.

cooperates with the product so that the outcome is an experience that is enjoyed because of its liberating and ordered properties.''

To introduce art appreciation bear in mind that children learn to appreciate art in the same way they learn other things. They learn to pound by pounding, to draw by drawing, to run by running. And they learn to appreciate art by seeing and understanding. Whatever the teacher does to help children increase their visual perception and understanding will lead toward appreciation. How successfully this can be done depends to a large extent upon the manner in which children are introduced to art and art objects. Care should be given to establishing a comfortable relationship, a familiarity, a friendship with art and art objects. Even the untrained and inexperienced can learn to talk intelligently about works of art if they take the time to examine them carefully. Because most of us are afraid of exposing our lack of knowledge we tend to shy away from the great potential for enjoyment that art offers.

A Foundation for Understanding Art

What relevant information might help us to establish the familiarity with art that leads to enjoyment? To begin with, every object can be identified—called by a name: It is a ceramic vase, a stone carving, a portrait, an etching, a cathedral, a batik, a costume, or a reproduction of a painting. Each object was made by a process or series of processes similar or related to ones that the children use. A ceramic vase is made of clay; it may have been made on a potter's wheel; it was fired in a kiln, glazed, and refired. The processes are technical, scientific, and historical—all aspects of which can provide interesting and useful information. An Indian war shield was made of native materials and required simple tools. Its rawhide surface was painted with special symbols that had religious or mystical significance to the maker. To begin to understand the shield helps children to understand the meaning of art in the Indian's culture.

When you and your class view an artist's work that none of you has seen before, what could you say, what kinds of questions might you ask? "This artist has made a painting. It is an unusually large (or small) painting. What is the shape of this painting? Is it a square or a rectangle? Can anyone tell what it is painted on (canvas, masonite, wood, paper, etc)? What colors seem to be used the most? Are these colors the same as those we use in our classes? If not, how do you think the artist made his colors brighter (or duller)? What do you suppose the artist is trying to show or say in this painting? Does this painting remind anyone of something you have seen before? What does it make you think of? Has anyone found the artist's name on the painting? We call that the signature. Who can pronounce the artist's name?" And so on.

With an approach as simple as this, even the least experienced teacher is able to open up an intelligent, honest, and objective way of looking. *Looking is the first step.* The next time the children see that particular work or a similar one, it will be like renewing an acquaintance. They have already been introduced; they are now fairly comfortable together; and they may even become lifelong friends.

If the art object is sculpture, the discussion could focus on the object's size, shape, kind of material and tools used, the color, texture, and what the children think of when they view it. These are all intelligent ways to approach art objects so that understanding and appreciation can follow.

Another useful approach that can help us appreciate an art object is to learn about its cultural background. Who made the object, at what time in history, in what place, for what purpose? With this kind of information the object immediately takes on added importance and begins to have meaning with which children may identify.

Enjoyment comes with understanding the meaning of art in other cultures.

Finally we need a set of reasonably stable principles and recognizable elements that occur in works of art so that we may have some criteria for examining a work of art. These criteria provide a common language for describing and recognizing. And,it is from the skillful, imaginative, and intuitive use of these elements and principles that most works of art are created. This does not mean that to be creative every artist must learn a set of rules, a formula, or a system which allows him or her to combine art elements and use art principles to guarantee a succesful art product. Many great artists never knew of these elements and principles, yet intuitively they used them to create their art. Interestingly, in a work of art the whole invariably turns out to be greater than the sum of its parts. That is because the artist always adds some intangible elements that may not be easily recognized or identified, and invests the art work with a personal spirit and style. That is really the difference between the artist and the craftsman. Of course, many people who work in the various so-called crafts are just as much artists as those who paint or sculpt. It is so also with children. Those children who invest their art productions with their personal feelings, style, ideas, etc. are functioning just like artists. Those who master the technical skills, the ability to utilize design elements and principles effectively, and invest their work with unusual sensitivity, intuition, and personal style are the ones whose work becomes outstanding and who may become artists as adults.

Although the nonspecialist may lack the ability to analyze the unique creative force in works of art, every teacher can learn to recognize the various design components and to utilize them in teaching. Even beyond the teaching role it is important to develop the ability to make reasonable assessments and personal judgments about art objects. For art plays a significant part in all our lives, whether we want it to or not, and regardless of whether we ever step inside an art museum or gallery. We choose our clothing to look attractive. We combine furniture, drapes, and carpeting the way an artist organizes colors and shapes. We landscape our homes to make our environments more pleasing and attractive. In our day-to-day lives we use artistic principles of balance, repetition, dominance, etc., without being aware that we are behaving like artists. Although each of us is not equally endowed, we can all improve our artistic faculties. Some individuals have an innate, intuitive sense of good taste—a feeling for what is fitting, harmonious, or beautiful. The special ability to make sensitive choices which show aesthetic excellence, is not given to everyone. Those who lack that special ability must depend more upon learning some of the principles that tend to improve the quality of their judgments.

It is important to know that there is no single aesthetic theory or set of rules that is universal. Theories have varied from one time period to another and from one culture to another. There is no formula for "good" or "bad." There is no agreed upon definition or standards for a "work of art." Some works that are treasured today were severely criticized and disapproved of as art in the past. In the end, we use our personal judgment based upon some acceptable standards and the ability to apply those standards with some objectivity and consistency.

The more exposure to a variety of art forms, the more we are likely to realize that the concept of prettiness or beauty applies to only a limited range of art works. There is no question that most of us now respond favorably to the visual beauty of the Impressionist painters, but when Impressionism first appeared, the critics were very severe in their judgment of its beauty.

But is it also possible to appreciate the work of artists whose styles are dramatically different—to enjoy the precise realism of one artist or the complete nonobjectiveness of another. It is possible to appreciate the strength of one artist's ideas in the way he portrays violence or misery; or in another to marvel at the technical virtuosity or quality of imaginativeness; and in still another to appreciate the inventiveness or the unusual use of materials. What we learn in time is to approach any art work, whether new or old, with an openness of mind and with a searching eye.

GUIDELINES FOR EXAMINING ART

There are several steps in approaching a work of art to increase enjoyment. *First: Examine it physically*. When working with children, describe its physical qualities—the most obvious ones. For example: "It is a painting. It is extremely large. It is a horizontal painting (or square or vertical). It appears to be painted on a fabric (canvas). The artist let his brush marks show (or she did not). Many (or few) colors are used." And so on. The painting itself may not be the main object of appreciating but it can be a primary source of stimulation for an experience in appreciation.

Second: Examine the work in terms of colors, lines, shapes, and whatever it represents that can be recognized. For example: "The artist has used his colors in an almost pure form—just like the colors we use in our classes. Or, the artist has dulled her colors or used a limited number of colors. See how the artist has separated this shape from the rest of the painting by using a line. See how that kind of line was used everytime he wanted to make a special shape? Notice that several shapes seem to dominate the picture. The artist has made them important by using colors also to define them. Notice that the shapes are different sizes. Do they seem to balance each other? Has he tried to get any kind of balance with his colors? What do we mean by balance? Who can point out how he achieves balance? Do you think he may have done that intentionally?" In this line of discussion, attention is directed to the relevant details. Each detail is really part of the organization and it is from the details that the art work gets its richness. At first glance, viewers may be unaware of the details in an art work. Examining art objects more frequently provides us the opportunity to add to the first perception. Little by little our perception becomes keener and richer.

Third: Examine the art work in terms of subject, content, meaning, mood, emotional quality, etc. Frequently the piece of art contains easily recognized objects or incidents which can be discussed by the children. They eagerly describe and interpret the lively horses of Remington and Degas, the scenes found in Currier and Ives lithographs, or the struggles of hunters and animals in the carvings of Eskimos. In talking about art objects children learn to identify the subjects: What is it? They learn to describe the work, and they learn its meaning as they discover the source and the context from which it came. In learning about context children are really engaging in the study of mankind. Art objects are among the most direct and tangible expressions of the philosophies and life styles of cultures. Every art object is replete with clues and questions: Who made it? For what purpose? How was it made? How was it used? What was its significance? What qualities does it have to make it a work of art? And so on. Teachers who seize upon this as a way of teaching discover how art can be a stimulus for logical thinking, for analysis, inquiry, and simple research. Occasionally, the teacher might ask: "Does this painting give you boys and girls any special feeling—like loneliness, emptiness, fear? Have any of you ever had an experience or a dream that gave you a similar feeling? Do you think that is what the artist may have been trying to show? Since we can't be certain exactly what the artist was trying to express through this painting, let us each imagine what it might be. . . ." In some cases the artist may have had *no* subject in mind—real or imagined. Such a work is called "nonobjective." Art leaves some things to be interpreted by the viewers.

Any examination of an art work which goes to that depth would begin to form a sound foundation for art appreciation for both the teacher and the children. Furthermore, if the teacher takes the time to gather available background material on the artist, the period in history, the culture from which the art work came, etc., this information can be easily and naturally woven into the classroom discussion and the questioning in a way far more effective than a mere recitation of facts. Bits of anecdotal information given from time to time are an excellent means for establishing identification and serve as an aid in remembering. For example, if you take your class to a museum to see the ceramics of the pre-Columbian cultures of Mexico, tell them the exciting story of how Cortez and a few hundred Spanish soldiers conquered the entire Aztec nation. This remarkable episode in history would capture their attention and imagination and bring excitement and meaning to everything pre-Columbian. If there is a clay sculpture of the Aztec priest Xipe Totec in the museum you might also point out that the priest is wearing the skin of a human who has just been sacrificed on the high altar, where the victim's heart was cut out and lifted to the sun god so that the sun would rise the next day. This would stimulate their imagination even further. You might go on to mention that the Aztec priest would later on shed the victim's skin as part of a ceremony of springtime and new birth. There are ceremonies symbolizing rebirth in many cultures—the Resurrection of Christ, for example. Although the Xipe Totec story is gory, it gives you the opportunity to add meaning to the ceramics of pre-Columbian Mexico. From that point on the students' interest and understanding will increase.

Art Appreciation in the Classroom

We all know that art appreciation begins "where the children are" in their development, in their interests, and in their tastes. From wherever you must begin, you build bridges to other art forms and other cultures. Children ought to learn to see and appreciate what is in their immediate environment regardless of its sparseness, and they should begin activities in which they can influence and improve their environment. Art appreciation might begin with one daffodil in a peanut butter jar, or it might begin by looking at the designs on the wing of a butterfly. What children see in their daily lives—houses, churches, pictures in magazines, flowers, weeds, motion pictures and slides, or pictures in the classroom—are all part of the wall-less museum that we as teachers must discover in the community. Art is everywhere—in the spirals of a seashell, in quilts, in architecture, in baskets, in sculpture, in books, in museums, in toys, and so on.

Children also need to be made aware of the aesthetics of their own environments and to have the opportunity to plan and think about ways to improve them. They need to become sensitive to what makes a pleasant environment and what destroys an environment. Very soon as adults they will have to deal with slum areas, decaying neighborhoods, and the problems of restoring and recovering good qualities that are being lost. A class might work on designs and models to show what could be accomplished to improve both the appearance and the function of areas that need help. Realistic problems and work toward their solution will bring a conciousness of the kinds of problems that can be conceptualized in design.

One of the best bridges to build in art appreciation is from children's work to the work of artists. Children and artists depend upon the same sources for inspiration—nature, people, fantasy, animals, conflict, etc. It is fun to introduce examples by artists who have chosen the same subject matter as the children are using. Sometimes the viewing of related art works may serve as motivation toward self-expression by children. This does not mean copying, for quite the opposite is desirable. A good experience in examining an art work leaves a greater residue than just a visual impression. It leaves a feeling *and* a meaning, both of which are part of creative production.

Art appreciation is an important part of childhood education and it should be part of a continuing and sustained program. In learning to see, to discriminate, to describe, to know art, the child comes closer to fulfilling his or her potential. Art appreciation is a useful and practical approach to education in which all learning is enhanced through the increase in verbal skills, information, and aesthetic values. It also serves as a stimulus for the children's creative development.

Perceiving a Work of Art

The first perception of a work of art for most people is that of an organization or composition of colors, lines, and shapes, which may or may not represent something recognizable. Usually as viewers we do not pay attention to the paint, canvas, or marble, but are attracted to the subject matter (if any), the colors, the shapes, and the way they have been arranged. If we have had any previous experiences at viewing, we may have some memories stored away and may already have begun to develop a system of perceiving that helps us to understand and appreciate what we are viewing. To improve our powers of perception we need to be familiar with certain characteristics of art works. The basic principles and design elements used by artists are discussed below.

ORGANIZING PRINCIPLES USED BY ARTISTS

Pattern or design is the means used to attain unity and variety in a work of art. The artist seeks to create a satisfactory relationship between monotony and chaos in order to have both visual excitement and visual order.

Balance is a means of maintaining visual equilibrium in a composition, design, or organization of an art work. An artist may achieve balance through the use of colors, shapes, or values. The most obvious example of balance is the use of equal weights on either side of a scale. Artists, however, utilize art elements to achieve optical equilibrium in much less obvious ways. For example, dark colors may appear "heavier" than light ones; large shapes appear "heavier" than small shapes; a smaller shape close to an edge may balance a larger shape on the opposite side closer to the center axis. An interesting object or shape may have greater "weight" than a less interesting shape of equal size.

While the instinctive natural feelings respond more satisfactorily to a sense of balance, there are many examples of art works that are not visually balanced and yet are aesthetically satisfying, particularly in the paintings from Japan and China.

Rhythm. Most people are familiar with the rhythms produced by musicians and the rhythms produced in poetry. A rhythm is a predictable pattern of strong and weak accents. In a work of art it may be obvious or it may be almost hidden, requiring a searching eye to find it, if it exists. The artist might have a rhythm of colors, of sizes, of shapes, of lines or dots, of lengths, or of darks and lights.

Repetition. An artist may choose to use the same shape, line, color many times within the same art work in order to stress or make dominant a particular visual idea. For example, a particular curve may be repeated a dozen times in a Renaissance painting.

DESIGN ELEMENTS USED BY ARTISTS

Line. A line is a visible mark made by a tool or instrument as it is drawn across a surface. Line usually suggests direction, orientation, motion, or movement. It may create a boundary separating an area of space from its surrounding background.

A line may be short or long, thick or thin, straight or curved. It may be predictable or unpredictable. It may be used to unify a composition or it may be used to divide one. Line may be used as the continuous edge of a figure or object, thus defining its shape. Such a line is called a *contour*.

Shape is determined by boundaries. The boundaries may be created by lines, colors, or values. Shapes may be simple or complex, two dimensional or three dimensional, clearly defined or vaguely defined, geometric or organic, active or static.

Texture relates directly to the surface quality of an object. The surface quality may be either seen or felt. The touching experience is referred to as tactile. Texture may be actual (having the physical quality that it visually appears to have) or simulated (having the illusion of a surface which physically does not exist). We may think of texture as the quality of a surface—its softness or hardness, dryness or wetness, smoothness or roughness, brightness or dullness.

Color is a sensation or a response to a visual stimulus recorded and interpreted in the mind of the observer. Color can be described only in terms of other colors. The color wheel is used to provide some kind of order to the study of color. The color wheel consists of primary, secondary, and intermediate colors arranged in a circle (Figure A). The *primary colors* are red, yellow, and blue; they are called primary because they cannot be produced by mixing, and they are the basic colors from which all the rest of the colors in the wheel are made. Violet (purple), orange, and green are *secondary colors* made by mixing pairs of the three primaries (red + blue = violet, red + yellow = orange, yellow + blue = green). Pigments that do not have a particular color, such as white or black, are called *neutrals.* Black and white when mixed together produce gray.

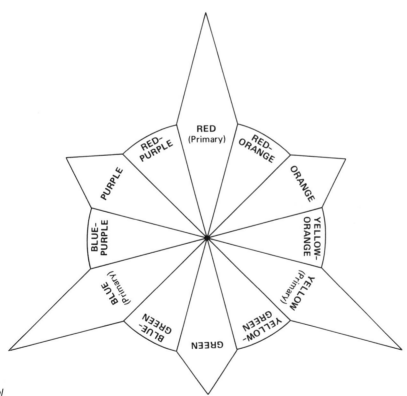

FIGURE A
The Color Wheel

Colors that are opposite each other on the color wheel are called *complementary colors* or *complements*. The mixing of one complementary color with another has an important effect on color, tending to neutralize it. The use of white or black with a color tends to change the relative lightness or darkness of the color, also tending to neutralize it. White added to a color produces a *tint* while black added to a color produces a *shade* (Figure B).

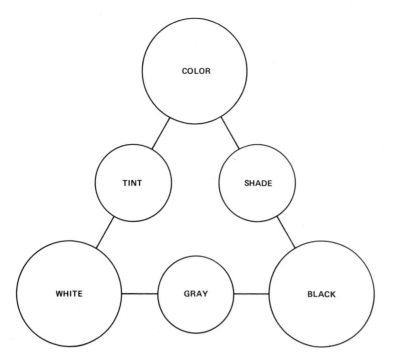

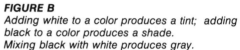

FIGURE B
Adding white to a color produces a tint; adding black to a color produces a shade. Mixing black with white produces gray.

Colors have three recognizable physical properties: *hue, value,* and *intensity.* Hue is the designated name of the color, for instance, red, yellow, green. The first thing we learn about color is its name—its hue.

Value and intensity are often confused. The *value* of a color refers to the amount of light that the surface reflects to the eye. For example, if an apple is viewed in bright light it reflects a lot of light and therefore has a light value. The same apple viewed in deep shade reflects less light and therefore appears as a darker value. That is why some leaves of the same tree appear dark while others appear light, depending upon the amount of light being reflected from the various leaves. An artist can change the value of a color by adding either black or white pigment to make it darker or lighter.

Intensity refers to the purity of the light reflected from the surface. For example, a red color coming directly from a tube of paint will appear very intense because it reflects only red wave lengths of light. If a small amount of another color is mixed with that red, the mixture appears less intense because it now reflects a combination of red wave lengths plus the wave lengths of the second color. The intensity is reduced whenever another color or black, white, or gray is added.

The way colors are used in combination can affect the way they appear. For example, if colors that are opposite each other on the color wheel (complementary colors) are used together (not mixed, but side by side) they will appear to make the greatest visual contrast.

Colors that are close to one another on the color wheel show less contrast. The least amount of contrast occurs in compositions using colors that are adjacent to each other on the color wheel. These are called *analogous colors* because they contain a common pigment. For example, yellow-green, green, and blue-green share green as a pigment in common and are therefore closely related.

These few color principles represent a beginning to the understanding of color and its use. Successful use of color does not always depend upon a conscious use of these principles, but an examination of the successful use of color will show that the artist never totally disregards such things as value, contrast, and intensity of color.

Selected References

BALLINGER, LOUISE BOWEN, and VROMAN, THOMAS F. *Design Sources and Resources.* New York: Van Nostrand Reinhold Co., 1965.

BEVLIN, MARJORIE ELLIOTT. *Design through Discovery.* New York: Holt, Rinehart and Winston, 1975.

BRUSH, KATHERINE F. *How to Look at Sculpture.* New York: Metropolitan Museum of Art, 1959.

CHANDLER, ANNA C. *Story Lives of Master Artists.* Philadelphia: J. B. Lippincott Co., 1953.

COLLIER, GRAHAM. *Form, Space and Vision: Discovering Design through Drawing.* Englewood Cliffs, N.J.: Prentice-Hall, Inc., 1967.

DAVIS, BEVERLY JEANNE. *Chant of the Centuries.* Austin, Tex.: W. S. Benson and Co., 1969.

ELSEN, ALBERT E. *Purposes of Art.* New York: Holt, Rinehart and Winston, Inc., 1962.

FAULKNER, RAY, and ZIEGFELD, EDWIN. *Art Today.* New York: Holt, Rinehart and Winston, Inc., 1969.

GETTINGS, FRED. *The Meaning and Wonder of Art.* New York: Golden Press, 1964.

GUYLER, VIVIAN. *Design in Nature.* Worcester, Mass.: The Davis Publications, Inc., 1970.

HASTIE, REID, and SCHMIDT, CHRISTIAN. *Encounter with Art.* New York: McGraw-Hill Book Company, 1969.

JANSON, HORST W., *Story of Painting for Young People.* New York: Harry N. Abrams, Inc., 1952.

KAINZ, L. C., and RILEY, OLIVE. *Understanding Art: People, Things and Ideas.* New York: Harry N. Abrams, 1966.

MOORE, JANET G. *The Many Ways of Seeing: An Introduction to the Pleasures of Art.* Cleveland: World Publishing, 1968.

MUNRO, ELEANOR C. *The Golden Encyclopedia of Art,* rev. ed. New York: Golden Press, 1964.

PAINE, ROBERTA M. *How to Look at Paintings.* New York: Metropolitan Museum of Art, 1959.

RUSKIN, ARIANE. *The Pantheon Story of Art for Young People.* New York: Pantheon Books, 1964.

SAUNDERS, ROBERT J. *Relating Art and Humanities to the Classroom.* Dubuque, Iowa: Wm. C. Brown Company Publishers, 1977.

SLIVKA, ROSE, and others. *The Crafts of the Modern World.* New York: The Horizon Press, 1968.

DRAWING
AND
PAINTING

3

To draw, you must close your eyes and sing.

               PABLO PICASSO

Understanding Children's Drawings and Paintings

In Chapter 1 we reviewed the creative development stages through which children pass. The various names ·given to these stages by the experts are of no great importance as long as the teacher recognizes and appreciates the changing qualities in children's drawing and painting as they grow and develop.

Before children attend school they begin activities having to do with control over their physical movements and the ability to provide sounds. Children's earliest uncontrolled marks on paper lead into a fairly predictable series of steps which become, in time, the first recognizable drawings. Generally the first marks, or scribbles, are disordered and uncontrolled. Soon the marks tend to repeat themselves as long horizontal strokes, long vertical strokes, or as circles or ellipses. In time, usually at about age 4 to 5, these marks are combined on one drawing and the child names it "mother," or "car," or "daddy." Although the nursery school or kindergarten teacher or parent may not recognize anything which seems to resemble mother, daddy, or a car, this is the first clue that the child has begun to associate mental images with the drawing.

During this whole scribbling period the child finds enjoyment in "kinesthetic activity"—the opportunity to make large motions—at first without control and later with greater control. As greater control is demonstrated, there is an increased relationship between the child's visual development and the child's motor, or muscular, development. Scribbles become increasingly complex and the child may use more time in creating them. During the later stages of scribbling, the child may even state in advance "I am going to make a car" or "I am making my house." Some parts of such scribbles may be identified while most parts still appear as unrecognizable marks.

Many children who have not had pre-school opportunities may begin with scribbles in school. *Scribbling is important.* The child learns to speak by making unrecognizable sounds first. The child learns to walk by first crawling, then stumbling and falling. The child misses his mouth often when learning to feed himself. Similarly, children need to scribble to gain the hand–eye control and coordination necessary to be able to draw and write. Scribbling is normal and natural, and a necessary part of the child's growth. Encourage young children to scribble freely and often. This is a key stage in developing the child's self-confidence.

Following scribbling, usually in kindergarten and first grade, children move into a conscious stage of making drawings and paintings. This stage is recognized by the generalization of objects and persons. Each child arrives at his or her own highly individualized style or formula for making a "woman," "man," "tree," "house," etc. For one child a "man" may consist of a circle for a head, a box-like form for a body, long rectangles for arms and legs, etc. A second child might use a square shape for the head, long strokes to represent the legs and arms, and dots for the eyes, ears, and mouth. Although there may be similarities among the drawings of a group of children, each child's concept is as individual as is his or her handwriting. At this stage of development when a child draws a series of "men" there is very little distinction between one drawing and the others. The same is true of the drawings of "women." In other words, they all have a very general quality about them. As time passes, the teacher can stimulate the children to form more specific images by asking questions that call attention to a particular body part. For instance: "What is the man doing," "where is the man going," "what is the man carrying?" Or perhaps as motivation for a drawing "I am kicking a ball," the teacher might ask: "Who can show us how to kick a soccer ball?" A lead-in such as this would bring about an awareness of feet, legs, bent knees, etc., and the children would begin to add these and other body parts in their drawings. A planned series of such focused lessons would result in increased richness of detail and inclusion of more body parts and their functions.

During this stage a phenomenon evident in the drawings of most children is that objects are drawn or painted on the paper in such a way that they often seem unrelated to one another either in location or in size. Very simply, important things may appear large, unimportant things smaller. One way to utilize this tendency is to call upon the child's still self-centered nature. The teacher can develop many good topics for drawing based upon what the children do and what they are interested in. "I am playing with my pet," "I am eating a Popsicle," "I am washing the car," "I am going to the store"—these are a few suggestions that elicit a good response.

The key at this stage, as in the scribbling stage, is to offer encouragement and sincere praise and to stimulate thinking. Children enter this stage with limited concepts of themselves and their environments. They should be given the guidance and stimulation to develop richer concepts, and to retain their confidence in their own highly individualized means of expression. By this time the children will be working with pencils, crayons, paints, and chalks. Usually, thick tempera paint is easier for children to control than watercolors. The children will for the most part use color in a very direct fashion, but in a highly personal way. It would be premature to try at this time to "teach color," because children are not yet very concerned about relating the color they use to the object they are portraying. Children will, of course, learn the names of colors.

A budding nonobjective artist.

Following the generalization period the children show evidence of a greater awareness of the relationships between the objects they draw and paint and the real objects or people from which their ideas derive. In simple terms, they now pay attention to and are aware of specific characteristics of a particular person or object and they include these essential characteristics in their art products. For example, if a child draws "Daddy and Mother," daddy may be shown larger than mother. Daddy may have black hair, a moustache or beard, and be wearing a brown suit, a colored sport shirt, a monogrammed belt buckle, perhaps eyeglasses, etc. Mother may be shown with curly hair (yellow, red, brown), wearing a necklace, bracelet, and ring, high-heeled shoes, etc. The child does not draw or paint these characteristics in a photographic manner. Rather by the inclusion of these characteristics, the child captures the qualities that make "Daddy and Mother." The same thing happens in the drawing of "my house" or "our car," etc.

An interesting phenomenon occurs during this stage if it hasn't already occurred during an earlier stage: the child begins to place all of the objects on a common line, generally referred to as a *base line*. This brings an orderliness into the child's drawing or painting, and also tends to bring a closer size relationship among objects. The practice of making the more important things larger and the less important things smaller becomes a less common occurrence. This also indicates, to some extent, the child's greater awareness of himself in relation to other people and other things. In other words, the self-centeredness of the young child is giving way to a greater awareness of living and working cooperatively within a group.

By this time the child is relating the colors he or she uses to the objects they portray. That is, if the child feels that trees characteristically have brown trunks and green leaves, then that is how he or she portrays them. The children will find colors that to them portrays flesh tones. The teacher now focuses upon providing lessons and individual stimulation to help the child perceive more and to include those perceptions in the drawings or paintings. The children will not yet draw "realistically," "naturalistically" or "photographically," and they should not be expected to. More of the lessons now focus on the word *we*. "*We* are camping by the lake," "*We* are sawing a log," etc. Children are now learning about space and distance, and still portray it in a child-like way. They still may exaggerate important things and neglect unimportant things. Good teaching will pay attention to helping each child develop richer concepts, not more realistic ones. By this stage the children can be working in crayons, temperas, chalks, watercolors, and a wide assortment of crafts. As their worlds grow larger, their interests widen. While their capabilities have expanded, they are becoming more sensitive, aware, and more critical of their personal creative products. Children need encouragement, direction, and a sense of accomplishment to keep their enthusiasm high and to keep them producing. This is a critical stage when many children cease to produce because of lack of confidence in their own style of expression, particularly if adult standards are applied to their art work.

The last stage in development that is likely to occur during the elementary or middle school years is the visualization stage. Not all elementary school children enter this stage. In fact, some people who are not by nature highly visually oriented may never work in a visual style in the arts.

Some children will have developed in their drawings or paintings a way of creating some illusions of space or distance. They may draw close objects larger and distant objects smaller. Close objects overlap or obscure parts of distant objects. Or, they may have learned to make the colors of close objects bright and intense while making distant objects pale or dull. Some children learn this naturally; others learn it from parents or teachers. Regardless, some of the children will now be seeing differently, paying attention to the way darks, shadows, and lights cause an object to seem to have volume, and to the way color changes in light and shadow, or if it is nearby or distant.

Although this visualization stage occurs naturally with a small percentage of children, others who are less visually oriented seem less inclined to draw or paint, exhibiting feelings of inhibition and usually extreme critical self-awareness. Here the teacher's support is essential.

Support is offered by the teachers' willingness to accept a great variety of forms of expression, recognizing each as having its own validity. During this period the crafts, which have been introduced along with drawing and painting at each level of development, may provide another supportive outlet for the nonvisual child. A further reinforcement for nonvisual children who think their drawings or paintings don't look "adult" enough to satisfy their critical nature, is to show them the drawings and paintings of well-known artists who do not depend upon visual reality to express their ideas. This tends to reinforce the nonvisual children.

In summary, the teacher who is aware and appreciates differences in children and children's creative drawing and painting will provide the climate where creativeness can flourish. The teacher will use art as a positive outlet for children's ideas and feelings and as a means of helping children to understand themselves and others. Art education will bring a greater appreciation of other cultures, past and present, and a knowledge of the processes through which man has made many different art forms to express ideas, imagination, and beauty.

Using the floor as a work surface allows big things to happen.

The Ways Artists Use Drawing

The word *drawing* refers in general to making images by marking upon some sort of surface which serves as a background. In this sense, drawing is the basis for almost every pictorial experience, particularly painting.

Although drawing seems to be the most fundamental means of artistic expression, it is not totally spontaneous. Even in the drawings of so-called "primitive" cultures, we can see at least two basic conventions. First, a line or stroke is used as a means to divide space; and second, drawing is used to give form to the artist's subjective image.

Earliest man created several distinct styles of drawing, some extremely sensitive. Some of these drawings remain on the protected walls of recently discovered caves or scratched on bones or stones. One style was extremely naturalistic, with fine illusionary effects, while another style was simplified and seems purely decorative. These same differences occur quite naturally in the drawings of present-day children. However, prehistoric man used art as part of his magic to try to control the forces of nature while children today use drawing as a means of visually expressing an idea or a fantasy.

The earliest cultures had very limited drawing materials. From the oldest remaining cave drawings in the Cantabrian Mountains of Spain and from other examples we know that early man, like all primitive peoples, used whatever was available. Eskimos scratched drawings on walrus tusks; Africans drew on the bark of trees; during the Bronze Age drawings were made on thin sheets of bronze; in Egypt men drew on papyrus or on clay tablets; in Greece and Rome drawings were done on wood or ivory tablets and on parchment made from the skin of animals.

It was during the Renaissance (fifteenth century) in Europe that Western drawing as we know it really became a major art form. Artists used charcoal, chalk, pastels, pen and ink, watercolor, and tempera for their drawings, which were usually done on sheets of paper. As drawing advanced as an art form, each artist seemed to develop a distinctive personal style. Drawings began to fall into three main groupings, each having its own validity. The first group reduces drawing to its essence—a simple outline with little or no indication of space, light, color, or texture. The second group represe ts a wide range of expressive styles. These drawings tend to be busy, intense, full of conflicting strokes and directions, more spontaneous and impulsive, full of energy and movement, and more expressive than descriptive. Line as used in expressive drawing tends to suggest movement, energy, and emphasis. The third major grouping is based upon the visual illusion of reality. Here the artists attempt to capture the qualities of distance, atmosphere, light—the careful interpretation of nature as the eye or the camera might view it. Some of these drawings are exact recordings of nature—every leaf, every blade of grass, etc. Some artists produce drawings that combine the visual illusions with very personal interpretations. Often these artists are the ones who make illustrations for books or newspapers.

Within these major categories hundreds of drawing styles have emerged, including those of the nonobjective artists such as Kandinsky, whose drawings seem to represent nothing recognizable but seem rather to be just great bursts of energy and motion.

Drawing, like painting and sculpture, has many valid directions; many are yet untried or not yet invented. One factor common to most artists who have achieved greatness is that they used drawing and worked hard at developing a technique which fitted their own style of thinking and expression.

The Art of Painting

Painting is the application of color to a surface for the purpose of creating some kind of image. Painting, like drawing, might be compared to writing in that it serves as the artist's means of communicating through symbols. It is the same for children.

In the most primitive cultures, where writing forms were non-existent, drawing and painting were often the only means of graphic communication. Art depended upon clear, understandable images. In most sophisticated cultures, where some form of writing developed, painting tended to become a more decorative and aesthetic experience. However, the need to communicate and the need of an aesthetic experience have been closely interwoven in many examples of art throughout history.

Many artists in the past have made their paintings on walls as part of architecture. The Greeks, Romans, Egyptians, Mayans, Aztecs, Renaissance artists, and others all found walls and ceilings perfect two-dimensional surfaces for their decorative, commemorative, or narrative paintings. During the Middle Ages and the Renaissance, painting was a major means of teaching Christianity to a population that had nothing to read. But later, as paintings became less important as simply a means of direct communication with the masses, they took on more importance as aesthetic objects. Painters began to work more on movable flat surfaces such as wood or canvas on stretchers. Artists have also painted on cardboard, paper, metal, leather, ceramics, and ivory.

The earliest wall paintings were painted either on wet plaster (fresco) which locked in the color forever, or on dry walls (secco) using color mixed with an emulsion consisting of glue, or a natural substance such as the yolk of an egg or casein. Sometimes the colors were mixed with hot wax and applied hot (encaustic). Later, in the fifteenth century, as oil paints were invented, a whole new approach to painting began. As colors became more brilliant, paintings could be retouched and more colors were available to the artist. Until the recent development of acrylic paints, artists had been using exactly the same materials and processes for hundreds of years.

Today, good quality artists' materials are available for the amateur as well as the professional. The artistic process is no longer limited to the artist whose livelihood depends upon his professional production. We are a nation of professional and amateur artists, finding pleasure in creative production, finding that the joy of the process of creating with paints often exceeds in importance the products which result.

Contemporary art, unlike the earlier art forms which were required to be clear and understandable, is now often focused upon experimentation in new materials, new aesthetic trends, new means of applying media to the surface. Subject matter may be simple and obvious, very complex, or nonexistent.

There simply is no way to briefly describe or to classify contemporary painting. For each individual viewer some art will be enjoyable, some confusing, some disturbing, and some repulsive. For the beginning viewer it is important to recognize that just being "beautiful" does not constitute the sole aim of art—or the arts. Every artist pursues his or her different goals by different means. The problem for the viewer is trying to find a quality of understanding in works of art to substitute for the obviousness of the beautiful, as each person has come to know beauty. That requires a lot of looking, an open mind, patience, and a willingness to learn.

Chalk and Pastel Drawing

Suggested Topics Camping in the forest. Traveling through the jungle. Scuba diving in the ocean. Prospecting for gold.

Primary Objectives

• To help children develop complex mental images through imagination or recall
• To organize a theme that is distributed to all portions of the working surface

Materials/Tools

Colored construction paper, 12″ × 18″
Colored chalks or pastels
Clear acrylic spray as fixative (optional)

The Lesson

Chalks and pastels can create appealing effects in drawing when used on paper which already has color or a gray value. Lighter pastel colors stand out against colored paper or gray values in ways quite different from the way they contrast with white or buff paper. Colored paper also creates an environmental quality—blue seems like water or sky; green seems like leaves or grass; black seems like night.

1. Choose a topic or a theme and stimulate class discussion with questions such as: Why are you camping in the forest? Who is with you? What special clothing are you wearing for protection? Are there animals in the forest? Do trees and wildflowers grow there? And so on.

2. Point out some of the ways that pastels and chalks differ from crayons. Pastels are soft and produce a dusty surface. They can easily be blended by rubbing one color over another. They are almost impossible to erase.

3. Have the children experiment with the pastels or chalks on several small pieces of colored paper before starting their drawings.

4. Suggest that everyone sketch the major parts of their drawing with a light-colored pastel.

5. As the children are working to finish their drawings, call attention to the importance of contrast—that is, getting strong darks against light areas and light colors adjacent to the dark areas.

6. The finished drawings need not be sprayed with a fixative unless they are to be stored in a pile or exhibited where they will be touched. Spraying should be done outside or in a well-ventilated area. This is a task for the teacher.

7. Pictures are enhanced by mounting or matting on a white or a contrasting paper or cardboard.
8. Show them off.

Useful References

LALIBERTÉ NORMAN, and MOGELON, ALEX. *Painting with Crayons: History and Modern Techniques.* New York: Van Nostrand Reinhold Co., 1967.

LINDERMAN, EARL W. *Invitation to Vision: Ideas and Imaginations for Art.* Dubuque, Iowa: Wm. C. Brown Company Publishers, 1967.

Felt-Tip Pen Drawing

Suggested Topics The teacher or a class member. Two bicycles. Three shoes. Six pencils.

Primary Objectives

• To use direct line as a tool for communication
• To learn through careful observation that even the most familiar figures and objects may become interesting through imaginative interpretation

Materials/Tools

Drawing paper or any large smooth drawing surface (the bigger the better)
Felt-tip pens or markers

The Lesson

Felt-tip pens create a thick or thin line, depending upon the size of the felt point. With thick blunt tips use large sheets of paper; with fine points use smaller sheets of paper. This type of pen is an ideal tool for contour drawing.

1. This is a good problem for helping coordinate eye and hand. Talk a little about how the eye can follow the outline of the person or object, and how a line can separate one shape from another.

2. For the subject of your drawing select one object in the room, such as a chair, and place it on a centrally located desk where it is easily seen. Have everyone make a drawing in the air with the finger tip—a drawing which follows the contour of every part in the subject.

3. Now select another subject, such as a seated model or a group of objects. This time the children draw directly on paper with a felt-tip pen following the contour. Emphasize the acceptability of "mistakes" in proportion, lines which do not meet, etc. This is a learning experience.

4. If you can find a reproduction of a Picasso lithograph of the period about 1954, show it to the class after completing one contour drawing. There is a great similarity to what the class is doing.

5. Display the work of the entire class. As an outside assignment, have the children make a contour drawing of a building in their neighborhood, using a pencil, ball point pen, or felt-tip pen on a plain sheet of typewriting paper.

Useful References

HERBERHOLZ, DONALD, and HERBERHOLZ, BARBARA. *A Child's Pursuit of Art: 110 Motivations for Drawing, Painting, and Modeling.* Dubuque, Iowa: Wm. C. Brown Company Publishers, 1967.

RÖTTGER, ERNST, and KLANTE, DEITER. *Creative Drawing: Point and Line.* New York: Van Nostrand Reinhold Co., 1964.

Tempera Painting

Suggested Topics   This is my daddy. This is my house. My mother in her garden. My cat in a fight.

Primary Objectives

* To help children enrich their concepts of familiar subjects
* To encourage bold, free painting as a balance for small, more restricted desk work

Materials/Tools

Liquid tempera paints

Easel paper

Bristle brushes, various sizes

Containers for paints

The Lesson

Because of the requirements of space, containers, brushes, and large flat surfaces, tempera painting is usually done individually or in small groups. For younger children the paints need to be pre-mixed to a thick consistency so they do not run excessively. Some classrooms have several easels; some have none. The floor serves adequately if no easels are available.

Tempera painting is very direct with young children. There may be little desire to mix or blend colors: red is generally used as red, blue as blue. Each container needs its own brush if colors are to remain clean. Otherwise each jar will soon be a muddy brown.

1. Talk with your group about the fun involved in making a large easel painting. Discuss what would make good subjects—tall buildings, trees, people, etc.
2. Tell them to make their pictures so complete that they touch all four edges of the paper—top, bottom, and sides.
3. While the children are painting, ask leading questions that might induce richer details. What is daddy wearing? What is mother carrying? Who is climbing up the tree?
4. When a painting is complete, look for its strength. Is it bright, is it bold, is it full of action, has the space been filled? Use this opportunity to give sincere praise for whatever good qualities are evident.

Useful References

COLE, NATALIE ROBINSON. *The Arts in the Classroom.* New York: John Day Co., Inc., 1966.

VIOLA, WILHELM. *Child Art.* London: University of London Press, 1952.

Tempera Painting

Group Project

Suggested Topic   A segmented painting of a landscape or a still life.

Primary Objectives
- To learn to observe carefully and with closer attention to detail
- To experiment in mixing colors to achieve differences in hue and value

Materials/Tools
Magazines, Sunday supplements
Liquid tempera paints
Paper plates for palettes
Soft brushes (camel's hair or similar)
Water containers
Drawing paper, 12″ × 12″

The Lesson
This project requires planning and preparation. It results in a large, dramatic group painting.

1. Find several large colored photographs of landscapes or still-life arrangements in magazines. Usually the best ones are advertisements. Carefully divide the pictures into 1½-inch squares (trim or crop the photograph so that it provides enough squares to give one to each child). Number the pieces on the back in sequence so they can be easily reassembled.

2. Provide each child with one 12″ × 12″ sheet of drawing paper for each small square from the photograph.

3. Give each child a palette (paper plate), a small brush, and a water container.

4. Review and demonstrate how colors may be made by mixing other colors: red and yellow make orange; red and blue make purple; blue and yellow make green.

5. Have each child lightly sketch with a pencil on the drawing paper the main areas or shapes he sees in the small segment of the photograph.

6. Begin to paint the sketches, interpreting color, line, texture, dark and light as they appear in the photographic segments.

7. Reassemble the small segments by their numbers. Using thumbtacks, assemble the large paintings in the same order on the bulletin board.

8. The differences in style and interpretation will be obvious. Some children are bold, others delicate. Point out that artists all see differently! You may

wish to illustrate this point by showing photographs of several landscapes by different artists. No two will be alike.

9. Tape the edges of the paintings together on the back. You will have a powerful group mural with every child represented.

Useful References

RANDELL, ARNE W. *Murals for Schools.* Worcester, Mass.: Davis Publications, Inc., 1958.

ROSENBERG, LILLI ANN KILLEN. *Children Make Murals and Sculpture: Experience in Community Art Projects.* New York: Van Nostrand Reinhold Co., 1962.

Watercolor on Wet Paper

Suggested Topics   A spring bouquet. In the football stands. The jungle. A flower garden.

Primary Objectives

- To work spontaneously, experiment, and make color discoveries
- To be imaginative in seeing subject matter that can be developed within "accidental" color patterns

Materials/Tools

White drawing paper
Watercolor paints
Brushes
Water containers
Sponges
Felt-tip markers

The Lesson

This project is more easily explained and understood by means of the following simple demonstration.

1. Place a piece of white drawing paper on a smooth surface and pour about one-quarter cup of clean water on the paper. Spread the water evenly over the entire paper using the palm of the hand. Sponge away all excess water from the surface of the paper and the adjacent table surface so that the paper is uniformly damp.

2. Moisten several colors in the watercolor box. With a clean brush, pick up a generous brush full of color and quickly apply it to the damp surface. Do not brush the paper; just touch the surface and let it run. Refill the brush and touch another area.

3. Clean the brush and choose a second color. This time cover areas not previously colored. Repeat with a third color. If the paper still is damp and "runny," you might try splashing the third color randomly over the paper. New colors will result as two moist colors touch and fuse together.

4. Now have the children write their names on their sheets of paper for later identification; then let them try what you have demonstrated. When their paper surfaces are colored, using the edge of a sponge have them blot up the puddles and any excess water. Place the paintings on the floor where they won't be walked over and allow them to dry for an hour or more. Try to keep the paintings flat when moving them so the colors don't run and fuse together, thus destroying their spontaneous qualities.

5. During the following class period encourage the children to think of appropriate subject matter. What do the colors suggest—forests, skies, underwater? The children can then lightly sketch their ideas directly on the watercolor painting and then go over their sketches with felt-tip markers or with additional watercolor paint. Let them paint until they feel that the pictures are completed.

Useful References

GREENBERG, PEARL. *Children's Experiences in Art: Drawing and Painting.* New York: Van Nostrand Reinhold Co., 1966.

MORMAN, JEAN MARY. *Art: Of Wonder and a World.* New York: Art Education, Inc., Publishers, 1967.

Watercolor Painting

Suggested Topics A neighborhood storefront. A view through the window. Boarding a school bus. Garage sale. Flea market.

Primary Objectives
- To learn to make careful visual observations
- To learn to record major shapes and colors to create a composition that is adaptable to the working surface

Materials/Tools
Drawing paper, 12″ × 18″, white or buff
Watercolor sets
Soft brushes (camel's hair or similar)
Pencils

The Lesson
1. Decide on a topic or choice of topics, and then discuss. What are the most important features? Are there people? What are they doing? Are there trees, cars, other buildings, and so on?
2. Have each child make a preliminary sketch with pencil defining the largest shapes. These will be the main areas to color first. After sketching the larger shapes, the children can lightly sketch additional details.
3. Work on a flat surface and use the paint in a free manner. Encourage each child to fill in the larger shapes with the color that seems appropriate. Some children will attempt to mix colors to achieve a special hue; others will use the colors as they come from the watercolor pan. Try to get the entire surface covered before concentrating on details.
4. Now work on the details, paying careful attention to specific colors and shapes.
5. Ask questions. Call attention to details the children may not be observing or recalling. Stress the importance of the background areas.
6. Mount or mat the watercolor paintings. Later let the group view them and talk about what they have painted.

Useful References

COLE, NATALIE ROBINSON. *Children's Art from Deep Down Inside.* New York: The John Day Company, Inc., 1966.

FEARING, KELLY, and BEARD, EVELYN. *Our Expanding Vision.* Austin, Texas: W. S. Benson and Company, 1960.

Crayon Resist

Suggested Topics Birds on a tree limb. Insects crawling through the grass. The aquarium. At the edge of space. The Fourth of July.

Primary Objectives

• To make visual discoveries through combining common media in experimental ways
• To develop a pattern and distribution of shapes that is complemented and "tied-together" by the background color or colors

Materials/Tools

Drawing paper

Wax crayons

Watercolors

Brushes

Slides from nature or a collection of *National Geographic* magazines

The Lesson

1. Choose a topic and discuss it with the group. Show some slides or colored photographs of the subject, for example, insects, fish, space, foliage, birds, etc.
2. Have each child make a drawing using the crayon colors intensely, but leaving large areas of the page not colored with crayon. If the crayon is applied lightly, have the child go over it a second time.
3. When all the crayon details are completed, mix a watercolor wash, or several colors, in large enough quantity to cover the entire page. The colors ought to be ones that are appropriate for the background of the picture. For example, green applied over insects might give the illusion of grass or foliage.
4. Cover the entire paper with the watercolor. Those areas colored with the wax crayons will resist the paint, but the uncolored paper will accept it. The crayon drawing remains virtually unchanged, but a dramatic change occurs since it is now contrasted against a colored background. Encourage further experimentation with the background color by dripping more intense color here and there on the damp surface, or by using a second color over the first one.

Useful References

Horn, George F. *The Crayon*. Worcester, Mass.: Davis Publications, Inc., 1968.
McGeary, Clyde, Jefferson, Blanche, and others. *My World of Art Series*. Boston: Allyn and Bacon, Inc., 1963–64.

Finger Painting Monoprint

Suggested Topics   Designs, free motions.

Primary Objectives
- To use the larger arm muscles in rhythmic, free motions
- To experiment with a variety of movements of arm, hand, and fingers

Materials/Tools

Formica, glass, or enamel surface

Liquid starch

Liquid detergent, to wash paint off hands

Tempera paint

Apron or smock

Newsprint paper

The Lesson

Finger painting provides an experience which encourages large free movements of the arm and hand without the restrictions of a preconceived outcome. Its primary value is in the doing, not in the painting that results.

For this activity it's important that every child wear an apron or smock. Good smocks can be made from men's shirts by removing the collars and shortening the sleeves. They should be worn buttoned in the back. Call on a few parents to make smocks for your class.

1. Early in the school term do at least one demonstration for all the children. Clear a formica-covered table on which to work. Gather the children about you. Pour some liquid starch on the table top. Start with about 3 to 4 tablespoonfuls. Sprinkle some dry tempera paint on the starch and a splash of liquid detergent. Mix and spread with the palm of one hand until an area about 20 inches square is covered.

2. Using the side of the hand, make a series of regular waves from right to left and left to right. Change the motion and move the hand like a saw, up and down. Wipe out what you have done and make a series of rhythmic wiggles with the finger tips. Try making a fist and repeating a new motion. Continue to experiment. Add starch and a splash of water if the surface becomes sticky.

3. At some point, place a plain piece of newsprint paper over the finger painting. Rub the back of the paper with a clean hand and pull it free from the surface. A mirror-image monoprint will be on the paper.

4. Add more starch and color. Let a child try it.

5. Only one or two children should be finger painting at a time. Help each child make the monoprint and assist with each addition of starch and tempera paint.

6. A bucket or basin of warm soapy water and a cellulose sponge are all that you need for cleaning the table top. Sponge the surface clean after each child has had a turn, so that the next child may start from a clean surface.

Useful References

HOOVER, F. LOUIS. *Art Activities for the Very Young.* Worcester, Mass.: Davis Publications, Inc., 1961.

MONTGOMERY, CHANDLER. *Art for Teachers of Children.* Columbus, Ohio: Charles E. Merrill, 1968.

Large Paintings

Suggested Topics This is how big Daddy is. This is a tall tree I am climbing. This is how I swing from a trapeze. This is how big our car is.

Primary Objectives
- To balance the constraints of small desk work
- To provide an opportunity for those children who think big to work big

Materials/Tools

Tempera paints

Cellulose sponge cubes (cut from a dry sponge with a mat knife)

Brushes, various sizes and types, including small house-painting brushes

Kraft wrapping paper or large paper sheets taped together to a size 28" × 36" or larger

The Lesson

From time to time it is useful to change the style of our classes. Most of the time class work is done at desks or tables. For this project push the desks aside and let the floor be a work surface that allows big things to happen. Some artists (such as the late Jackson Pollock) use the floor as a primary work surface.

1. Cut enough pieces of wrapping paper to provide one for each child. Mix a variety of tempera paints in plastic or tin containers so there are a few more containers of paint than children. Place them all in the center of the room with enough brushes for everyone and a bucket of soapy water for brush cleaning.

2. Place the wrapping paper pieces around the perimeter of the room and have the children choose a work space. Ask the children to think of what they want to paint big, but tell them not to start until they have a good idea.

3. Instruct the children to go to the center of the room and choose one brush and one color as soon as they have a good topic and to paint with that color until they need a second color. Then they must wash their brushes, choose another color, and continue to paint until their idea is completed.

4. The sponge cubes work well to apply paint for large areas.

5. Stimulate the thinking of individuals with leading questions, and call attention to those who are working freely, using their colors interestingly, working boldly, and so on.

6. Stress the importance of using the space—that is, making the painting touch all the edges of the paper.

Useful References

Bannon, Laura. *Mind Your Child's Art.* New York: Pelligrini and Cudahy, 1952.

Bland, Jane C. *Art of the Young Child.* New York: The Museum of Modern Art, 1958.

Crayon Sgraffito

Suggested Topics   Nightime at the shopping mall. Night on the freeway. In the sports arena. In the depths of the ocean.

Primary Objectives

- To learn to take advantage of the unpredictable or the element of discovery in art
- To enrich visual imagery through observation, imagination, or recall

Materials/Tools

Smooth drawing paper, 9″ × 12″ or smaller

Wax crayons

Sharp points (scissors, pins, pens, nails, etc.)

The Lesson

1. Choose a topic and discuss it. What can you see in a darkened area? How does this differ from how it appears in the daylight?
2. Using wax crayons, randomly cover the entire page with various colors. Make each color intense.
3. Cover the first layer of colored crayons with a layer of black crayon.
4. Using the point of a scissor or other sharp point, create the drawing by scratching through the black crayon, exposing the bright colors beneath.
5. The finished sgraffito drawing creates the reverse effect of a direct drawing and gives the illusion of a vision of darkness.

Useful References

GREENBERG, PEARL. *Art and Ideas for Young People.* New York: Van Nostrand Reinhold Co., 1970.

HORN, GEORGE F. *The Crayon.* Worcester, Mass.: Davis Publications, Inc., 1968.

Drawing Caricatures

Suggested Topics   Famous people: politicians, movie and TV stars, world figures, etc.

Primary Objectives

- To learn and perceive facial parts
- To observe and stress the special characteristics of a person
- To look at the way some artists have been able to capture the character of an individual by focusing on only a few features

Materials/Tools

Drawing paper

Pencils

Felt-tip pens

The Lesson

In preparation, clip some cartoons of famous people from newspapers and magazines. Use the library as a source of earlier caricatures. Also clip photographs of TV and movie stars, politicians, and other well-known people.

1. Talk about what an artist looks for. What makes a person stand out? What physical or facial characteristics do we remember about a particular person? Does he have an unusually broad grin, prominent ears, a beard or mustache, bushy eyebrows, a space between the front teeth, etc.? Is she "known" by her sunglasses, long dangling earrings, wide-brimmed hat, Afro hairdo, double chin, almond eyes, full lips, etc.?
2. Let everyone choose a photograph of someone well known. What facial features stand out—a large nose, a "toothy" smile, arched eyebrows, a frown, etc.?
3. Draw the features selected, keeping them simple and *exaggerated*.
4. Re-draw the caricature, eliminating everything unimportant and over-emphasizing everything important. Go over the pencil drawing with a dark felt-tipped pen.
5. Exhibit the caricatures. Number them and let the children try to match the photographs with the drawings.

Useful References

COHEN, ELAINE PEAR, and GAINER, RUTH STRAUS. *Art: Another Language for Learning*. New York: Citation Press, 1976.

LINDERMAN, EARL W. *Invitation to Vision: Ideas and Imaginations for Art*. Dubuque, Iowa: Wm. C. Brown Company Publishers, 1967.

Drawing from Various Angles

Suggested Topics   360 ways to draw a still life or a live model.

Primary Objectives
• To learn of the many ways to view any subject
• To relate learning about the degrees in a circle to a drawing activity

Materials/Tools
Drawing paper
Cardboards (about 12″ × 18″) to serve as drawing boards
Pencils
Erasers
Masking tape
Magnetic compass (borrow one from a Boy Scout)

The Lesson
1. Draw a circle on the blackboard and mark it at 90°, 180°, 270°, and 360°, to show the relative location of degree markings as they appear on a magnetic compass.
2. Clear a large working space so the children can sit on the floor in a circle.
3. Set up a still-life arrangement or pose a model in the center of the room. Using the magnetic compass, mark four positions on the floor: 90° (East), 180° (South), 270° (West), and 360° (North).
4. On slips of paper mark 10°, 20°, 30°, etc. Put them in a box. Let each child select a number randomly from the box and find his or her approximate location on the floor corresponding with the degree number chosen.
5. Talk about how each young artist will now see the subject differently because each views it from a different angle. Therefore, there is no chance that two drawings will be exactly the same.
6. Have the children begin to draw whatever can be seen from each vantage point.
7. When the drawings are completed, tape or thumbtack them on the walls, windows, doors, at or near the position from which they were drawn; or lay them on the floor in a circle so everyone can walk around and view them.

Useful References

PATTEMORE, ARNEL W. *Art and Environment: An Art Resource for Teachers.* New York: Van Nostrand Reinhold Co., 1974.

TRITTEN, GOTTFRIED. *Art Techniques for Children.* New York: Van Nostrand Reinhold Co., 1964.

Life-Size Action Figures

Suggested Topics   Action sports, dancing, changing a tire, lifting a log, carrying a heavy weight, chopping a tree.

Primary Objectives

- To provide a starting point for drawing for students who are losing confidence in their ability
- To call attention to how parts relate to the whole
- To reduce the "stiffness" that occurs in the drawings of pre-adolescents

Materials/Tools

Slide or overhead projector or flood lamp
Kraft wrapping paper cut in 6 ft. lengths
Felt-tip marking pens
Tempera paints or other color materials
Scissors

The Lesson

This lesson provides a "crutch" which the teacher would not want to use repeatedly. It is useful in providing a starting point for students who have become timid about their ability to communicate visually.

1. Clear a wall where the 6 ft. lengths of wrapping paper can be thumbtacked and where the light from a flood lamp, overhead projector, or slide projector can be thrown.
2. The students work in teams. One child poses close to the paper "in action"—shooting a basket, firing a rifle, roller skating, chopping a log, water skiing, etc. The teammate quickly but carefully outlines the shadow on the paper. Then the two exchange roles.
3. After everyone has a penciled outline, decisions are made about those body parts that are hidden due to overlapping and those parts that are visible. All the major lines which separate parts are sketched in pencil.
4. Take time to talk about clothing. Observe what is worn—its color, texture, etc. Encourage everyone to re-take their original poses and study their own body positions. Have children model for each other to see how things appear.
5. Use tempera or other color materials to complete the figures.

6. Trim away the excess paper and assemble all the figures on one wall. Group them so they each are partially hidden by overlapping. This will provide an "instant" group mural, or the drawings may serve as a first step for a more comprehensive mural project.

Useful References

LALIBERTÉ, NORMAN, and MOGELON, ALEX. *Silhouettes, Shadows and Cut Outs.* New York: Van Nostrand Reinhold Co., 1968.

SHESSLER, B. *Sports and Games in Art.* Minneapolis: Lerner Publications, 1966.

Film Strip Illustrations

Suggested Topic   Story illustration of current classroom reading.

Primary Objectives
- To stimulate mental images through recall
- To develop sequential thinking
- To depict the images that communicate most effectively

Materials/Tools

Used, outdated, or discarded 35 mm film (sometimes available from commercial suppliers)

Liquid household bleach

Sharp-pointed felt-tip pens that mark on acetate (Marks-A-Lot, Design, or similar)

Paper rectangles, $1'' \times 1\frac{1}{4}''$

Film strip projector and screen

The Lesson

1. Unroll the film and soak it in bleach until the emulsion is loose. This takes only a few minutes. Wipe clean with paper towels.

2. Have each child think of a story to illustrate, and then write a list of 10 to 20 scenes or episodes that illustrate the story. For example, using the story of Jonah and the whale, the first drawing might be a ship at sea, the second the ship being tossed in a storm, the third the crew surrounding Jonah, the fourth showing him being thrown overboard, the fifth the whale, the sixth the whale seeing Jonah, the seventh Jonah being swallowed, etc.

3. Give each child a small rectangle of paper $1'' \times 1\frac{1}{4}''$ to use as a guide for the size limit of each drawing.

4. Allow 5 or 6 inches of blank film before the first drawing. Images must be drawn from side to side between the film sprocket holes (that is, the film is unrolled vertically).

5. Using felt-tip pen, draw the first scene directly on the film. Complete it with additional colors if colored pens are available.

6. Using the small paper rectangle as a guide, begin the second drawing directly below the first drawing.

7. The third follows the second, and so on, until all frames of your story are completed.

8. Major mistakes can be removed by washing with bleach, then drying. But avoid any changes except to correct major errors.

9. When the drawings are completed, darken the room, project them on the screen, and have each child narrate his or her story. This is a good opportunity to combine oral and visual communication.

Useful References

Cohen, Elaine Pear, and Gainer, Ruth Straus. *Art: Another Language for Learning.* New York: Citation Press, 1976.

McFee, June K., and Degge, Rogena. *Art, Culture and Environment.* Belmont, Calif.: Wadsworth Publishing, 1977.

Cut Paper Group Mural

Suggested Topics   The International Airport. A horse and cattle ranch. Our town (city). Our neighborhood. The harbor.

Primary Objectives

- To learn the value of cooperation through the group process of a team approach
- To understand visual overlapping of objects in space
- To understand the visual illusion of diminishing size as it relates to distance

Materials/Tools

Colored construction paper

Paste

Scissors

Large sheet of wrapping paper, approximately 3′ × 5′

Tempera paints

The Lesson

1. Have the class decide on a topic based upon a group experience or the common knowledge of the group about a specific environment.

2. Say, for example, the theme is "Our Town." Discuss the most important parts—the business district, civic buildings, churches, schools, stores, apartment houses, shopping centers, residences, the airport, etc. List these on the chalkboard.

3. Let each child choose a building—church, school, factory, apartment house, residence, etc. to make. "Big" buildings might be no larger than 8″ × 10″; "little" buildings proportionately smaller. Don't be too fussy about size.

4. Give each child a pair of scissors, some paste, and an assortment of colored construction paper. Have children plan their buildings by lightly sketching the main shapes with pencil, then cutting them out of the colored paper. Details are added with other colors. Make details with colored paper rather than drawing with pencils or crayons. While the children are making their individual projects, begin to prepare the wrapping paper on which all the parts will soon be assembled.

5. Staple or thumbtack a large piece of wrapping paper on the wall. Assign one or two children to plan and make appropriate background, streets, grass, and the sky. This can be done with large sheets of construction paper, colored tissue paper, or tempera paint.

6. When children finish their buildings, have some of them make people, trees, cars, buses, airplanes, clouds, birds, etc.

7. Have each child temporarily place her or his building somewhere on the background with a bit of tape. In the process they will discover that many things have to "give" a little to include everything. Overlapping is discovered as a visual phenomenon.

8. When everything is included and in the best location, have two or three children begin to paste everything to the background.

9. The finished mural will surprise everyone with its charm and beauty. Everyone will learn that this could be accomplished only through group effort. For each child this is *our* mural.

Useful References

RANDELL, ARNE W. *Murals for Schools.* Worcester, Mass.: Davis Publications, Inc., 1958.

TEMKO, FLORENCE. *Paper Cutting.* Garden City, N.Y.: Doubleday and Company, Inc., 1973.

MODELING
AND
SCULPTURE

4

*I want to make things that are fun
to look at.*

ALEXANDER CALDER

Background Information about Sculpture

Fifty years ago a visitor to a major art museum would have been exposed to many pieces of sculpture: statues of saints, kings, heroes, nymphs, mothers with children, classical nudes, romanticized lovers, cupids, etc. The visitor probably would have been able to recognize the subject matter of most of the sculpture and probably would have understood what the artists were trying to express through their work. A museum visit today to view the work of contemporary sculptors is something different! It is far less easy to understand the mysterious intentions of the contemporary artist, and the art forms often seem unwilling to surrender their meanings. As viewers we need not be distressed if the art is difficult to understand. That is a common experience.

Contemporary sculpture falls into numerous categories. Some of it is based upon the easily recognized classical naturalistic traditions, some upon surrealistic tendencies, some upon abstractions of the human figure or other natural forms, and some—the so-called "nonobjective" sculpture—is based upon pure abstraction. Whatever the form, a work is considered to be sculpture if it is a representation with a three-dimensional quality. If it has form and can be examined from all sides, it is called sculpture "in the round." If it projects from a flat surface or is carved into a flat surface, it is called "relief" sculpture.

Traditionally, people have been taught to think of sculpture as having been carved from a solid material with sharp tools such as chisels. Modeling was thought of as shaping and forming plastic materials, such as clay, with the hands or with modeling tools. Today's· artists continue to use all of the traditional materials such as stone, marble, clay, wood, wax, etc., but they have added many new materials to their repertoire and also the industrial techniques of welding, casting, joining, etc. Just as quickly as industry develops a new process, some artist finds a way to use it. Newer industrial materials such as fiberglass, acrylics, polyurethane, stainless steel, concrete, and others are commonly used by today's sculptors. In other words, no limits are placed on the contemporary artist. Thus, today's sculptor freely uses any materials and any means, including light, energy, and motion, as legitimate processes of sculptural expression.

Subtractive sculpting on a block of plaster.

Traditional sculpture is relatively easy to understand, because there has been plenty of time for study and contemplation by scholars. Their studies have helped to give meaning to much of the work produced in the past. To cite a few examples, scholars tell us that the Venus of Willendorf, chipped from a hard stone about thirty thousand years ago, was undoubtedly used for magical purposes or fertility rites. Carved statues of Greek gods were placed in great temples, to be worshipped as though they were the living gods themselves. The so-called primitive sculptures of Africa and New Guinea were thought to contain the spirits of ancestors and played significant roles in the ritual ceremonies. The religious statues of Christ, Mary, and the saints were objects of great respect for Christians, as were the Buddhas of the East and the sphinxes of Egypt. Later sculptures honored kings, princes, and heroes. These sculptures all communicate their meanings in obvious ways and seem easy to understand.

But by the beginning of the twentieth century, sculptors had begun to break with classical tradition. They were tired of the numerous monuments which filled every public space. Artists wanted to express their interpretation of people and their environment in a more direct and more personal way. Some began to parallel the movements that were occurring in painting. Both painting and sculpture changed rapidly and dramatically around the beginning of the twentieth century. Sculptors were incorporating impressionism, expressionism, cubism, abstraction, and even borrowing directly from the so-called primitive work of Africa.

Today there is an even greater freedom and range of expression. It often tends to leave the older viewer puzzled at the meaning, materials, or form. What is often forgotten is that although many of us have been conditioned traditionally, children today are growing in a period of time when dramatic change and the unusual is commonplace. Contemporary styles and materials are easier for the young to assimilate and enjoy. Enjoyment is the most important step toward appreciation. For the young who daily experience new concepts in music, packaging, architecture, transportation, food products, etc., the newer concepts in art are far less abstract and confusing than they are to their parents and grandparents. Children have a great capacity to assimilate the ideas, emotions, and feeling of contemporary art, and seem to have the added capacity for enjoying the various aesthetic forms of today's artists.

Modeling and Sculpture in the Classroom

The acceptability of virtually any material or process for the creation of sculpture opens many new opportunities for working in sculpture with children. Perhaps today's sculptors are only re-discovering some of the processes that have been used in the past, as well as utilizing every new material and process as quickly as it becomes technically feasible.

Historically, sculptors have used all sorts of materials: stone, wood, clay, bone, ivory, leather, feathers, fibers, shells, even human hair, bones, and teeth. Sometimes they dressed their sculptures in clothing or armor. Many found it useful and even more expressive to decorate their sculptures with paints, enamels, or precious gems. Today too there are no restrictions other than safety on either the materials or the processes used. (Perhaps there never were any except for those imposed by the purist, classical art academy tradition.)

The earliest art inspirations probably came from magic, from man's desire to exercise some control over the forces of nature. The forms in nature that were used in art often came directly from the immediate environment. Some forms appear close to visual reality while others are simple abstractions.

In a sense, the child and the artist have always approached art in similar ways. Both interpret their visual and tactile impressions of their world through very personal imaginations. They select materials and a style suitable to express themselves as individuals. Although many cultures and periods in art have had strict formulas and systems for the artist to follow, today's artist, like a child, is free to develop a style as personal as his own handwriting.

No art program could ever be complete without the opportunities for a variety of three-dimensional or sculptural experiences. Many children who have difficulty conceptualizing with two-dimensional media may find themselves more readily when working in three dimensions. For example, a child might not understand perspective or foreshortening in drawing, yet can immediately solve problems in a material that permits a three-dimensional solution.

It is also stimulating to work with materials that are new and different. They present new challenges, new limitations, and open new possibilities. This causes new ideas to develop and new solutions to result. Some children respond tactilely to materials, that is, they respond to how the materials *feel;* others respond visually, that is, to how they *look.* Every condition that opens another outlet for creativity ought to be explored.

Modeling in Clay

Suggested Topics I am on my knees planting, digging, etc. Campers (cowboys, scouts, Indians, forest rangers) huddling close to a campfire. Animals I have petted. Portrait of my mother, father, or other relative.

Primary Objectives

• To develop a greater awareness of parts of the body, especially joints such as knees and elbows
• To create figures that capture the basic postures of the body

Materials/Tools

Moist clay (if you have a kiln) or Plasticine (if no kiln available), baseball size lump per child
Newspapers
Plastic bags
Pieces of cloth
Water containers

The Lesson

Use this opportunity to show photographs of earlier cultures such as the early ceramics of Greece or the pre-Columbian clay figures of Western Mexico. Talk about how clay figures were used to depict the daily activities of the people and how these objects now serve as a record about them.

1. Stress the importance of forming the figure from one lump of clay by squeezing, shaping, etc. Demonstrate how parts may be joined with moist clay ("slip") and by "scoring" (dragging clay from one surface to another with a pencil point to make a strong joint). Stress compactness so parts don't stick out too far, thus drying too fast and breaking easily.
2. Talk about the positions we take when we kneel or huddle. Have the children demonstrate some positions they might assume for the subject they have chosen.
3. With wet clay, work on a damp cloth or table top covered with newspapers. If using Plasticine, the work can be done on any surface covered with newspapers.
4. Stress again the importance of making the figures compact. Thin parts or details that stick out will dry fast, become brittle, and may be easily broken before firing.

5. Pay attention to the basic posture, less attention to small details on this project.

6. If the modeling is not completed in one session, wrap each clay figure in a damp cloth and store it in an airtight plastic bag.

7. When the figures are completely modeled, let them begin to dry in the air. They may be rubbed or burnished while still slightly damp, and may easily be carved with a sharp tool at this stage.

8. When the pieces seem very dry, avoid handling them until they are ready to place in the kiln. Firing the clay will harden it permanently. If your school has a kiln, fire the pieces and use the opportunity to make the experience also a science lesson. Explain that the physical property of clay changes when it is exposed to temperatures above 1000°F. and thus it can no longer be returned to a plastic condition by adding water. (For further information, see the introduction to Ceramics, Chapter 9.)

9. It is not absolutely necessary to have a kiln. Dried clay objects can be painted with acrylic or tempera paints. Without firing, however, they are fragile and impermanent.

Useful References

DIMONDSTEIN, GERALDINE. *Exploring the Arts with Children.* New York: The Macmillan Co., 1974.

HAUPT, CHARLOTTE. *Beginning Clay Modeling.* Palo Alto, Calif.: Fearon Publishers, 1969.

Sand Casting

Outdoor Project

Suggested Topics   Sea creatures. The sun. Designs from found objects.

Primary Objectives
- To create a design for relief sculpture
- To use materials common to the construction industry as an art medium

Materials/Tools

Sand (ordinary construction type)

Heavy cardboard boxes for holding the sand

Plaster of Paris (see below)

Plastic bucket or basin

Plastic spoons

Sticks, shells, etc.

Wire, 10″ pieces bent into loops for hangers

The Lesson

Before beginning the activity with children, become acquainted with the procedure for mixing plaster of Paris. Prepare a simple sand mold in a small box. Measure one quart of water and put it into a plastic basin or bucket. In a dry container, measure two quarts of dry plaster. Add the dry plaster to the water a handful at a time; then mix the plaster and water with the hand until no lumps remain and the mixture is smooth and creamy. Spoon some of it into the mold to avoid damaging the sand image and then gently pour in the remainder. Wash the container while the plaster is still damp. Allow the plaster to dry for several days before removing it.

1. Talk about and experiment with the designs children create with their hands, feet, buckets, bottles, shells, sticks, etc. when playing in damp sand.
2. Have the children divide into teams, each to plan one sand casting.
3. Have the children partially fill the boxes with three inches of damp sand. Compress or tightly pack down the sand. Sprinkle or spray with water to keep it damp. Let the designing begin.
4. The designs are created by pressing objects into the sand or by scooping away part of the surface, causing a depression. When something is pressed in, usually some sand must be removed to accommodate it. If these depressions are organized and not chaotic, they form a composition. The design that will be the mold for the liquid plaster might be a recognizable form, for example, a sun with a face and radiating rays, or a fish with textured scales

and fins, or simply a design whose elements are rhythmic, repetitive, or contrasting. The shapes must be large and obvious.

5. When several designs have been achieved to the satisfaction of the teams, mix a container of plaster of Paris and scoop some of it gently into the boxes, covering the design with a layer about 1½ to 2 inches thick.

6. Before the plaster hardens, insert several loops of wire in the back to use as hangers. These can be suspended from the box with string so they will not sink and disappear into the moist plaster.

7. After several days, when the plaster is hard, gently lift it from the sand and carefully brush away the excess sand.

Note: Plaster relief sculptures must be kept indoors. They will slowly deteriorate if left outdoors in the sun and rain.

Useful References

Andrews, Michael. *Sculpture and Ideas.* Englewood Cliffs, N. J.: Prentice-Hall, Inc., 1965.

Leyh, Elizabeth. *Children Make Sculpture.* New York: Van Nostrand Reinhold Co., 1975.

Assemblage I

Suggested Topics Flowers from the Planet Z. A make-believe bouquet.

Primary Objectives
- To stimulate imaginative use of scrap or discarded materials
- To learn to organize or compose in space with three-dimensional materials

Materials/Tools

Plastic cups, paper cups, egg cartons

Modeling clay

Scrap materials—Popsicle sticks, ribbons, weeds, seed pods, buttons, soda straws, beads, junk jewelry, coffee stirrers, feathers, felt, etc.

Decorative scrap paper—tissue, Christmas and gift wrappings

Florist's wire

Stapler

Scissors

White glue

The Lesson

1. Check your library for a book on twentieth century sculpture. Show the work of some artists who use all sorts of materials in different ways. Suggestions: Larry Rivers, Claus Oldenberg, Louise Nevelson, Pablo Picasso, etc.
2. Encourage the children to talk about what they believe people would be like on a strange planet. Would their plants and animals be different? What would their flowers be like?
3. Give each child a paper or plastic cup and a walnut-size piece of modeling clay to press into the bottom of the cup's interior.
4. Have each child make a "flower" by combining paper scraps, feathers, ribbons, etc. and gluing them onto a coffee stirrer, soda straw, or Popsicle stick. Push the end of the stirrer into the clay so that it stands like a flower in a vase.
5. Make a second, third, and fourth flower, so that soon each child has a bouquet in the cup.
6. When the bouquets are completed, use them as a means of encouraging the children to talk to the class about "their" planet.

Useful References

D'AMICO, VICTOR, and BUCHMAN, ARLETTE. *Assemblage.* New York: Museum of Modern Art, 1972.

LORD, LOIS. *Collage and Constructions in Elementary and Junior High Schools.* Worcester, Mass.: Davis Publications, Inc., 1958.

Plaster Carving

Suggested Topics   Dogs, cats, birds, bears, buffalos, etc.

Primary Objectives
- To conceive and carve a three-dimensional representational figure
- To try to recognize large characteristic forms and eliminate all unnecessary detail
- To maintain an interest over several work sessions

Materials/Tools
Plaster of Paris (see below)

Plastic bucket or basin

Cardboard boxes, 6″ or smaller

Drawing paper

Mat knives (X-Acto or similar)

Hand coping saw

Sandpaper

The Lesson

This project requires considerable advance preparation. Learn to mix plaster of Paris. Measure one quart of water and pour it into a plastic basin or bucket. In a dry container, measure two quarts of dry plaster of Paris. Add the dry plaster to the water a handful at a time; then mix the plaster and water until no lumps remain and the mixture is smooth and creamy. It is now ready to pour into a form.

For forms, find as many small-size gift boxes as possible, 6 inches square or smaller. Seal any open corners with tape so they don't leak. Liquid plaster poured into these boxes will quickly harden, retaining the shape of the box. These need to dry about two days before peeling away the cardboard boxes. They are then ready to carve.

It will be helpful to have some illustrations of bulky sculptures with simple forms. Select several from a sculpture book borrowed from the library to show the class. Photographs of animals can be found in old issues of *National Geographic* magazine. Show a few examples from the Visual Alphabet Appendix in this book.

1. Discuss the two primary methods of sculpture: the *additive*, which involves building up or joining on parts as in modeling, and the *subtractive*, which involves removing parts by carving, cutting, or sawing, as in carving marble statues. This project is subtractive.

2. Provide every child with several pieces of drawing paper on which to make sketches.
3. Have the children decide on their animals. Explain the need to keep it simple, because small delicate parts that protrude may easily break off. Talk about making the ears lie back against the head, or the tail or trunk turn back against the body.
4. Make preliminary sketches and discuss them.
5. Sketch the main form directly on the plaster. Begin to cut or saw away the larger areas. At this time the plaster is quite soft and easy to cut. Stop the work at this point and allow the plaster to dry for several more days.
6. When the plaster is almost dry, finish the carving. The details will be easier to make at this time. For a very smooth surface, sand lightly with fine sandpaper.

Useful References

ANDREWS, MICHAEL. *Sculpture and Ideas.* Englewood Cliffs, N.J.; Prentice-Hall, Inc., 1965.

LEYH, ELIZABETH. *Children Make Sculpture.* New York: Van Nostrand Reinhold Co., 1975.

Assemblage II

Suggested Topics   A treasure box.   A box full of surprises.

Primary Objectives
- To stimulate imaginative thinking through the unusual use of common materials
- To use some of the elements of design in developing a three-dimensional composition

Materials/Tools

Cardboard boxes, shoe box size or smaller

Discarded items—spools, buttons, junk jewelry, feathers, keys, paper fasteners, bottle caps, small containers, etc.

Colored papers

Tempera or fast-drying house paint

Brushes

White glue

The Lesson

1. Have the children paint the interior and exterior surfaces of their boxes with tempera or quick-drying house paint.
2. From the scrap collection, have each child select a few objects that contrast—small/large, rough/smooth, bright/dull, hard/soft, etc.
3. Now discuss composition. Composition is an organization of forms, colors, shapes, and textures. It is not chaos—thrown together like trash in a wastebasket.
4. Have each child move, manipulate, arrange, and rearrange the objects chosen to make a personal composition that is pleasing to the child.
5. Using white glue, fasten all parts to the interior of the box.
6. Display the boxes for all to admire.

Useful References

D'AMICO, VICTOR. *Experiments in Creative Art Teaching.* New York: Doubleday & Co. Inc., 1960.

REED, CARL, and ORZE, JOSEPH. *Art from Scrap.* Worcester, Mass.: Davis Publications, Inc., 1960.

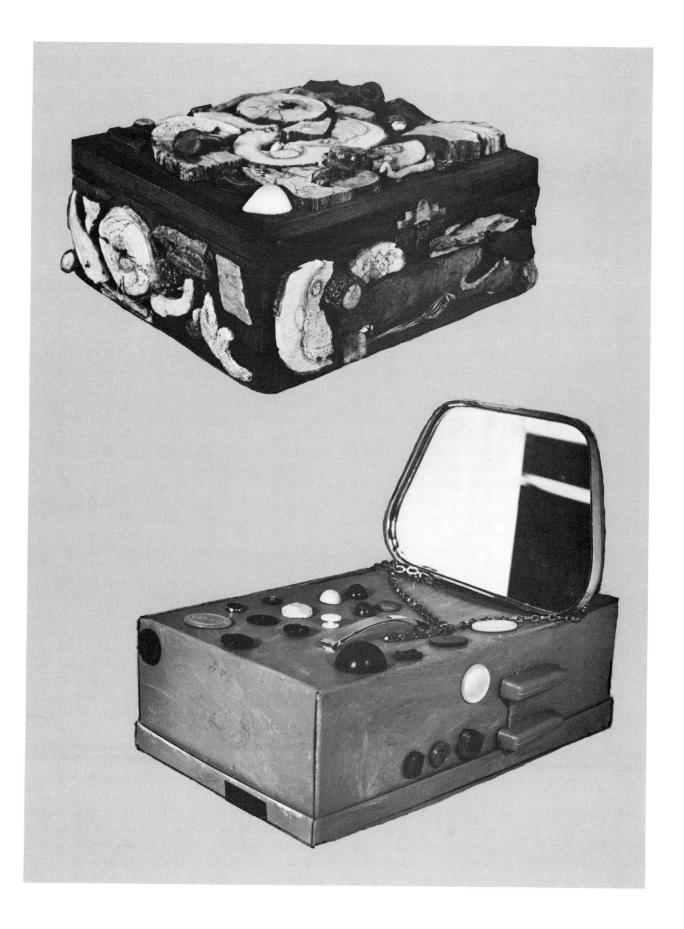

Cast Relief Sculpture

Suggested Topics   Animals in action—walking, running, flying, pouncing, climbing or fighting.

Primary Objectives
• To develop a composition in relief within the confines of four walls
• To learn the process used to make molds and casts

Materials/Tools
Modeling clay
Popsicle sticks or coffee stirrers
Petroleum jelly (Vaseline)
Plaster of Paris (see below)
Plastic bucket or basin
Shoe boxes or other small boxes
Newspaper or a drop cloth
Colored paints—tempera, acrylic, or watercolor
Polyurethane or shellac
Brushes
Sandpaper

The Lesson
Before beginning this project, learn to mix plaster of Paris. Measure one quart of water and pour it into a plastic basin or small bucket. In a dry container, measure two quarts of dry plaster of Paris. Add the plaster to the water a handful at a time; then mix thoroughly with the hand until the mixture is free of lumps and has a smooth, creamy consistency. It is now ready to pour into a mold.

Find an art book in the library with illustrations of Egyptian relief sculptures, and borrow some old issues of *National Geographic* magazine for good photographic examples of animals.

1. Propose the topic "Animals in action," and show some of the animal photographs you have collected illustrating animals running, fighting, etc.
2. Have the children decide on an animal and then make profile contour drawings that fit the size of their boxes. This is the time to help get the special characteristics of the animal. What makes a horse different from a cow? How does a buffalo differ from a leopard?

3. Cover the bottom of the box with a layer of modeling clay about one-half inch thick.

4. Trace or draw the outline of the animal with the point of a pencil.

5. Scoop out the clay within the outline by using the fingers, a Popsicle stick, or any small, rigid object. Remember that the figure will end up in reverse; where you dig deepest it will protrude the most.

6. When the details are completed and the surface has been smoothed or textured as desired, smear a very thin coating of petroleum jelly over the entire surface.

7. Cover an area on the floor with newspapers or a drop cloth, and place all the relief modelings there in readiness for pouring the plaster.

8. Prepare plaster of Paris as described above. Pour some plaster into each box to at least three-fourths inch deep. Allow it to dry and harden for several days.

9. Carefully remove the box. The plaster will be fragile while damp. Gently pull the modeling clay free from the plaster. Allow to dry several more days.

10. Gently remove any excess clay and wipe away any petroleum jelly. If any areas need to be smoother, sandpaper the areas gently.

11. Paint with tempera, acrylic, or watercolor paints—whatever is available. A coat of shellac or polyurethane will give a shiny finish.

Useful References

ANDREWS, MICHAEL. *Sculpture and Ideas.* Englewood Cliffs, N.J.: Prentice-Hall, Inc., 1965.

MEILACH, DONA Z. *Creating with Plaster.* Chicago: Reilly and Lee, 1966.

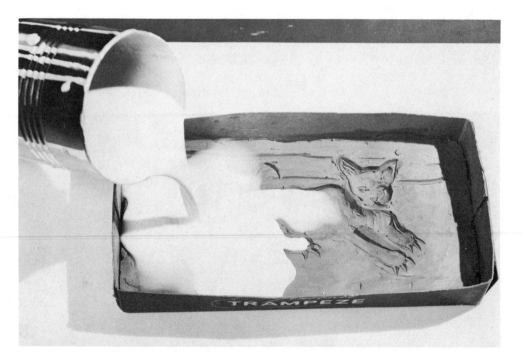

Metal Foil Repoussé

Suggested Topics   Jungle animals in combat.   An insect feeding on a leaf.

Primary Objectives
- To engage in a traditional, multi-step process which requires planning and execution from the reverse side of a sheet of thin metal
- To experiment with surface textures that add interest to the composition

Materials/Tools

Copper or aluminum foil, 36-gauge or heavier

Repoussé tools made by sharpening and sanding a tongue depressor or Popsicle stick

Heavy cardboard or plywood, for mounts

The Lesson

1. Explain the meaning of *repoussé:* pushed out from the back. Show photographic examples of relief sculptures, including some work of silversmiths.
2. Give each child a piece of metal foil approximately 5″×5″ or larger. Have the children plan a design to fit the exact size of the foil.
3. Call attention to developing sketches which are adaptable, that is, simple, clear forms without much detail that will fill the piece of foil from side to side and top to bottom. Don't let the process of repoussé become more important than the concept the child desires to express with it.
4. When the ideas are well developed as sketches, provide each child with a half-inch thick pad of newspapers for use as a work surface. (The surface on which metal is tooled has to "give.")
5. Lay the sketch over the foil and trace it carefully with the point of a pencil or a ball point pen.
6. Using a tool made by pointing then sanding a tongue depressor or Popsicle stick, begin to push out the design, going over one shape at a time with light pressure. As you move to another shape or area, ridges are formed which separate the shapes. Remember, you are working on the back; the other side will be the finished side.
7. Some shapes or areas require repeated rubbing to increase their depth; others may require some type of texturing to visually separate shapes.
8. The metal repoussé can be turned over and pressed from the opposite side to better define shapes.

9. The completed repoussés are enhanced by mounting. Attach them to cardboard mounts by means of staples, or mount them on plywood, using small nails (sometimes called escutcheon pins) available from craft stores.

10. Copper foil repoussé can be oxidized or darkened before mounting by using a small pellet of liver of sulphur (available at a craft store or drug store) dissolved in a cup of boiling water. This solution will blacken the surface of the copper. After a day, the surface can be rubbed with steel wool. The high spots will glisten as shiny copper, the low spots remain a deep contrasting dark color.

Useful References

MATTIL, EDWARD L. *Meaning in Crafts,* 3rd. ed. Englewood Cliffs, N.J. Prentice-Hall, Inc., 1971.

WACHOWIAK, FRANK, and RAMSAY, THEODORE. *Emphasis: Art*, 3rd ed. Scranton, Pa.: International Textbook Co., 1976.

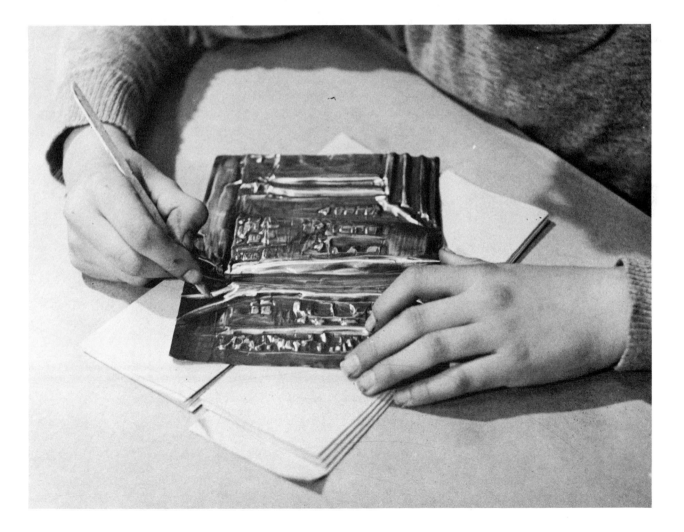

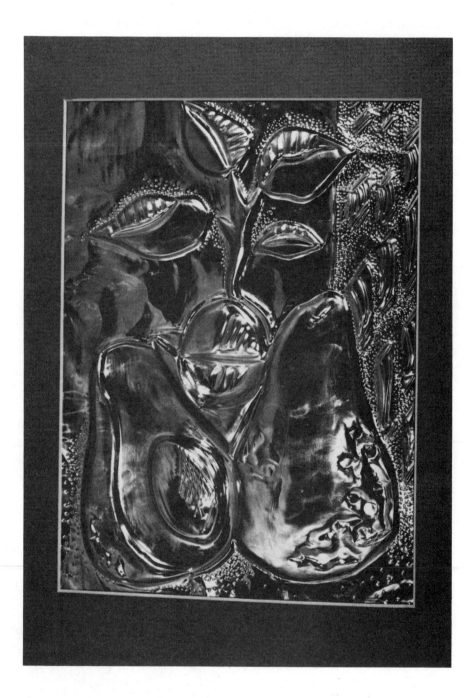

Salt Ceramic Modeling

Suggested Topics   A circus. A zoo. A jungle. A crèche.

Primary Objectives
- To think and work in three dimensions
- To understand movement and action in a figure
- To work through several steps to achieve a finished product

Materials/Tools

Table salt

Cornstarch

Double boiler

Annealed iron wire (stovepipe wire)

Paints

Brushes

Shellac or polyurethane

The Lesson

To prepare salt ceramic (which is not a true ceramic), combine 1 cup of table salt, ½ cup cornstarch and ¾ cup of water. Heat the mixture in the top of a double boiler over boiling water, stirring constantly. In about two to three minutes the mixture thickens and reaches the consistency of unbaked bread dough. Remove from the heat and allow it to cool; then knead for several minutes. It is then ready to be used, or it can be stored for several days if kept airtight in a plastic bag. Because salt ceramic does not shrink or swell in the drying process, it can be applied over a wire armature or framework. This allows children to have more flexibility in their designs than is possible with natural clay. Make up a test batch and then write out the directions for parents to make at home, where such cooperation is practiced.

1. Spend some time in discussion to develop rich ideas. Talk about what makes an elephant different from a cow or pig. What are the characteristics of the animal each child chooses to make?

2. For the armature, give everyone a wire about 40 inches long which has been bent double at its mid-point. Have each child attempt to make a skeleton, without cutting the wire, of the neck, four legs, the body, wings, etc. The armature must be able to stand alone.

3. Give each child a baseball size quantity of salt ceramic, and have the children begin to model it around the wire armature. Salt ceramic is not plastic

like natural clay. It requires more nudging, pushing, and pinching to shape it. A drop or two of water may help in joining pieces.

4. When the entire figure is complete, allow it to dry. Drying may take days, depending on the humidity. When absolutely dry, it is rock-hard and very strong.

5. Paint the sculptures with any kind of paint. Then coat them with polyurethane or shellac if a shiny surface is desired.

Useful References

HAUPT, CHARLOTTE. *Beginning Clay Modeling.* Palo Alto, Calif.: Fearon Publishers, 1969.

MATTIL, EDWARD L. *Meaning in Crafts,* 3rd ed. Englewood Cliffs, N.J.: Prentice-Hall, Inc., 1971.

Scrap Wood Constructions

Suggested Topics Land vehicles, airplanes, space vehicles, buildings, toys, etc.

Primary Objectives
• To use scrap material in an imaginative way
• To combine a variety of pieces into an organized form

Materials/Tools
Small pieces of wood from a carpenter or cabinet shop

White glue or carpenter's glue

A variety of circular wood pieces cut from tree branches, approximately 1" to 3" in diameter and ¼" to ½" thick

Tempera paints (optional)

Small wire nails (brads)

Hammer

The Lesson
In this lesson the materials are the primary motivators. In advance, have a classroom father with a home shop cut tree branches into circular pieces.

1. Tell the children that they may choose pieces and assemble them to construct anything they wish. Because the disks of wood cut from the branches will immediately suggest wheels, lots of vehicles will result.

2. Pieces of soft wood such as pine can be joined with small nails. Larger pieces can be joined with white glue or carpenter's glue.

3. When the objects are assembled, allow them to dry overnight and paint them the following day—or leave them unpainted.

4. Exhibit the constructions on a table top or window ledges before they are taken home.

Useful References
Accorsi, William. *Toy Sculpture.* New York: Van Nostrand Reinhold Co., 1965.

Röttger, Enrst. *Creative Wood Design.* New York: Van Nostrand Reinhold Co., 1961.

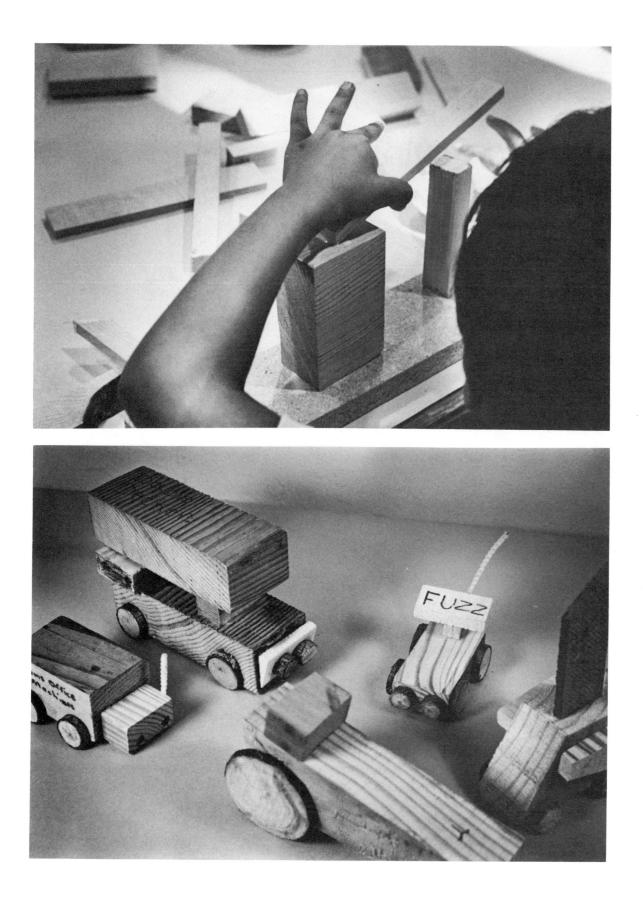

Styrofoam Sculpture

Suggested Topics   Simplified abstractions based on the human figure or animal forms.

Primary Objectives

- To learn about stylized or abstract forms used in contemporary sculpture and in sculpture from past cultures
- To observe the main characteristics of an object and interpret them in a personal way
- To learn to simplify forms

Materials/Tools

Styrofoam packaging (large chunks can be cut up with a carpenter's saw)
Mat knives (X-Acto or similar)
Hand jig or coping saw
Sandpaper, coarse and medium grit
Blocks of wood, for bases
White glue

The Lesson

1. Bring art books from the library to show the class examples of Henry Moore, Jacques Lipshitz, Archipenko, African sculpture, Cycladic sculpture, Eskimo sculpture, pre-Columbian sculpture, etc. Choose examples where forms and shapes have been simplified or treated abstractly.
2. Discuss some of these works, pointing out, for example, what body parts have been emphasized, what parts have been eliminated. How has the artist simplified or changed a figure to achieve the finished sculpture?
3. Let each child choose a piece of Styrofoam and make several sketches of forms which could be carved from that piece. If available, show the children some of Henry Moore's sketches so they may see the way he conceived of his sculpture before he carved or modeled it.
4. Encourage the children to design so that their sculptures will look interesting from all vantage points, not just from the front.
5. Sketch the design lightly on each side; then begin to cut away pieces with the jig or coping saws and knives.
6. When the cutting is completed, sand the surfaces and round any surface which requires it.

7. Sand a piece of wood for a base and then attach the sculpture onto it with white glue.

8. Exhibit the pieces and have a class discussion on abstraction in art.

Useful References

ANDREWS, MICHAEL. *Sculpture and Ideas.* Englewood Cliffs, N.J.: Prentice-Hall, Inc., 1965.

JANSON, HORST W. *History of Art.* Englewood Cliffs, N.J.: Prentice-Hall, Inc., 1962.

Assemblage III

Suggested Topics   Imaginary space equipment.

Primary Objectives
- To invent new uses for discarded or waste materials
- To create interesting designs in three dimensions

Materials/Tools

Discarded hardware, clocks, radios, kitchen items, nuts, bolts, pipe, hinges, knobs, light bulbs, hoses, wire, batteries, etc.

Screw drivers

Pliers

Wood scraps, various small sizes and shapes

Boxes from shoes, small gifts, etc.

Epoxy glue or electric glue gun

The Lesson

This project requires an advance search by the children for discarded items which can be disassembled and parts of them used to invent imaginary space equipment. The children can make up new names for their inventions and can describe what they do and how they work.

1. After a healthy discussion, have the children select items from the general collection or use what they have found. The items should be assembled to give the impression of a machine, tool, or some kind of equipment. Some parts may be fitted into a container and some may be joined together.

2. When the children have achieved the desired organization, the parts can be joined either with the glue gun or with epoxy glue. The electric glue gun is a most versatile tool that joins almost anything quickly and easily. The teacher should monitor its use, however, as accidents may cause painful burns.

3. Epoxy glue usually comes in two tubes. On a disposable jar lid, squeeze out about one inch from each tube, side by side. Mix them together with a toothpick and apply the mixture with the toothpick to the surfaces to be joined. Avoid getting epoxy glue on clothing or the skin. It can be removed from the skin with alcohol on a soft cloth.

4. The glue from the gun hardens immediately, but the epoxy requires a day to set. It should then be strong and secure.

5. Have a show and talk about the session. You will learn a great deal about outer space from the children.

Useful References

LEYH, ELIZABETH. *Children Make Sculpture.* New York: Van Nostrand Reinhold Co., 1975.

LIDSTONE, JOHN. *Building with Balsa Wood.* New York: Van Nostrand Reinhold Co., 1965.

Wire Sculpture

Suggested Topics   Doing gymnastics. A ballerina. Action sports.
An athlete.

Primary Objectives

• To use wire to create forms which enclose space, thus creating volume
• To capture the feeling of movement or action in a sculptured figure

Materials/Tools

Annealed iron wire (stovepipe wire), 2 yards per child
Wire cutters
Small wood scraps, for bases
Wire brads (small nails)
Hammer

The Lesson

Working with flexible wire is like working with a pencil line on paper. However, because wire can be bent in any direction, it is possible to create a form with volume, not just a two-dimensional shape.

1. Begin this lesson by showing photographs of people doing something that requires a special physical skill such as a person skiing, a dancer kicking, a cheerleader jumping, etc. In discussion, point out how legs bend at the knees, and how the body bends forward, backward, and sideways. Talk about volume; indicate that the wire ought to give a sense of enclosing space. Illustrate balance. What will make an athlete fall? Lack of balance will also cause a wire sculpture to topple. Encourage some experimental positions before settling on a final one.

2. Have each child serve as her or his own model and try to create an action figure out of the wire. Urge children to plan and make some type of foot which can be fastened to the base.

3. When the figures are completed, have children nail them to the wooden bases, using the wire brads. Pound the brad in about halfway, then bend it over the part of the wire sculpture that represents the foot. Repeat this with several more brads until the figure is securely fastened to the base.

4. Display and discuss the children's work, if time permits. Children learn from each other as well as from the teacher.

Useful References

BROMMER, GERALD. *Wire Sculpture and Other Three-Dimensional Construction.* Worcester, Mass.: Davis Publications, Inc., 1968.

LIDSTONE, JOHN. *Building with Wire.* New York: Van Nostrand Reinhold Co., 1973.

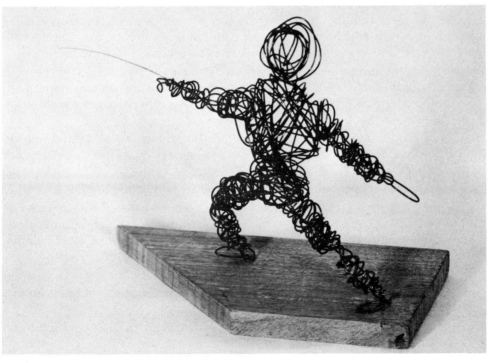

Toothpick or Coffee Stirrer Constructions

Suggested Topic   Working like engineers or architects.

Primary Objectives
- To design using a single element (toothpick, coffee stirrer) to construct a volume
- To create a three-dimensional form from a single element, with emphasis on balance

Materials/Tools

Fast-drying model cement

Wood toothpicks, coffee stirrers, paper cups, cardboard tickets, playing cards, paper clips, or any item available in quantities of the same size and shape

Electric glue gun (see below)

The Lesson

Have a discussion on how people have learned to take simple single elements and combine them into complex three-dimensional forms. Logs go together to form cabins; girders go together to form bridges and skyscrapers; boards go together to form houses, etc. With the use of one element, each child is to create a structure which can represent something, or which can simply be a new form that has no function other than its own beauty and uniqueness.

1. Demonstrate joining elements with model cement. Pieces have to be held together with the fingers until joined; or they can be laid on wax paper with edges touching. The cement must be fast drying; otherwise the construction is too slow.
2. If an electric glue gun is available, almost anything can be joined quickly and easily with this tool. Use with caution, however, as the tip is very hot and careless use may result in burns.
3. Tickets, cards, paper cups, etc., may be joined with slots, or slots and glue.
4. Let the structures grow and grow. The problem of balance will be faced as things topple. Then new solutions will come forth. Some children become so challenged by this problem that the structures rise to remarkable heights.

Useful References

Horn, George F. *Art for Today's Schools.* Worcester, Mass.: Davis Publications, Inc., 1967.

Lidstone, John. *Building with Balsa Wood.* New York: Van Nostrand Reinhold Co., 1965.

Life-Size Stuffed Paper Figures

Team Project

Suggested Topics   Dressed for a party, sports, church, cold weather, etc.

Primary Objectives
- To call attention to the details of clothing
- To lift the restrictions of small, tight, desk-size art work
- To encourage making figures with action or movement

Materials/Tools
Kraft wrapping paper cut in 10 ft. sheets
Soft lead pencils
Scissors
Stapler
Paste
Colored tempera paints
Mirrors
Newspapers

The Lesson

1. Fold each sheet of kraft wrapping paper in half so it is a 5 ft. length when double.
2. Tape the kraft paper sheets to the walls (with the fold at the top) so they reach the floor. (Or, if you have room, lay them on the floor.)
3. Have one child stand in front of a folded sheet while a second child quickly outlines his or her body, using the soft lead pencils. Advise the children to hold the arms free of the body and to separate the feet.
4. The children can work at a table or on the floor to complete details of their life-size portrait, checking their appearance in a mirror or by using a mental image.
5. Paint the figure, clothes, features; then trim away the excess paper with scissors.
6. Holding both pieces of the paper together, begin to staple the edges of the head. Lightly stuff the head by pushing crumpled newspaper through the opening at the neck. Then staple the sides of the neck, the shoulders, and part of the upper arms. Stuff any parts that have both sides stapled. Don't staple too far before stuffing. Continue to staple and stuff until the entire figure is complete.
7. Fasten completed figures to the wall all around the room on an evening when parents will visit the school.

Useful References

LEYH, ELIZABETH. *Children Make Sculpture.* New York: Van Nostrand Reinhold Co., 1975.

MEILACH, DONA Z. *Soft Sculpture and Other Soft Forms.* New York: Crown Publishers, Inc., 1974.

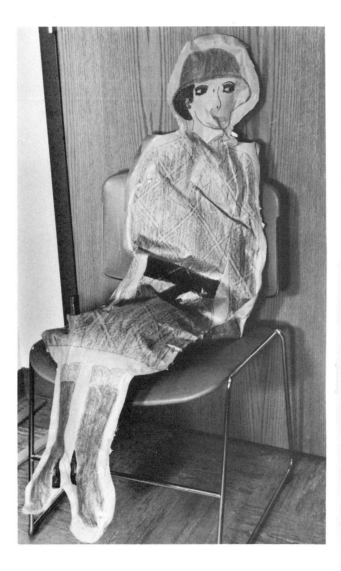

Aluminum Foil Sculpture

Suggested Topics   Beasts, birds, and bugs.

Primary Objectives
- To observe the various shapes and characteristics which combine to form the subject
- To observe the way parts relate to the whole design
- To manipulate a material not commonly used for sculpture

Materials/Tools

Aluminum foil (odds and ends and used pieces)

Newspaper

Annealed wire (any soft, flexible wire)

The Lesson

1. Decide on a range of subjects, and then look at pictures or preferably the real thing.
2. Look at the subject from the side, front, back, top, and bottom. How many ways can you look at a beetle?
3. If appendages such as long arms, wings, thin legs, etc. are needed, it may be necessary to make an armature or framework of wire before beginning to form the larger body parts with crumpled paper and foil.
4. Crumple some newspaper to form the shapes of the larger parts, then cover the parts with foil. Keep the work fairly small to conserve foil.
5. More foil is used to combine the parts. As the foil is added, the children quickly learn that it can be pressed, pinched, folded, etc. to create the desired shapes.
6. Use the last layer of foil to try to capture the texture of the bug, beast, or bird.
7. How can these sculptures be best displayed? Talk it over and set up an exhibit.

Useful References

RASMUSSEN, HENRY, and GRANT, ART. *Sculpture from Junk.* New York: Van Nostrand Reinhold Co., 1967.

TRITTEN, GOTTFRIED. *Art Techniques for Children.* New York: Van Nostrand Reinhold Co., 1964.

Cardboard Animals

Suggested Topics   Zoo animals, domestic animals, pets, insects, etc.

Primary Objectives
- To improve the ability to perceive and recall
- To pay attention to details
- To understand the concept of volume

Materials/Tools

Cardboard pieces, approximately 8″ × 10″, 3 per child

Metal snips (sometimes called tin snips or plate shears)

Scissors

Mat knives (X-Acto or similar)

Tempera paint and brushes

The Lesson

1. Prepare in advance one profile view of a horse cut from cardboard (Figure A). As you talk with the children about animals and how they look, show them this one; then try to make it stand. Since it won't, ask the children why it won't. Why can a deer stand on such tiny feet? Because it has four legs and they are spread apart, giving a broad supporting base. How can we make the cardboard horse stand?

2. Prepare in advance a front view of the horse's shoulders, body, and two legs (Figure B) and a back view of its rump and back legs (Figure C).

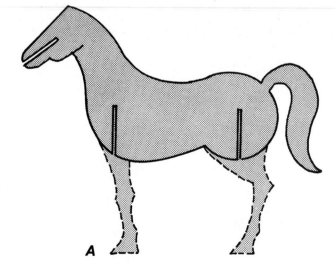

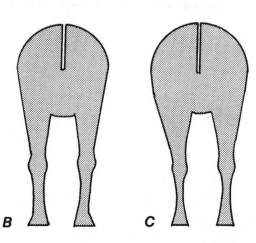

A   B   C

3. Cut the legs away from the first two-dimensional example, leaving only the body, neck, and head (Figure A).
4. With the tin snips, make a cut about halfway up the front part of the horse's body and another halfway up the back part (Figure A).
5. Make a cut about halfway down the frontal view between the shoulders (Figure B) and one halfway down the rear view, bisecting the rump (Figure C).
6. Slip the two pieces into place and the horse stands securely (Figure D).
7. Now, what other part might be added? We can cut a front view of the horse's face and ears, make a slit in it, and slip it on the profile head (Figure E).
8. Every animal will have a different set of problems and solutions. Look carefully at pictures of rhinos, hippos, giraffes, caterpillars, lizards. You'll find others in the Visual Alphabet (see Appendix). Choose an animal and make it three-dimensional from flat cardboard.
9. Paint the animals and show them off.

Useful References

ASPDEN, GEORGE. *Model Making*. New York: Van Nostrand Reinhold Co., 1964.
LIDSTONE, JOHN. *Building with Cardboard*. New York: Van Nostrand Reinhold Co., 1965.

Mobiles

Primary Objectives

- To use the principle of balance in a three-dimensional object
- To create a balanced form which moves in response to air currents
- To use materials selectively and imaginatively

Materials/Tools

Lightweight springy wire
Nylon thread and needle
White glue
Styrofoam balls, cubes, plates, meat trays, etc.
Scissors
Mat knife (X-Acto or similar)

The Lesson

The development of the mobile as a sculptural form has been credited to Alexander Calder, a leading American sculptor of the twentieth century. Many cultures have attached or hung lightweight objects such as feathers to larger objects to add a decorative element and to obtain interest through movement. Calder combined balance, movement, and color to create sculpture that appears lightweight, although it is not, and that moves and dances through space as a result of air movement. Calder wanted his art to be playful and enjoyable.

In making classroom mobiles the unfortunate tendency is to abandon the principles of balance and movement and simply hang clusters of objects from a stiff support such as a coat hanger. Avoid this.

1. Cut a length of wire about 8 to 10 inches long. Push a small ball or cube of Styrofoam onto each end of the wire.

2. Find the point along the wire where it balances the Styrofoam objects. Put a dab of glue on that point and wrap, then tie an 18-inch nylon thread to the spot. Suspend the wire by the thread to see if it balances. If it doesn't, move the Styrofoam until it does.

3. Take another wire, add Styrofoam objects at each end, and attach (glue and tie) a thread at their balance point. Tie this thread to the balance point on the first wire. Suspend the whole thing from the top thread and adjust the balance. You now have a simple mobile that balances and moves (Figure A).

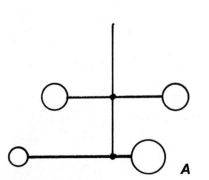

A

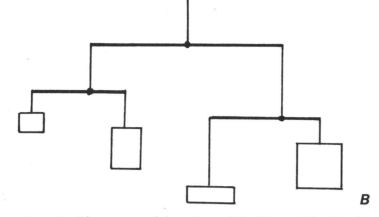

B

4. Now experiment with a more elaborate mobile (Figure B). Cut flat shapes out of Styrofoam plates or meat trays. Using a needle and nylon thread, pierce the edge of each piece and attach a 12-inch length of thread. By this thread hang a Styrofoam piece to one end of an 8- to 10-inch wire. Tie another shape to the other end of the wire. Now find the point along the wire where one Styrofoam shape balances the other. Attach a 15-inch thread at that point. Repeat this with two more shapes and a second wire.

5. Take a third wire about 15 to 20 inches long. To one end attach the balance-point thread from one assembled set of Styrofoam objects. Tie the second set by its thread to the opposite end of the wire. Hold up the wire from which both assembled sets are now suspended. Find the balance point and attach a 10- to 12-inch thread. Suspend the entire mobile by that thread. Everything should balance and move freely.

6. Additional parts may be attached, as long as matching weights are added to the opposite ends of each wire. The Styrofoam shapes may be colored in many ways, either before being attached or when the mobile is complete.

7. Thumbtack the mobiles to the ceiling by their main thread, and enjoy the playful movements.

Useful References

ANDREWS, MICHAEL. *Sculpture and Ideas.* Englewood Cliffs, N.J.: Prentice-Hall, Inc., 1965.

D'AMICO, VICTOR, and BUCHMAN, ARLETTE. *Assemblage.* New York: Museum of Modern Art, 1972.

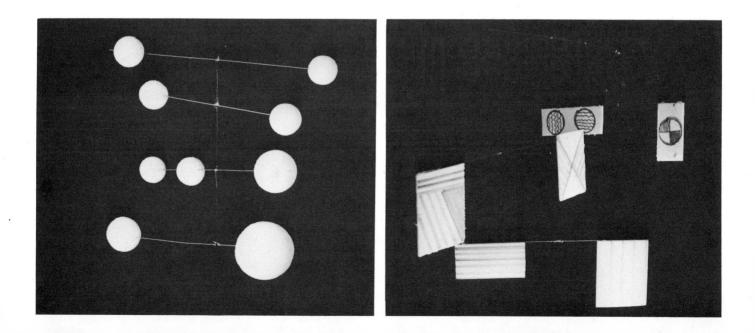

Folded Paper Buildings

Suggested Topic   Our house, our neighborhood.

Primary Objectives
- To increase the ability to perceive and recall details
- To develop an understanding of volume
- To create a three-dimensional object from flat paper

Materials/Tools

Strips of construction paper, approximately 3″ × 18″

Scissors

Pencils

Paste

Watercolors, felt-tip markers, crayons

Transparent tape

The Lesson

1. Talk about the building you are in. How many sides does it have, how many corners, how many floors, how many windows?
2. Talk about our homes. Can you remember what your house looks like from the front? Is the back different? Is it made of brick or wood? Are there many windows or few? Does it have a porch? And so on.
3. Give each child a 3″ × 18″ piece of paper and have them fold it in half so it is now 3″ × 9″. Fold it again and now the paper is divided into four equal panels, each measuring 3″ × 4½″ (Figure A).

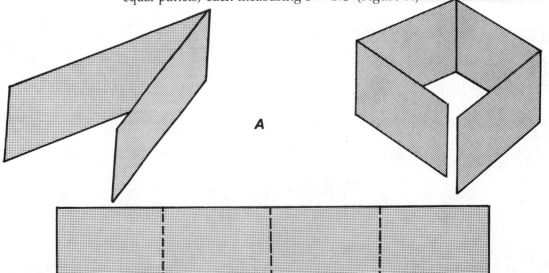

A

B

4. Have the children recall the front of their house and draw that on the first panel on the left of the paper.

5. When that is completed, tell them to imagine that they have gone to the right side of the house. Remember what that looks like and draw it on the second panel.

6. Now imagine going to the back of the house. Remember what that is like and draw it on the third panel. Draw the other side of the house on the last panel (Figure B).

7. Suggest that the children color these drawings with watercolors, felt-tip markers, or crayons.

8. When the coloring is completed, fold the panels to form a square, and tape the two end edges together with transparent tape so that the house now stands alone and encloses space (Figure C). A roof is optional. If the children want to make a roof, encourage them to do so.

9. Group all of the houses together to form a friendly neighborhood.

C

Useful References

MONTGOMERY, CHANDLER. *Art for Teachers of Children.* Columbus, Ohio: Charles E. Merrill, 1968.

TROGLER, GEORGE E. *Beginning Experiences in Architecture: A Guide for the Elementary School Teacher.* New York: Van Nostrand Reinhold Co., 1972.

TEXTILES 5

*The object of teaching a child is
to enable him to get along
without his teacher.*

ELBERT HUBBARD

Background Information about Textiles

How or when people first began to create textiles will probably remain a mystery. Through carbon dating, scientists have found evidence of basket weaving as far back as 5000 B.C. But archeologists and anthropologists can only speculate on the steps that led to the making of actual textiles as they are known today. Undoubtedly the struggle to survive in a hostile environment caused early humans to seek some means of covering their bodies as protection from the cold, and it is likely that they began to use the furs and skins of animals for this purpose. In time they invented ways to attach one skin to another. This attaching probably took the form of primitive sewing by making a long, thin strip of skin and passing it through holes in each of the hides to be joined.

Weaving most likely came out of the need for a means to store and carry foodstuffs. By intertwining flexible natural fibers such as branches, rushes, or grass, it was possible to create some form of woven basket. From the layers of rubbish which have lain untouched for thousands of years, scientists have determined that as early as the Stone Age, man had discovered the principle of weaving.

With the domestication of animals, people started to maintain herds of deer, goats, and sheep to provide food and clothing. Somewhere back in history people learned to remove the fur from animals and then spin the hairs into thread. Later on, many thousands of years ago, they wove the thread into fabric. Long before the birth of Christ, in Egypt, India, Norway, Peru, and China, people had mastered the art of weaving and were making fine textiles of wool, linen, cotton, and silk. In the dry areas of Egypt, China, and Peru, many fine examples of textiles have been discovered intact in ancient tombs and grave sites, where they have not suffered the ravages of moisture, wear, light, or polution.

Only three hundred years ago the people who colonized America were forced to learn to spin their own yarns from sheep wool and to learn from the Indians to make dyes from natural materials. In those days every household had its spinning wheel, and most households owned a homemade loom for weaving cloth. A weaving industry grew quickly in New England to provide much-needed cloth for the independent colonists.

Today most fabric is produced by machine in high-speed industrial factories. However, there is a serious and talented group of craftsmen who still produce textiles by hand, using the same simple methods that have been used for thousands of years. Science and industry have done astonishing things to improve the production of textiles, but the creative craftsperson working alone on a hand loom or with needle and yarn continues to create equally astonishing works of art with fibers.

Weaving, stitchery, appliqué, dyeing, and other textile crafts are just as important today as mediums of creative expression as they were in ages past. Fibers and textiles offer an opportunity for creative exploration and production using texture, color, line, and shape to develop a unique means of expression for the child and the artist alike.

Cardboard Loom Purse

Primary Objectives

- To learn about weaving as a craft linking many cultures
- To learn the basic principles of weaving
- To learn to follow directions carefully

Materials/Tools

Cardboard pieces about 5″ × 8″ or 6″ × 9″ (one for each child)

Rulers

Pencils

Scissors

Weaver's warp or kite string (13 yards per child), wound on individual cards or spools

Yarns

Tongue depressor shuttles or needles with very large eyes

Masking or transparent tape

The Lesson

This project may be started in class and worked on intermittently or taken home to complete. It utilizes the weaving process as practiced for thousands of years, yet permits experimentation.

Making the Loom. Start everyone together with clear, specific instructions. Demonstrate the difficult steps. If the loom is not properly made, success is not likely.

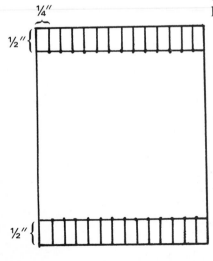

1. Give each child a piece of cardboard and a ruler. Let the children decide which shape their purse will be—long or wide—and hold the cardboard either horizontally or vertically.
2. Rule a line one-half inch from the top edge of the cardboard and another line one-half inch from the bottom edge. These lines are called *margins*.
3. Starting on the left edge, make marks one-quarter inch apart along the entire length of the top margin (Figure A).
4. Move the ruler down and do exactly the same thing on the bottom margin.
5. Place the ruler along the first ¼″ mark, top and bottom. Rule a line from the top edge to the top margin and from the bottom margin to the bottom edge.
6. Do the same thing with the second and third marks, etc., continuing until the entire margin, top and bottom, is divided by lines one-quarter inch apart.

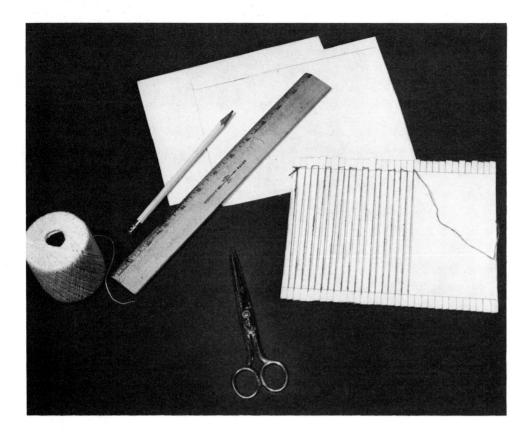

7. With scissors, cut along these lines from the edge to the margin, both top and bottom.

8. Distribute the warp (string).

9. Now comes the tricky part. Everyone watches and follows the teacher's demonstration and explanation! Taking the end of the string, loop it around the first cut at the top left and knot it in place, with the spool of string in front.

10. Bring the string down to the first cut on the bottom left. Run it into the cut and bring it up the back. Run it into the first cut. You have made a trip completely around the cardboard loom and are back where you started!

11. Carry the string over to the right and run it through the second cut at the top. Now the string is on the back of the loom. Carry it down to the bottom and put it in the second cut. That puts the string on the front again. Carry it up and go into the second cut again. Another round trip! That places the string on the back again. This time carry it over to the third cut on the back. Run it through the cut, and once again the string is on the front. Down to cut #3 on the bottom, up the back to #3, through #3 to the front. Carry it over to #4, through it, down the back, and so on.

12. When the last cuts are reached and the warp run through them, one more thing must be done. Because there is a warp on the front to match every one on the back, an even number exists. This loom needs an *uneven* number. So wherever the last "round trip" ended, carry the warp down one more time and tie it off on the last bottom tab. That should be diagonally opposite the starting point. This causes two warp threads to exist on that spot. Now there are an uneven number of warp threads.

13. Run masking or transparent tape across the front and back of both rows of tabs so the tabs will not break off during the weaving process.

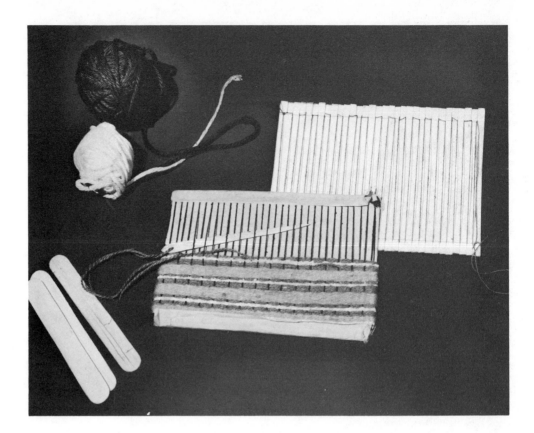

Weaving the Weft. The weaving tool can be made by splitting a tongue depressor lengthwise, sharpening one end to a point, and drilling a hole in the opposite end. Or you may use a large embroidery or darning needle.

14. Thread about one yard of yarn into the needle or tongue depressor shuttle. Starting about the middle of the bottom, run the yarn under three or four warp threads; then begin to go over, under, over, under, etc.

15. When the edge is reached, remember whether the last warp was over or under. Turn the loom over and keep on going across the back in the same sequence.

16. When the double warp is reached, treat it as two separate warp threads. Go over one, under the other, or vice versa, depending on the sequence when you reach it.

17. The uneven number of warp threads will automatically cause the sequence to be reversed on the second trip around. That is, this time "overs" will be "unders," and "unders" will be "overs." If that does not happen, a warp thread probably was missed somewhere in the weaving. Don't panic—go over two or under two (not both), and pick up the under, over, under, sequence again.

18. After several rows the yarn (weft) comes to its end. Tuck the final inch under three or four warps. Cut a new yard length of yarn and run it under three or four warps, as when starting. Pick up the sequence where you left off.

19. After five or six rows are completed, front and back, use the fingers or a comb to pack the rows of weft tightly together. Do this at regular intervals for a tightly woven purse that will not expose the warp.

20. Change colors as your design demands. Try some variations: over two, under one, over two, under one, etc. Do 12 or 15 rows in a changed sequence, and it will begin to have a new texture.

21. When the top is reached, pack the weft together as tightly as possible, using fingers or the tines of a fork or comb. Complete the last few trips around with a needle rather than the tongue depressor shuttle.

22. Remove the tape; then tear off the tabs, one by one. Gently loosen the loops at the top so that the cardboard will slip out. The top is open; the bottom is closed!

23. Add a lining and a zipper or snaps, and you have a lovely handwoven clutch purse. A simple braided strap may be added as a modification.

Useful References

CREAGER, CLARE. *Weaving: A Creative Approach for Beginners.* New York: Doubleday & Co., 1974.

RAINEY, SARITA R. *Weaving without a Loom.* Worcester, Mass., Davis Publications, Inc., 1966.

Embroidery or Mock Weaving on Burlap

Suggested Topic   A new interpretation of a crayon drawing.

Primary Objectives
• To learn to adapt ideas to a new process
• To develop imaginative interpretations with fibers

Materials/Tools
Burlap, cotton mesh, or onion bags
Small, picture frames or embroidery hoops
Felt-tip pens
Embroidery needles
Cotton or wool yarn
Stapler
Cardboard or construction paper
Masking tape

The Lesson
This project requires a small frame or set of embroidery hoops for each child, so you may have to work with a few children at a time.

1. Save several drawings from each child which have large, well-defined images of a house, boat, car, tree, cat, person, etc. With the child, decide on one of these to be interpreted by embroidery.

2. Stretch burlap or cotton mesh across a small picture frame and staple it in place; alternately, secure between embroidery hoops.

3. Have the child sketch the image onto the burlap, using a felt-tip pen.

4. Thread a blunt needle and demonstrate on a practice fabric how to go over, under, over, under, etc. Then reverse the next line.

5. On a piece prepared for demonstration, draw a simple image, such as an animal, with a felt-tip pen. Demonstrate a running stitch that follows the outline. Go under one thread then over two, under one and over two, etc., until the outline is complete. If the figure has details or parts, draw them and then outline them in the same way. Perhaps some parts lend themselves to being filled in with stitches that go back and forth until the area is solidly filled.

6. Have the children begin to outline their drawings. Encourage them to stitch the details and to fill in open areas.

7. Cut mats from cardboard or construction paper and attach the embroideries with masking tape.

Useful References

LANE, ROSE WILDER. *Book of American Needlework.* New York: Simon and Schuster, 1963.

RAINEY, SARITA R. *Weaving without a Loom.* Worcester, Mass.: Davis Publications, Inc., 1966.

Box Loom Weaving

Primary Objectives
- To learn the basic principles of weaving
- To use fibers creatively to make a small fabric
- To learn some of the vocabulary and history of weaving
- To recognize textiles as a universal art form

Materials/Tools
Frame

Ball of cotton string for warp

Yarns, fibers for weft

Scissors

Nails

Hammer

Tongue depressor shuttles

Mat knife (X-Acto or similar)

Sandpaper

The Lesson
This project allows children to experience the basic method of weaving as used for thousands of years to create fabric by means of interlocking fibers or threads. Give a short explanation of weaving to the entire class even though only one child at a time can use the loom.

Making the Box Loom
1. Construct, or have constructed, a simple frame of soft wood, approximately 15″ × 20″. Stretchers used to attach canvas for oil painting are excellent. The stretchers must be nailed or glued so they remain rigid.
2. Across the shorter ends, hammer in ¾″ finishing nails at half-inch intervals.
3. Attach the warp string to one of the corner nails, stretch the string to the opposite end, and go around two nails. Return to the opposite end and go around two nails, back to the opposite end, and so on.
4. Tie the warp onto the last nail that remains

Weaving
5. The weaving can be done with the fingers or with a shuttle made by splitting a tongue depressor lengthwise and drilling a hole in one end. Smooth

the edges with a mat knife and sandpaper. The shuttle guides the weft over and under the warp.

6. Select a colored yarn, cut about a one-yard length, and thread it through the hole in the tongue depressor shuttle.

7. Begin to weave at one end, going over, under, over, under, the warp until you reach the opposite side. Carefully pull the weft across, leaving about one inch hang out from the starting edge.

8. Reverse the direction of weaving, going around the last warp thread. Be careful not to pull the weft so that it distorts the parallel warp threads.

9. On the return, the weft goes under each warp thread that it went over during the first trip across, and it goes over each warp thread that it first went under.

10. When the beginning side is reached, go around the last warp thread and reverse direction. By this time the principle of weaving will begin to be evident.

11. Change colors and textures as the design calls for, or simply experiment randomly to see what happens.

12. When the loom is full and the weaving completed, carefully release the warp threads by slipping them over the nails.

Useful References

BIRRELL, VERLA. *The Textile Arts.* New York: Harper & Row, Publishers, Inc., 1959.

WILSON, JEAN. *Weaving Is Fun.* New York: Van Nostrand Reinhold Co., 1970.

Trapunto Pillow Cover

Suggested Topics A self-portrait. A cat, bird, flower, insect, etc.

Primary Objectives
- To plan a multi-step design
- To create an aesthetic but utilitarian object
- To recognize textiles as a universal form of art

Materials/Tools
Fabric squares 14″ to 18″. For the front use thin, smooth, plain colored shirt weight (cotton, muslin, percale). For the back use any sewable fabric, since it will not be seen.

Padding: polyester or cotton batting

Small toss pillows, if available

Pencils or dressmaker's chalk

Needles and thread

Straight pins

Scissors

The Lesson

If children can bring in a small discarded toss pillow, use it. Adapt the fabric size and shape to fit the pillow. Otherwise decide upon a size between 14 and 18 inches square.

1. First plan a simple design on paper, essentially a contour drawing of the subject (portrait, animal, flower, etc.). Work to get the design to fill in and fit the square. Don't be afraid to let children look at photographs. They can't copy; they can only interpret them. Get good designs! Help the children to simplify their design through discussion.

2. Sketch or trace the design very lightly on the top fabric with a pencil or, on darker fabric, with dressmaker's chalk.

3. Using thread that matches the color of the fabric, stitch along the outline of the design with small, tight stitches. The stitches should go through the two layers of fabric, holding them together while creating a visible outline of the design.

4. When the stitching is completed, the design is ready to be stuffed. A small scissor cut is made in the back fabric within the stitched outlines of a section of the design. Stuff polyester or cotton batting into the hole, pushing it in with a small stick or watercolor brush handle. When the portion of the design looks puffed out, stitch the hole to close it.

5. Fill all the design areas with padding. Any additional details can be sewn through the fabrics and the padding.

6. The finished trapunto cover is now ready to be attached to the pillow. This can be done by simply sewing it on to the existing face of the pillow or by using another piece of fabric of equal size to make a complete pillow cover. If circumstances permit, enlist the aid of class parents to finish the covers on sewing machines at home.

Useful References

MEILACH, DONA Z. *Creating Art from Fibers and Fabrics.* Chicago: Henry Regnery Co., 1973.

MORGAN, MARY, and MOSTELLER, DEE. *Trapunto and Other Forms of Raised Quilting.* New York: Charles Scribner's Sons, 1977.

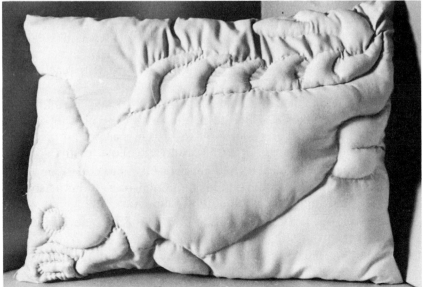

Appliqué Wall Hanging
Group Project

Suggested Topics   Vegetables from the garden. My house. A forest. Fruits.

Primary Objectives
- To compose a design from fabric pieces in a group situation
- To allow each individual to construct a segment of the whole design
- To learn the craft of appliqué and to appreciate it as a universal art form

Materials/Tools
Paper and pencils
A variety of scrap fabrics gathered by teacher, parents, children
Felt scraps
Rick-rack
Straight pins
Needles, yarn, thread
Scissors
Muslin or old bed sheets cut into 12" × 12" squares
Large backing sheet of muslin or other fabric

The Lesson
Appliqué is the process of creating a design by sewing or gluing one material onto another. This favorite American craft (also popular in many other countries) developed because our ancestors couldn't bear to see scraps of fabric go to waste. The appliqué process allows the designer to use curves and straight lines to create images with cloth in the way a painter creates images with brush and paint.

1. Plan a large wall hanging for the classroom, with each child having a square to complete.
2. Each child decides upon one image to portray—a building, person, or event—and makes a sketch to fit the size of the muslin square. Have the children make paper patterns of the larger parts. The patterns should be about one-quarter inch larger all around to allow for the seam.
3. Using scrap fabrics, each child cuts out pieces to correspond with the parts of the sketch. Things have to be simplified—a fact that is soon discovered. Designs change to accommodate the new material.
4. If possible, turn the edges under and press flat before pinning the pieces to the muslin square.
5. Pin the largest pieces onto the muslin square first.

6. Demonstrate how to thread a needle (a threading device is helpful) and how to stitch the edges onto the muslin.

7. Sew, sew, sew.

8. When all the squares are completed, let the children decide how they would like them to be assembled for the hanging.

9. With the help of a parent and a portable sewing machine, sew all the squares together. Attach the hanging to a backing sheet, and machine stitch between the squares. For greater effect, add a solid border of an appropriate color around the entire hanging.

10. Display the completed hanging on a wall by means of thumbtacks, push pins, or staples. It will be a source of pride and admiration for everyone.

Useful References

BIRRELL, VERLA. *The Textile Arts.* New York: Harper & Row, Publishers, Inc., 1959.

LANE, ROSE WILDER. *Book of American Needlework.* New York: Simon and Schuster, 1963.

Embroidery Emblem

Suggested Topic   My mark, symbol, emblem: This stands for me.

Primary Objectives
- To learn the craft of decorating with needle and thread
- To become familiar with examples of needlework as an art form
- To learn to work over longer periods of time and to persist until a task is complete

Materials/Tools
Denim or other solid colored fabric, about 10" × 10"
Paper and pencils
Embroidery hoops, 8" diameter
Dressmaker's carbon
Cotton embroidery floss, six-strand
Straight pins
Crewel needles
Scissors
Steam iron

The Lesson
Except for early and primitive societies where little clothing was worn, almost every culture has used needlework to add interest to fabrics. This project will make a personalized embroidered emblem that can be used to adorn a shirt, blouse, etc.

Anyone who can thread a needle and push it through fabric is capable of some form of decorative embroidery. For the advanced embroiderer, dozens of different stitches may be used. For the beginner, any stitch that shows up and covers is enough. Practice a few basic stitches before beginning the lesson.

1. Prepare designs, each child making his or her personal symbol. Start with a small design, 3 to 4 inches in diameter.
2. Pin the design over dressmaker's carbon and trace it firmly with a pencil onto the fabric. Be sure the fabric is large enough to be held with the embroidery hoops.
3. Demonstrate a few simple stitches such as outline stitch, lazy daisy, satin stitch, running stitch (see Figures A to D).

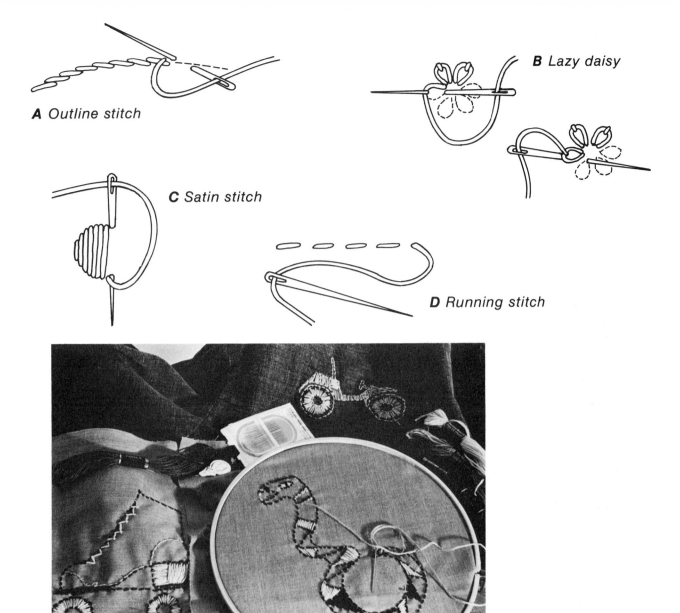

A Outline stitch

B Lazy daisy

C Satin stitch

D Running stitch

4. Let the children make some practice stitches on fabric scraps.
5. Begin to embroider. As occasion arises, discuss ways to stitch for better coverage.
6. Trim away excess fabric from around the finished design, leaving only about one-half inch of fabric extending beyond the embroidery design.
7. Fold most of the excess under and press with a steam iron to get a sharp edge.
8. Using a needle and thread, sew the emblems on a shirt, jacket, or pair of jeans.

Useful References

ENTHOVEN, JACQUELINE. *Stitchery for Children: A Manual for Teachers, Parents and Children.* New York: Van Nostrand Reinhold Co., 1964.

LANE, ROSE WILDER. *Book of American Needlework.* New York: Simon and Schuster, 1963.

Wax Crayon Batik

Suggested Topics   Things that live in the ocean. Things that fly through the air. Things that crawl on the ground.

Primary Objectives

- To work in materials that afford only partial control of the final product
- To appreciate "accidental" effects and learn how to repeat them
- To recognize batik and appreciate the craft as a universal art form

Materials/Tools

Wax crayons

Cardboards

Plain unprinted cotton fabric pieces, 10″×12″ (preferably used), white or a light color

Commercial dye, dark color

Bucket or container for the dye bath

Newspapers

Electric iron

The Lesson

Wax crayons when applied heavily to fabric will resist dyes in the same way that hot wax applied in the traditional batik methods of Indonesia, China, and India resists dye. This method avoids the problems of working with hot wax.

1. Stretch the fabric over a piece of cardboard and secure with tape.
2. Have the children draw directly with wax crayons onto the fabric, making sure that the crayon is applied in an extraheavy manner. Weak or light pressure on the crayon will not put down enough of a coating to prevent the dye from coloring those areas.
3. Use the crayons only where the major images are to remain, allowing the other areas to remain open and ready to accept the dye.
4. The teacher must prepare a dye bath in advance. One dark color in a bucket should be enough. Spread several layers of newspapers on the floor next to the sink and place the bucket on them.
5. When the crayoning is completed, the fabric is submerged in the dye bath until the dye has saturated all uncrayoned areas. The fabric looks darker when wet, so often additional dyeing time is necessary to get a really intense color. *Always follow the manufacturer's directions.*

6. When the dyeing is completed, the fabric is rinsed in cold running water until little color comes from the fabric. Rinse in warm soapy water and hang to dry.

7. With a warm iron, press the design between layers of newspaper. This will remove most of the wax from the crayon, leaving a residue of color in the fabric.

Useful References

BELFER, NANCY. *Designing in Batik and Tie Dye.* Worcester, Mass.: Davis Publications, Inc., 1972.

KREVITSKY, NIK. *Batik Art and Craft.* New York: Van Nostrand Reinhold Co., 1976.

Textile Marker Design on Shirts

Suggested Topics Vehicles I like to ride. Sports I like to watch. Animals I like to touch.

Primary Objectives

- To plan a personal design that can serve as an emblem or symbol to be worn on clothing
- To simplify the design so it can be interpreted with felt-tip textile markers and still retain its identity

Materials/Tools

Textile markers
T-shirt or plain cotton or synthetic blend shirt
Cardboard
Electric iron (optional)

The Lesson

Textile markers come in various colors and apply easily to fabric in a manner similar to other felt-tip pens. They are easy to handle and make a strong, indelible mark. Because they apply easily, the designs might be adapted almost directly from drawings or paintings made earlier, or a new design can be developed specifically for this project.

1. Stretch the shirt over a cardboard and fasten the buttons. If using a T-shirt, slip cardboard into the shirt.
2. Draw directly onto the fabric, using the painting or drawing as the model. It is a good idea to sketch the entire design in a light color which can later be covered with a darker color. This way minor slips are not noticeable.
3. Finish the design with darker colors. Work the color into the fibers by slowly building up color, using repeated marking with light pressure rather than one heavy marking.
4. Allow the designs to dry thoroughly. Pressing with a warm iron helps set the colors and makes them stay bright longer. This is optional.

Useful References

LAVOOS, JANICE. *Design Is a Dandelion.* San Carlos, Calif.: Golden Gate Junior Books, 1966.

LINDERMAN, EARL W. *Invitation to Vision: Ideas and Imaginations for Art.* Dubuque, Iowa: Wm. C. Brown Company Publishers, 1967.

Tie-Dye and Mark Wall Hanging

Suggested Topic   What does this remind me of?

Primary Objectives

- To design combining some controls and some "accidents"
- To find ways to create varieties of designs through discovering different tying arrangements and the way colors are used

Materials/Tools

Clean white cotton fabric squares, approximately 20″ × 20″ (synthetic fabrics will not hold the dyes satisfactorily)

Twine

Commerical fabric dyes (Rit, etc.) in primary colors

3 large plastic buckets for dye baths

Felt-tip pens (Marks-A-Lot, etc.)

Newspapers

Electric iron (optional)

The Lesson

1. Demonstrate the tie-dyeing process with several examples. Begin by grasping the fabric at its center. About an inch down from the point, wrap it securely with twine and then tie it. Move down the fabric an inch or so and wind more twine around that section, making sure the wrapping is very tight; then tie it.

2. Spread out the unwrapped fabric and grasp it by one corner. Move down several inches from the corner and tightly wrap with twine. Repeat on all corners.

3. Dip a portion of the tied off fabric into one color for a short time. Remove it and let the excess drip off.

4. Put another portion of tied fabric into a second color. Remove it and let the excess drip off.

5. Dip a portion of the remaining tied fabric into the third color. Remove and drip. It is important not to dip an already dyed section of fabric back into another color, because this would diminish the intensity of the color and make it "muddy." Be sure to stress this point.

6. Allow the tie-dyed squares to dry for at least two days. Then cut and remove the twine and unfold the fabric.

7. If an iron is available, press the squares, then stretch them on cardboard or lay them flat on newspapers.

8. Have each child use a felt-tip pen to add whatever seems appropriate to make these somewhat similar designs become highly personal ones.

9. Teach the children to sew a simple hem or call on some parents to sew hems on sewing machines at home.

10. Fasten each finished square along the top to a small stick, and use them as wall hangings.

Useful References

BELFER, NANCY. *Designing in Batik and Tie Dye.* Worcester, Mass.: Davis Publications, Inc., 1972.

HARTUNG, ROLF. *More Creative Textile Design: Color and Texture.* New York: Van Nostrand Reinhold Co., 1964.

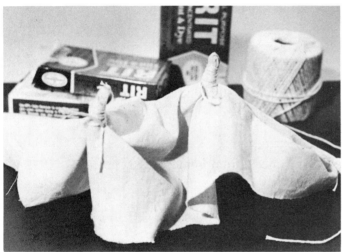

Stenciling on Fabric

Suggested Topics Making an abstraction using geometric shapes. A floral design. Fruits. Insects.

Primary Objectives
- To learn to simplify or abstract designs from nature
- To learn the craft of hand stenciling
- To carefully plan and execute a simple stenciled design and apply it to fabric

Materials/Tools
Drawing paper

Waxed stencil paper, or backing sheets from mimeograph stencils

Stencil brushes

Water-soluble textile paints

Muslin cut into 15" squares

Cardboards

Mat knives (X-Acto or similar)

Masking tape or straight pins

The Lesson
Since this may be a first experience in stenciling on fabric, take the time to explain and demonstrate each step.

1. Draw a simple design with at least three shapes on a piece of drawing paper. These shapes may overlap each other but overlapping isn't essential.
2. Place the design on a cardboard surface and lay the stencil paper over it. If the stencil paper is not transparent, sketch the largest shape directly on the stencil paper.
3. With the X-Acto knife, cut around the edges of the shape until the section can be removed.
4. On the remaining stencil paper (or on a fresh sheet), outline and then cut out the second shape.
5. Repeat the process with the third shape. If more than one shape is cut from the same piece of paper, allow plenty of space between openings.
6. Stretch muslin cloth over the piece of cardboard that was used as a cutting surface, and pin or tape it in place.
7. Put a small dab of the first color on a scrap of stencil paper; dip the bristles of the stencil brush in it and practice brushing on a piece of scrap paper.

8. Place the first stencil over the fabric. Hold it in place with the fingers of one hand. Begin to brush gently from the outside edge of the design toward the center. Brush completely around the design, slowly building color by brushing the color over the fibers. Avoid using too much textile paint as it will smear when the next stencil is laid on it.

9. Remove the stencil for the first color and put the second stencil in place. Repeat the brushing technique with a second color. Repeat with the third stencil, using still another color.

10. Allow the stenciled fabric to dry. To set the colors, follow the instructions given for the type of textile paints used. Some of the newer paints require no additional steps and will remain quite colorfast.

Useful References

HARTUNG, ROLF. *More Creative Textile Design: Color and Texture.* New York: Van Nostrand Reinhold Co., 1964.

KAFKA, FRANCES. *The Hand Decoration of Fabrics.* Bloomington, Ill.: McKnight and McKnight Publishing Co., 1959.

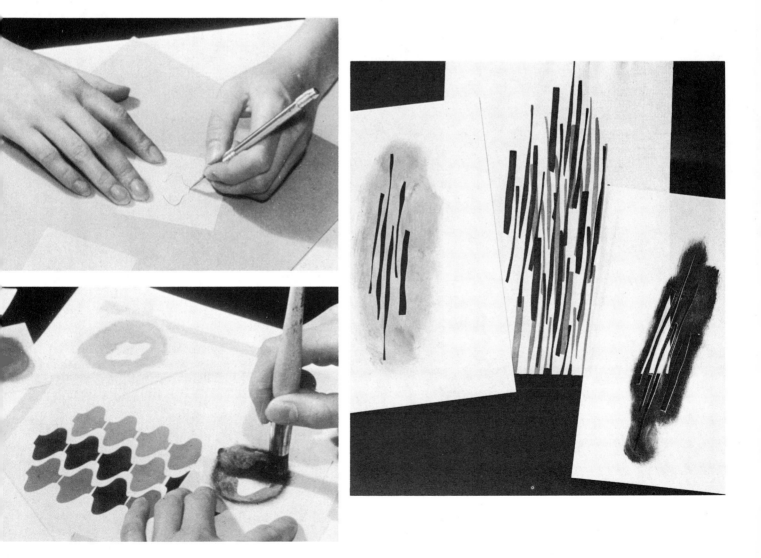

PUPPETS AND MARIONETTES

6

The Art of Puppetry

A puppet is a small-scale figure of a person or animal, usually hollow, and manipulated by the hand or fingers. The word *puppet* is derived from the French word *poupée*, meaning doll. A marionette, one form of puppet, is usually a complete figure with arms and legs, normally manipulated by strings from above. These basic distinctions do not take into account the wide array of puppets and marionettes that do not fall precisely within one category or the other.

Puppets and marionettes have been used for centuries to present various types of theatrical performances in Europe and Asia. The earliest known written record of puppets and marionettes dates to the fifth century B.C. in Greece, but there are also ancient traditions of puppetry in China, Java, and India. Even among the American Indians a form of puppetry was used in ritual ceremonies.

The essence of puppets and marionettes is the fact that they replace live actors. The viewers know it is theatre; it is make-believe. Because of this sense of unreality, puppets can do outrageous things that actors may not or will not do. In the old Punch and Judy shows, for example, Punch was always beating Judy over the head with a club, and would often throw the baby out the window.

Some puppets and marionettes are so intricately made as to be almost life-like. Yet many of the best puppets ever made were quite crude, capturing only the most elementary qualities of the character they portrayed. The Indonesian shadow puppets and the parchment cut-out puppets of Thailand are very stylized and, in both countries, puppetry is a superior art form.

Other puppets are equally admired when their accuracy in detail makes them appear as miniature people or animals. People are charmed by being able to look at the world in miniature.

The modern puppet as most people know it evolved in Italy, where it was used for religious drama. Later, in addition to religious drama, puppets were used in satirical plays and to enact tales of chivalry and comedy. Puppets gained such popularity that some of the finest writers and artists began to write the plays and to carve and costume the figures. The great composer Haydn wrote music for five marionette operettas for the private theatre in the palace of Prince Esterhazy.

In this country puppets have been used largely for the entertainment of children. A generation ago children (and grownups) were fascinated by the puppets of Burr Tillstrom. Everyone knew Kukla, Fran, and Ollie, who entered their homes through the television tube. More recently the Muppets of Jim Henson have captivated audiences throughout the world, first on Sesame Street, a children's series on public television, and later on "The Muppet Show," an adult/child program on commercial television. Interestingly, the most successful of contemporary puppet shows use live actors who interact with the puppets.

Puppets continue to hold the interest of audiences in Eastern Europe and Asia, where some puppet theatres employ as many as sixty performers and technicians. Puppets have been part of both Eastern and Western cultures for at least twenty-five centuries. It is likely that new forms will emerge and traditional forms continue to be used in the future by both professionals and amateurs, and especially by children, to act out their fantasies in a theatre of make-believe.

Using Puppets with Children

Puppets are widely used in teaching because they provide many opportunities for personal development through their designing, building, and operation. One of the great thrills a teacher can have is the

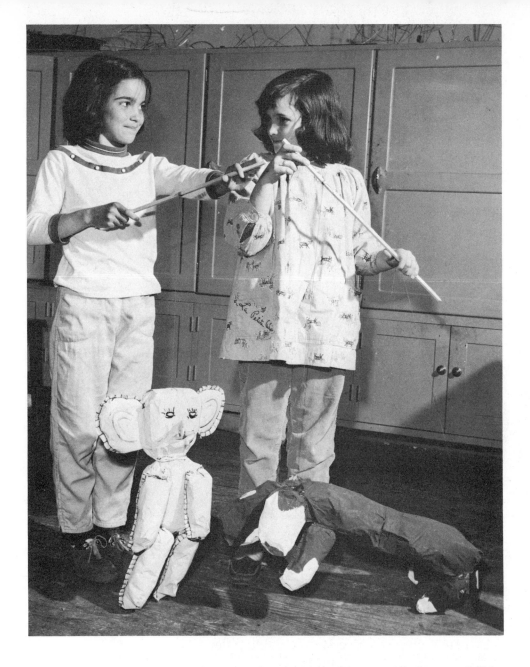

satisfaction of getting a shy or withdrawn child to open up and begin to express qualities that may not even have been suspected. Children who lack self-confidence are unable to communicate their thoughts or feelings unless they find the right medium. For them, puppetry may be the answer. In puppetry many opportunities exist for enriching a variety of educational situations. Through a puppet the child may feel free to express ideas and feelings which otherwise may remain dormant.

Speaking through puppets children also develop language skills. And working in a group they learn the significance of sharing, cooperation, teamwork, and the meaning of human interaction.

In some instances the puppet may serve as a therapeutic aid, providing that extra measure of courage which the shy child needs in order to get up before the class and say something. Using the puppet as a prop, the sensitive child may be able to take the first step forward.

As a teaching tool, puppetry can be used at every age level and in every environment, from the most elaborate to the poorest classroom facility. Great flexibility is possible. There is no set method of making or using puppets, no right or wrong way, although there may be a best way for each individual teacher or a best way considering the available resources. It is important, however, that teachers vary the methods used at different age levels and that they avoid repeating the same puppet types year after year in all grades.

Puppetry is a good means to relate creative art activities with other studies in the curriculum, such as literature and history. However, find the ways to use the imagination and creative abilities of the children. Don't begin writing scripts and directing plays in which the children become the paint and brushes used to carry out an adult's idea in the classroom.

Puppetry can turn a child's imagination on. We have all seen children pick up a stick and pretend it is a sword or rifle, or maybe a horse to ride or a spear to throw. In the same way, a puppet can turn the child into a pirate, a queen, a clown, a tiger, an astronaut, etc. Transformed via the puppet, children invent new words and new ways of speaking. If a script evolves and a show is undertaken, many skills must be coordinated: reading, remembering, speaking, acting, and learning to listen while others speak.

Puppet-making has special appeal as well as great potentials for education. Make it an activity in which everyone grows, everyone has an important part, and where whatever we produce is both "mine" and "ours."

Paper Bag Puppet

Suggested Topics   Neighbors. Somebody special. Relatives.

Primary Objectives
- To call attention to the special qualities or characteristics of individuals
- To enrich the existing style (schema) of individual children
- To use "throw away" materials in imaginative ways
- To encourage verbal expression

Materials/Tools
Brown paper bags, various sizes
Newspaper
Sticks about 20 inches long
Colored paper
Transparent tape
Scissors
Paste
Crayons

The Lesson
This is an easy first puppet which can be made in 20 to 30 minutes and then used for some spontaneous improvisations.

1. Ask the children to see how long a list they can make of face and head parts. Write them on the blackboard: eyes, ears, nose, mouth, lips, tongue, teeth, hair, nostrils, eyebrows, eyelashes, pupils, eyelids, moustache, beard, freckles, glasses, etc.

2. Everyone is going to make somebody special. What makes "our person" special—big eyeglasses, a large nose, freckles, curly hair, etc.?

3. Holding the open edge of the bag at the bottom, draw, paint, or cut and paste a special face on the bag.

4. To support the puppet head, a long "neck" is needed. If sticks are not available, roll two double pages of folded newspaper to make a tight roll about 20 inches long and 1 inch in diameter; fasten with tape to keep it from unrolling.

5. Insert the stick or the paper roll in the bag and add crumpled newspaper to fill out the bag.

6. Close the bag's opening around the paper roll and tie or tape it securely.

7. Send three children with their puppets behind a desk or the piano. Develop a situation: Two children were running across a flower garden when an old man came out and saw them. He said, "Who are you and what are you doing here?" Let the three children pick up the dialogue and carry on with it. After a few minutes, send up another group with a new situation.

8. As an alternative, for several days allow the children to make any announcements to the class using their puppets.

Useful References

CURRELL, DAVID. *Puppetry for School Children*. Newton, Mass.: Charles T. Branford Co., 1970.

SCOTT, LOUISE BINDER; MAY, MARION; and SHAW, MILDRED. *Puppets for All Grades*. Dansville, N.Y.: The Instructor Publications, Inc., 1972.

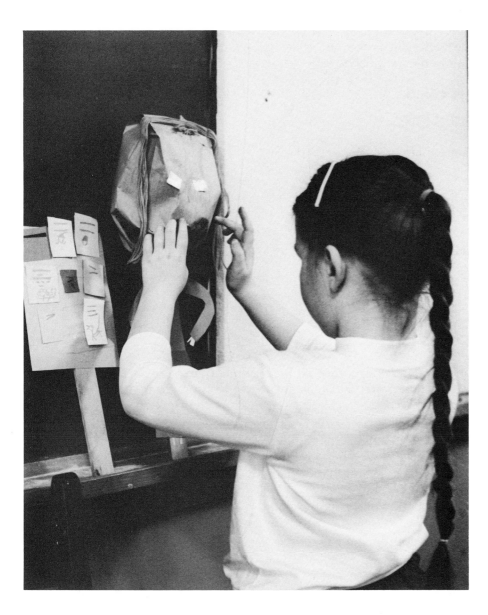

Paper Bag Marionette

Suggested Topics   A self-portrait. Grown-ups (father, mother, teacher, preacher, policeman, cowboy, etc.). Animals.

Primary Objectives

- To recognize and portray the special characteristics of individuals
- To develop richer concepts for self-expression visually and orally
- To develop manipulative skills

Materials/Tools

Paper bags of various sizes
Stapler
Transparent tape
Scissors
Large-eye darning needles
Colored paper
Paste
Kite string or twine, about 3 yards per child
Yarn
Sticks, 1″ thick, about 18″ long
Newspaper
Tempera paints and brushes

The Lesson

Marionettes differ from other puppets primarily in the way they are manipulated. Marionettes are usually suspended by strings from a stick or a combination of sticks, held from above. The marionette is given movement or action by moving the stick, or by moving the strings attached to the various part of the marionette. In this lesson large movements of the whole figure will provide all the action necessary.

1. Talk about what the marionettes are to represent. What main parts will they need? A body, head, arms, legs, etc.
2. Select a bag to serve as the body, fill it with crumpled newspaper, and neatly staple or sew it closed with yarn, using large stitches.
3. Select an appropriate bag for the head, stuff it and sew or staple it closed.
4. To make arms and legs, cut a paper bag lengthwise and sew up the open sides. Stuff and then sew or staple to close.
5. What else is needed? Cut a bag to create a nose, eyes, tail, wings, etc.

6. Attach the head, arms, and legs to the body by sewing; then paint with tempera paints. Other parts can be sewn or stapled in place and details and decorations added made from colored paper and paste or painted on with tempera paints.

7. With large-eye darning needles attach 15- to 20-inch lengths of string to the top of the head, the shoulders, the hands, and any other spot that seems appropriate. These areas can be reinforced with pieces of gummed tape before sewing, to avoid tearing the bags.

8. Tie the strings to several places on the stick which, when held horizontally, maintains the marionette in the proper position.

9. Have the children practice "walking" their marionettes across the floor. Soon the children will focus so much attention on the marionette that they will lose awareness of their own presence.

10. Plan some simple skits and perform them with the children in full view—no stage, no props, no self-consciousness.

Useful References

CURRELL, DAVID. *Puppetry for School Children.* Newton, Mass., Charles T. Branford Company, 1970.

ENGLER, HARRY, and FIJAN, CAROL. *Making Puppets Come Alive.* New York: Taplinger Publishing Company, 1973.

Paper Bag Hand Puppet

Suggested Topics   Talkers (people, animals, creatures).

Primary Objectives
- To increase oral communication and reduce self-consciousness
- To use commonplace materials in an imaginative way

Materials/Tools

Small or medium-size paper bags

Colored paper

Scissors

Paste

Scraps of yarn, straw, felt, etc.

The Lesson

1. Slip the hand into a paper bag with the fingers bent around the folded bottom portion so as to make this flap act as the puppet's mouth when the hand is opened and closed (see Figure A).
2. Have each child manipulate the bag before designing the face.
3. Using colored paper, scissors, and paste, create the face, hair, ears, hat, etc.
4. Use the puppets to enact simple, spontaneous skits; or let the puppets read aloud during the reading lesson; or let them deliver the announcements to the class from time to time.

Useful References

Editors of Sunset Books. *Children's Crafts.* Menlo Park, Calif.: Lane Publishing Co., 1976.

SCOTT, LOUISE BINDER; MAY, MARION; and SHAW, MILDRED. *Puppets for All Grades.* Dansville, N.Y.: The Instructional Publications, Inc., 1972.

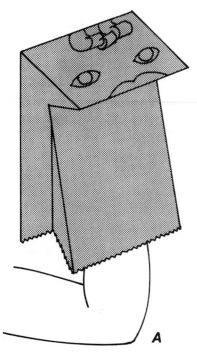

A

Stocking Puppet

Suggested Topics   Animals, people, reptiles, imaginary creatures.

Primary Objectives
- To improve oral communication and reduce self-consciousness
- To use commonplace materials in a new and creative way
- To develop skills of sewing, cutting, and manipulating

Materials/Tools

Felt squares 4" to 5"

Stockings or socks

Scissors

Needle and thread

Yarn, buttons, fabric scraps

The Lesson

The stocking puppet was popularized on television over a decade ago by Shari Lewis and her interesting, friendly characters (notably Lambchop).

1. Fold a square of felt or other heavy fabric in half, and cut it into a semi-circular shape, leaving the folded edge uncut. This piece will serve as the mouth, which the puppeteer's fingers will open and close.

2. Cut a slit in the toe of a sock, just wide enough to accommodate the folded mouth.

3. Insert the folded mouth into the slit, with the curved edges towards the toe. Using needle and thread, sew the mouth in place. Don't worry too much about precise fit, as any gathering and puckering will add character.

4. What else is needed, and what can be formed to create those parts? Some suggestions are buttons or badges for eyes, fabric for ears, yarn for hair, and so on. Maybe the creature needs spots or stripes, fur, or whiskers.

5. Although all children may receive the same instruction, their individual interpretations soon evolve and cause each puppet to be different. Don't be afraid to call attention to details, to raise questions, and to push for greater richness.

6. Children respond immediately to this puppet. Somehow it lends itself to use in the way a ventriloquist works. Children talk to their stocking puppets, and the puppets talk back in new voices.

Useful References

CURRELL, DAVID. *Puppetry for School Children.* Newton, Mass.: Charles T. Branford Company, 1970.

LATSHAW, GEORGE. *Puppetry: The Ultimate Disguise.* New York: Richard Rosen Press, 1978.

Papier-Mâché Puppet

Suggested Topic   Characters from a favorite television series.

Primary Objectives
- To plan and construct a multi-step project
- To translate images into a three-dimensional form
- To learn the values and problems of group activity

Materials/Tools

Newspaper
Construction paper
Gummed tape
Paper towels
Wallpaper paste
Plastic containers for paste and water
Fast-drying house paint
Tempera paints and brushes
Fabric for a costume
Needles and thread
Cardboard
Stapler

The Lesson

This puppet is usually constructed as part of a carefully-planned unit in which children write or interpret short plays and perform them before an audience. Puppet and costume construction usually require several concentrated work sessions plus at least one rehearsal period.

1. Divide the children into groups, each of which is to plan and present a short play or skit using themes from favorite television series. After each child has volunteered or been assigned to create one character, the children work as a class in the initial stages of constructing the puppet.

2. To begin the head, crumple a single page of newspaper into a ball about the size of a tennis ball.

3. Cut a strip of construction paper about 4×8 inches. Roll it around the middle finger to form a tube, and wrap it with moistened gummed tape. This tube is the neck of the puppet.

4. Cut four strips of gummed tape about 12 to 15 inches long. Moisten a strip and run it lengthwise along the tube. Holding the ball of newspaper on the end of the tube, bring the sticky tape over the paper ball and down the other side of the tube. Repeat this with three more strips, until the ball sits firmly on the tube like a head sitting on a neck.

5. To make the arms, roll two tubes of construction paper, one that fits the thumb and one that fits the little finger. Draw two hand or mitten shapes on a piece of cardboard. Leave enough cardboard to serve as a wrist and arm about one inch in length. Cut out the two hands and wrists. Slip each of them into one end of each tube, pinch the tube flat against the wrist extension, and staple in place.

6. The teacher should prepare several quarts of wallpaper paste and distribute it at this time in plastic containers (empty margarine cups are ideal for this).

7. Tear small strips of newspaper, dip them into the wallpaper paste, and apply them to the head and neck. Cover everything with two layers. In the same way, cover the arms and hands with several layers of papier-mâché to reinforce these parts.

8. Now add special features to the head. Small wads of crumpled paper might serve for cheeks, nose, chin, bulging eyes, etc. Several thicknesses of paper may be cut to form ears, eyes, a tongue, etc. These features are attached with paste and additional strips of paper. (As the children work, they will explore possibilities and invent solutions. There is no "right way" of doing it.)

9. When all parts have been attached, a final layer of either small pieces of torn newspaper or paper toweling dipped in paste is applied over the entire surface and smoothed so there are no loose edges.

10. After drying for several days, the puppet is ready for painting. Apply one coat of fast-drying house paint over the entire surface and let it dry before using the tempera paints. The base coat will seal the surface and require less tempera to cover.

11. The fabric costume should be loose fitting, with openings for each of the arms and the neck. It should be long enough to cover the child's arm at least to the elbow. Details can be sewn on or otherwise attached to add special characteristics, for instance a necktie or collar, an apron, spots or stripes on an animal, etc.

12. The puppet is ready for performing.

Useful References

BEAUMONT, CYRIL W. *Puppets and Puppetry.* New York: Studio Publications, 1958.

BODOR, JOHN. *Creating and Presenting Hand Puppets.* New York: Van Nostrand Reinhold Co., 1968.

Rod Puppet

Suggested Topics   Caricatures of famous people—movie and television stars, sports figures, politicians, world celebrities, etc.

Primary Objectives

• To capture the most prominent facial features of a well-known person
• To learn to exaggerate or distort facial characteristics
• To role-play in spontaneous drama

Materials/Tools

Magazine pictures of famous people (full figure)
Oak tag or used manila folders
Pencils
Paper punch
Paper fasteners (round heads)
Colored marking pens
Scissors
Thin dowel rods or soda straws
White glue, tape
Electric glue gun (optional)

The Lesson

1. Show the class cartoons of well-known personalities collected from magazines and newspapers. Discuss how artists create caricatures of their subjects by making an oversized nose, large teeth, bushy moustaches, big eyes, etc., to emphasize particular characteristics of that individual.
2. Let children choose their subject from among the magazine pictures.
3. Have them sketch on oak tag a simple caricature of the subject, with an enlarged head, smaller body, arms and legs.
4. Cut out the head and body in one piece and the arms and legs separately.
5. Join the arms and legs to the body by punching holes and attaching parts with paper fasteners.
6. With marking pens, color in the clothing and facial features. Additional parts can be made from colored paper, yarn, buttons, etc.
7. Attach one rod to the back of the body of the figure with tape and white glue. This must be strong enough to support the whole figure and to control the main movement of the whole figure.

8. Attach a second rod either to one arm, or a leg, or the lower jaw, using both tape and white glue. (An electric glue gun is excellent for attaching the rods. The teacher should monitor its use to prevent burns.) This rod will control one body part only, while the other rod controls the entire figure. With the second rod the figure can either wave its arm or appear to walk or talk. The child has to decide which of these motions is preferable.

9. When the glue is dry and the rods secure, practice with the puppets; then create some simple situations in which the characters play different roles.

Useful References

BAIRD, BILL. *The Art of the Puppet.* New York: The Macmillan Company, 1966.

CURRELL, DAVID. *Puppetry for School Children.* Newton, Mass.: Charles T. Branford Company, 1970.

Puppet Stage
Group Project

Primary Objectives

- To plan and construct a workable stage in a team or group approach
- To listen to and work with the ideas of others and to help make group decisions
- To learn by experience the importance of cooperation

Materials/Tools

Large cardboard box measuring about 36″ × 30″ on one side

Mat knife, (X-Acto or similar)

Colored construction paper

Scissors

Tempera paints

Brushes

Gummed kraft tape

Photo flood lamp on a tripod

The Lesson

Plan a simple stage that can be built quickly and discarded after the puppet show. A cardboard carton from a large appliance is ideal for this purpose. This size permits cutting an opening about 18″ × 24″, which will accommodate about three to four hand puppets at one time—the limit of the number of children who can squeeze behind the stage.

1. In the longest side of the box, cut an opening approximately 24 inches long and 18 inches high.
2. Remove the box top, the bottom, and the side opposite the cut out opening. This leaves only the walls of the opening (i.e., the proscenium arch) and two side walls.
3. Place the stage on top of a desk, table, or piano and tape the side walls securely to the supporting surface. Use masking tape, which is easily removed and will not harm the furniture.
4. Decorate the stage front. Give the theatre a name, and with cut-out paper and tempera paints transform the cardboard box and give it new meaning.
5. Locate the flood lamp so that it lights the stage opening. Darken the room.
6. Have the puppeteers huddle behind the stage and practice their performance. Stress large, exaggerated gestures; stress loud stage voices that project; stress becoming the character.

7. If this puppet stage does not suit your purposes, design one that does. Any available materials may serve satisfactorily. Plain brown wrapping paper stretched across a doorway or the corner of a room will serve excellently. Fasten the paper with tape or staples, cut out a stage opening (proscenium arch) with scissors, reinforce the corners with tape, decorate the front, and perform.

Useful References

BODOR, JOHN. *Creating and Presenting Hand Puppets.* New York: Van Nostrand Reinhold Co., 1968.

ENGLER, HARRY, and FIJAN, CAROL. *Making Puppets Come Alive.* New York: Taplinger Publishing Co., 1973.

Shadow Puppets

Suggested Topics Cowboys and Indians. Cops and Robbers. Space Men and Humans. Dogs and Cats.

Primary Objectives

- To work in a group situation in order to learn the importance of cooperation
- To learn to plan a multi-step project
- To learn about another culture through an art form

Materials/Tools

Old X-ray film or used manila file folders
Drawing paper and pencils
Sandpaper
White glue
Scissors
Dowel sticks, 18″ long, small diameter
String
Needle and heavy thread
White bedsheet
Photo flood lamp

The Lesson

If possible, find a book in the library that has illustrations and information about Indonesian shadow puppets. Prepare an example of a shadow puppet in advance and demonstrate how it is used.

1. Divide the class into four or five groups. Let each group choose a theme for its puppet show, and each child decide on what puppet to make.
2. Establish some size limits: figures 12 to 14 inches high; animals in proportion.
3. Have the children draw a profile sketch of their puppet on drawing paper. On another sheet of paper draw the side view of one arm and a side view of one leg. These will be the movable parts.
4. Lightly sandpaper the X-ray film.
5. Cut out the head and body, then the legs and arms from the sketch. Glue them to the X-ray film or file folders with white glue.
6. With scissors, cut out the head, body, arms and legs. Using a nail or other pointed object, punch tiny holes where the arm and the leg attaches to the body. Knot a string and thread it through each hole; then re-knot it on the other side so it can't slip through. These two parts are movable.

7. Make a series of five or six parallel holes about one-quarter inch apart through the main part of the body and a similar series through the movable arm and movable leg.

8. With heavy thread and a needle, attach three lightweight dowel sticks, each about 18 inches in length, one to the body, one to the movable leg and one to the movable arm. The one attached to the body is used to hold the puppet upright and move it left or right. Using one rod at a time, the child can either move an arm or move a leg to create an illusion of walking. The unused rod simply dangles while the other two are in use and it is unnoticed because it hangs behind the main body of the puppet.

9. These puppets can now be used behind a sheet flooded with light to cast shadows on the sheet. Use a table or desk to block the puppet manipulators from view.

10. Have each group practice operating the puppets, and then perform an improvisation.

Useful References

Engler, Harry, and Fijan, Carol. *Making Puppets Come Alive*. New York: Taplinger Publishing Company, 1973.

Correll, David. *Puppetry for School Children*. Newton, Mass.: Charles T. Branford Company, 1970.

PRINTMAKING 7

Background Information about Printmaking

If you have ever stepped into wet paint, the next step you took produced a print of your shoe sole. As you continued to walk, you made multiple prints.

Most people associate the word "print" with the mechanical process used in publishing to produce type on a page. In art, printmaking refers to a method used by artists to make more than one impression of a picture. Each print is considered to be an original. The first artists to experiment with printmaking were looking for a way of reproducing drawings. They soon discovered that each method of printmaking has its own characteristics. A groove cut into the surface of linoleum does not print to look like a line drawn with a pen point.

Each printmaking technique has its own style, resulting from the kinds of tools the artist uses, the surface printed on, and the printing method used.

Basically, there are three kinds of processes by which prints can be made: *intaglio*, *relief*, and *surface*.

INTAGLIO METHOD

In the intaglio process a smooth surface or plate is engraved, etched, or scratched so that a shallow groove results. The grooves serve as the design or picture. The plate, usually of copper, zinc, aluminum, or plastic, is then covered with a sticky ink. Then the surface is wiped clean, leaving ink deposited in the grooves.

Using a press with great pressure, paper is pressed down, forcing it into the grooves. The ink in the grooves sticks to the paper, and this becomes the print.

The intaglio process includes *etching, engraving, dry-point* and *mezzotint*. Each of these processes requires special equipment and materials. These processes were used by Rembrandt, Goya, Picasso, and many other famous artists.

RELIEF METHOD

The relief process does the reverse of intaglio in that the surface which is cut away does not print. In relief printing the design is drawn onto the surface of a block of wood or linoleum. Portions of the design are carved out or cut away with sharp metal gouges or knives.

Printing of reliefs is a fairly simple process because great pressure is not required. In fact most relief prints are made by simply rubbing the back of the paper with something hard and smooth. A thick, tacky ink is rolled onto the surface of the wood block by means of a brayer, or is applied with a dabber. Paper is laid on the inked surface and rubbed with a smooth object such as the bowl of a wooden spoon. When the paper is removed, the print is a mirror image of the block. If additional colors are desired, additional blocks are cut, inked, and printed.

In addition to wood and linoleum blocks, printing surfaces can be made of cardboard, metal, and plastics. Recently rubbings have been made from a great many sources, from temple walls to tombstones. These rubbings are another type of relief prints.

SURFACE METHOD

The technique of surface printing is closely allied with commercial printing processes in which the image or picture is printed from the flat surface of stone or metal onto a flat surface such as paper or fabric, or in which the image or design is applied to the paper or fabric surface by a stencil. Apart from this similarity, these processes differ greatly and are not otherwise related.

Lithography is an old process requiring a high degree of skill and special equipment. An image is drawn on a stone or zinc surface with a grease crayon. The surface not covered by the grease crayon is etched with acid and then treated with gum arabic. The greasy image holds ink; the etched area is kept moist with water and it resists ink. The resulting print is a perfect mirror image of the original drawing.

In *silk screen,* or *serigraphy,* the image is created by forcing paints or inks through the open meshes of a silk fabric stretched over a rectangular frame, or screen. A portion of the mesh is closed or blocked by means of a lacquer film, leaving only the design area open. Paper or fabric is then placed beneath the screen, and by means of a squeegee, paint is dragged across the screen's surface and forced through the open areas of the mesh onto the surface below. The paint deposited on the surface is the print. A separate screen is required for each color.

Contemporary artists may combine all three basic methods, and are always inventing new variations of older methods. Prints, or *graphics,* to use a popular term, have made it possible for people of modest means to own original works of art. Artists generally sign their works either on the print itself or in pencil at the lower right-hand edge of the paper, just below the print. If the edition is limited in number, they usually number the prints. For example, "7/50" would indicate that the print was the 7th of a total printing of 50.

Rubbing

Suggested Topic A design from raised surfaces or textures.

Primary Objectives
- To increase visual awareness
- To recognize and use existing design from unexpected sources
- To organize unrelated parts into a harmonious composition

Materials/Tools
Magazine covers
Wax crayons or soft pencils
White glue
Ditto or typing paper

The Lesson

This lesson enlarges upon the common experience of placing a coin under paper and gently rubbing the paper with a pencil to create an image. If appropriate, the lesson may be used as an out-of-doors assignment to search for raised or lowered surfaces with a pattern or design, for example, manhole covers, a tile wall, a radiator cover, etc.

1. Display a rubbing from a coin, medal, embossed book cover, or a piece of wood with raised grain.
2. Encourage the children to find surfaces which can be rubbed to capture an impression.
3. Have the children tear or cut pieces of magazine covers and place them randomly or selectively on a page. Cover them with a clean sheet of paper and gently make a rubbing.
4. Demonstrate how to use the side of the pencil or crayon to get varieties of dark and light values.
5. Have the children move the pieces about and continue the same rubbing.
6. Some children may want to control the shapes beneath the rubbing to "make a picture." Let them do it.

Useful References

BODOR, JOHN. *Rubbings and Textures: A Graphic Medium.* New York: Van Nostrand Reinhold Co., 1968.

BROMMER, GERALD F., and HORN, GEORGE. *Art: Your Visual Environment.* Worcester, Mass.: Davis Publications, Inc., 1977.

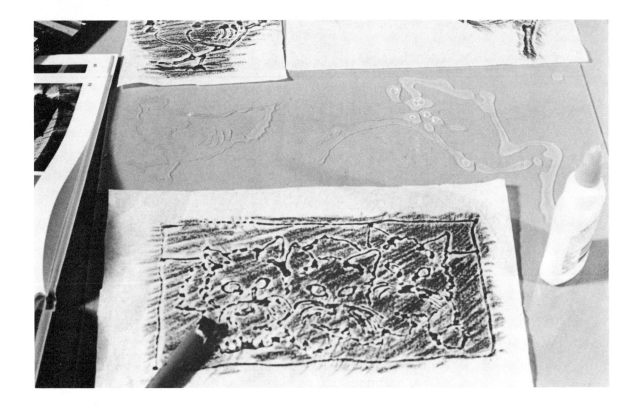

Metal Foil Print

Suggested Topic Close-up view of insects, flowers, leaves, shells, etc.

Primary Objectives

- To increase awareness of design as it is evidenced in the details of nature
- To adapt design motifs from nature sources to a relief printmaking process
- To learn a printmaking process and some appropriate vocabulary

Materials/Tools

Heavy aluminum foil (TV dinner trays, frozen food trays, etc.)
Pencils
Water-base printer's ink
Pie pan or cookie sheet
Brayers
Newspaper
Thin paper (tissue paper, onion skin)
Drawing paper

The Lesson

Focus on the complex and interesting patterns that occur in nature. Show some photographic examples of butterflies, insects, etc. Let the children search for things in their environment which can be drawn enlarged as though looking through a microscope or a magnifying glass.

1. Have each child make a drawing about 9″ × 12″ with a pencil or pen.
2. Cut a rectangular opening about 5″ × 8″ in another piece of paper and have the children move it about over the drawing until they find the most interesting area. In a simple way, they are searching for good composition.
3. Lay a piece of aluminum foil about 5″ × 8″ on a pad of newspapers. Place the selected segment of the drawing over the foil, and trace over it with a pencil, using heavy pressure.
4. Remove the drawing and go over the indented lines again until they protrude well above the level of the flat surface. Advise the children that too much pressure will result in a hole or tear.
5. Place some water-base printer's ink on an inking slab (cookie sheet), and roll through it with a brayer until it sounds tacky.
6. Gently roll the brayer across the raised lines of the foil design.
7. Place a thin sheet of tissue paper over the foil, and rub the back of the paper with the palm of the hand or another smooth surface.

8. "Pull the print" (printmaker's language), and share the results.
9. The teacher can select one or two prints from each child. These can be mounted on construction paper and displayed in the classroom.

Useful References

LINDERMAN, EARL, and LINDERMAN, MARLENE. *Crafts for the Classroom*. New York: The Macmillan Company, Inc., 1977.

WACHOWIAK, FRANK, and RAMSAY, THEODORE. *Emphasis: Art*, 3rd ed. Scranton, Pa.: International Textbook, 1976.

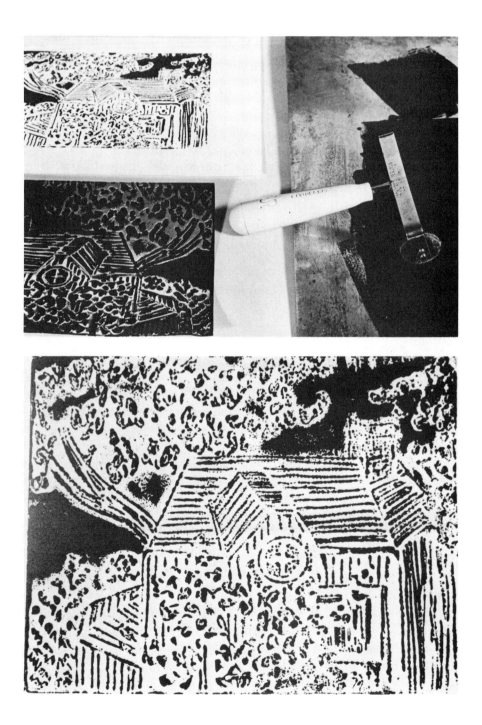

Stencil Print with Chalk

Suggested Topics Insects with wings. Flowers and blossoms. A bowl of fruit. A city skyline.

Primary Objectives

• To develop designs based upon objects from the environment
• To recognize and draw the primary shapes of the object
• To complete the several steps in stenciling in order to produce a complete stencil design

Materials/Tools

Colored chalks or pastels
Facial or toilet tissue
Scissors, mat knives, or single-edge razor blades
Paper, small pieces for stenciling, about 6" square
Paper, large sheets for the print

The Lesson

1. Bring a group of colored photographs of insects for the class to examine. Point out the shapes of the head and bodies; examine wing shapes; look at the antenna, legs, mandibles, etc. Talk about color.
2. Fold some small pieces of paper. Demonstrate how to sketch one-half of an insect body along the fold. Cut it out.
3. Make a small wad of facial or toilet tissue. Rub it vigorously on a colored chalk. When it is charged bright with color, place the unfolded stencil representing the insect body on top of the large sheet. Hold it firmly in place. Rub the chalked tissue across the opening, depositing chalk on the paper below. Always rub from the edge toward the center of the opening, as this will help avoid tearing the stencil.
4. Fold another smaller piece of paper and sketch one-half of a head along the fold. Cut out the head shape and place the stencil opening in a likely position in relation to the body. Prepare the tissue wad with more color, hold firmly and rub again.
5. Repeat this process for the wings, legs, antenna, wing patterns, etc.
6. Any part can be stenciled a second or third time if desired.
7. After each child has made a good print to take home, have everyone do a print for display as part of a group picture or mural.

Useful References

HARTUNG, ROLF. *More Creative Textile Design: Color and Texture.* New York: Van Nostrand Reinhold Co., 1964.

TISON, ANNETTE, and TAYLOR, TALUS. *The Adventures of the Three Colors.* New York: World Publishing, 1971.

Stencil Spray Print

Suggested Topic   Designs in nature and in man-made objects.

Primary Objectives
- To recognize design elements such as line, shape, texture, and pattern in both natural and man-made materials
- To combine various elements into pleasing compositions
- To make a monoprint by a stencil spray process

Materials/Tools
Flat nature materials—leaves, ferns, grasses, etc.

Man-made objects—plastic spoons, forks, thread, string, buttons, lids, keys, hardware, etc.

Can of spray paint

Paper, any plain paper, white or colored

Newspaper

The Lesson
1. Have the children make individual collections of natural and man-made items with interesting items such as those listed above. Suggest that the children keep their finds in a small paper bag.
2. Plan the lesson around *composition*, i.e., organizing the combined shapes into an interesting, pleasing arrangement.
3. Work in an open, well-ventilated area or out-of-doors if possible.
4. Cover the floor or ground with newspaper to catch any over-spray.
5. Each child makes a "composition" of some of the objects available. Stress keeping the objects as flat as possible to the paper surface. This will prevent the spray from getting under the objects and changing the design. If more items are needed, cut out or tear paper shapes to add to the composition.
6. Spray the arrangement lightly, holding the spray can about 20 inches from the paper.
7. Ask the children to remove a few items from their composition and add other items.
8. Spray again, this time with a heavier spray.
9. Allow the stencil prints to dry. Remove the items and behold nature's and man's beautiful shapes combined.

Useful References

GUYLER, VIVIAN. *Design in Nature.* Worcester, Mass.: The Davis Publications, Inc., 1970.

MORMAN, JEAN MARY. *Wonder under Your Feet.* New York: Harper & Row, Publishers, Inc., 1973.

Paraffin Block Print

Suggested Topic   Nature designs in close-up.

Primary Objectives
- To increase the awareness of designs in nature
- To learn to select smaller, interesting patterns from nature for adaptation to creative designs
- To increase manual skill in working small and in detail

Materials/Tools

Blocks of household paraffin (used for canning and candle making)

Small V-gouges (used for linoleum cutting)

Drawing paper

Water-base block printing ink

Brayers

Tissue paper sheets, white or colored (gift wrapping)

Magnifying glass

The Lesson

Because paraffin is relatively inexpensive and can be used over and over, it is very suited to this printmaking process. Paraffin may be purchased commercially in 1 lb. packages, each divided into four or five blocks. Thus one package provides eight or ten flat sides on which to cut designs. If only a few small V-gouges are available, the children will have to take turns working on this project.

1. Bring a selection of natural materials such as weeds, seed pods, shells, etc. and photographs from nature that show detail. Have the children look at some of the materials through a magnifying glass.
2. Have each child choose an interesting section from one of the materials and draw an enlarged image of it on a piece of 9″ × 12″ paper.
3. From that drawing let each child decide on what portion of the drawing is most successful. Lay a paraffin block over the portion selected and trace around its edges. In this process, the children have determined the composition to transfer to the paraffin block.
4. Re-examine the nature materials with the magnifying glass to study the appearance of the section chosen. New lines may be added to the design.
5. Working from the drawing, gently sketch the drawing onto the smooth surface of the paraffin.

6. With a V-gouge, carefully carve away the design.

7. Ink the carved surface of the block, using the brayer and printing ink.

8. Lay a sheet of tissue paper on the inked surface and rub the paper with the fingertips until the image is visible through the paper.

9. Lift the print, place it flat to dry, then repeat the process until an ''edition'' of 5 to 10 prints has been ''pulled.''

10. Sign each print at the lower right edge on the border close to the inked surface. If desired, number each print, using the numbering system described in the introduction to this chapter.

11. The teacher can select one print from each child to mat or mount and display in the classroom.

Useful References

Andrews, Michael F. *Creative Printmaking.* Englewood Cliffs, N.J.: Prentice-Hall, Inc., 1964.

Gorbaty, Norman. *Printmaking with a Spoon.* New York: Van Nostrand Reinhold Co., 1960.

Stamp Prints

Suggested Topic   Making a pattern based upon a repeat.

Primary Objectives

- To use some of the organizing principles of design such as pattern, balance, repetition, and rhythm
- To discover design motifs in commonplace items
- To produce some simple printed designs

Materials/Tools

Suggestions for the stamps: small cubes of Styrofoam, corks, small blocks of wood, cubes of cellulose sponge, pencil erasers, bottle caps, small jar lids, etc. Search for a variety of objects with distinctive shapes—circles, squares, triangles—or interesting surface textures. Each object should leave a clear impression of its shape or texture.

Drawing paper

Tempera paints

Newspaper

Stamp pads (see below)

The Lesson

If you don't have commercial stamp pads (the kind used with rubber stamps), a satisfactory substitute can be made as follows: Fold three or four paper towels and saturate with water. Drip some tempera paint on and spread it evenly. Another way is to brush the paint directly on the stamp for each print.

1. Demonstrate the use of various stamps. Stress pressing the stamp onto the stamp pad for each print. In doing the first print, experiment. Pay special attention to developing a pattern through a regular repeat.
2. Before printing, have the children put some newspapers for padding beneath their drawing paper to make it softer and more receptive to the print.
3. Print a regularly repeated design until the entire sheet of paper has been filled. The design might repeat in all sorts of ways—in even or "odd" rows, with reversed images, overlapping, spiraling, in a concentric pattern, etc.
4. Try another sheet, this time combining two stamps of different shapes and two colors.
5. Encourage the children to see what kind of pattern they can invent with the added color and shape.

Useful References

BROMMER, GERALD. *Relief Printmaking.* Worcester, Mass.: Davis Publications, Inc., 1970.

COX, DORIS, and WARREN, BARBARA. *Creative Hands.* New York: John Wiley & Sons, Inc., 1951.

Mirror Image Prints

Suggested Topic   Symmetrical designs.

Primary Objectives
- To create designs based upon symmetry
- To experiment with "accidental" shapes and colors
- To be selective in choosing designs or patterns that have visual appeal

Materials/Tools

Tempera paints
Drawing paper
Magazine pages (not colored)

The Lesson

This project relates to the kind of earlier experiments most children have made with inkblots or Rorschach design, but requires that the children add something additional of their own.

1. Fold in half a sheet of paper or a page from an old magazine. Unfold.
2. Drip or apply paint on the surface of one half in a random manner.
3. Refold the sheet, pressing surfaces together on the desk top. Rub the hand over the paper several times to insure a good transfer of the paint.
4. Drip on another color, fold, and open again.
5. If the print begins to "look like" something to the child, it is perfectly all right to let him finish painting it to be whatever he chooses. If it remains a design, don't force the child to see what doesn't come out naturally.

Useful References

JABLONSKI, RAMONA. *The Paper Cut-Out Design Book*. Owings Mills, Md.: Stemmer House Publishers, Inc., 1976.

RÖTTGER, ERNST. *Creative Paper Design*. New York: Van Nostrand Reinhold Co., 1961.

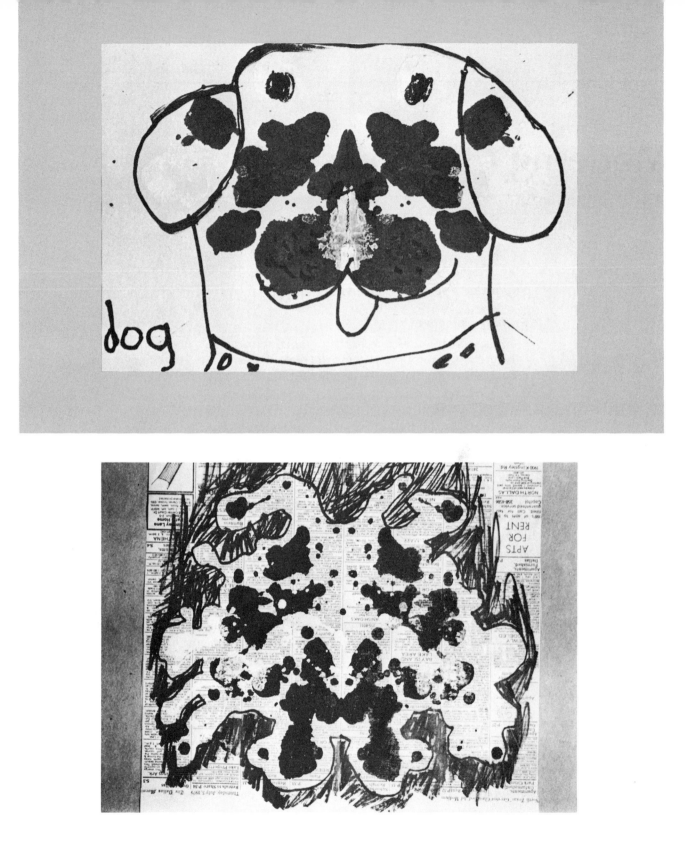

Modeling Clay Prints

Suggested Topic   A repeated design.

Primary Objectives
- To use repetition as one of the organizing principles of design
- To utilize commonplace items to create designs
- To produce several pages of relief design based upon a repeated motif

Materials/Tools

Modeling clay, oil base (Plasticine, Plastilene, Modelo, etc.)
Newspaper
Tempera paint or printing ink
Newsprint
Found objects—paper clips, bottle caps, plastic forks, nuts, screws, etc.

The Lesson

1. Have each child pat or press a lump of modeling clay into a square or rectangle or a circle about 3 inches in diameter and 1 inch thick.
2. Using found objects, press an object into the clay until the clay's surface retains a good impression of the object. Choose another object and repeat until an interesting arrangement of shapes is obtained. If the child is not satisfied with the design, let her smooth the clay and try again.
3. To make the printing pad, fold many layers of newspaper into a pad 6 to 8 inches square and about ¼ inch thick. Saturate the pad with water until it is well soaked. Put tempera paint, liquid or dry, or printing ink on the surface of the pad and smear it around until it is evenly spread.
4. Press the modeling clay block, design side down, into the printing pad. Lift and press on a clean sheet of paper which is laid on newspapers to allow it to "give" a little.
5. Return the modeling clay block to the stamp pad and make a second print adjacent to the first one. Repeat until the page is full.

Useful References

ANDREWS, MICHAEL. *Creative Printmaking*. Englewood Cliffs, N.J.: Prentice-Hall, Inc., 1963.

GORBATY, NORMAN. *Printmaking with a Spoon*. New York: Van Nostrand Reinhold Co., 1960.

Cardboard or Styrofoam Print

Suggested Topics A portrait of my face. A portrait of daddy or mother.

Primary Objectives
- To create prints using only shapes as the design element
- To find the essential characteristics of the subject and define them as shapes
- To understand the process of relief printing

Materials/Tools
Cardboard
Styrofoam trays or packaging (from meats or fast foods)
Tissue paper
Water-base printing ink, light and dark colors
Brayers
White glue
Inking slab—cookie sheet or heavy glass
Scissors
Tablespoons
Mat knives (X-Acto or similar)

The Lesson
This project will produce results quite different from those obtained with crayons, paints, or pencils. This print will have large, bold, flat shapes which define the various components of the picture.

1. Discuss the problem of making a portrait. Talk about the shapes of eyes, ears, nose, mouth, etc.
2. Have each child make a drawing of a head that fills a 5″×8″ sheet. With scissors, cut out the shape. This will serve as the pattern for the first printing surface. Next cut out shapes to represent eyes, nose, mouth, hair, ears, etc. These will be the patterns for another printing surface.
3. Trace around the pattern of the head on a larger piece of cardboard or on the smooth surface of a Styrofoam tray. Cut around it with a mat knife or similar tool. Glue the piece representing the head to another sheet of cardboard, using white glue. This will serve as the first printing surface.
4. Trace the patterns of the eyes, nose, mouth, ears, hair, etc. onto a piece of cardboard or Styrofoam and cut them out. Trace the head pattern from step 3 on another sheet of cardboard and on that attach the cut-out pieces representing eyes, nose, mouth, etc. in their appropriate locations. This will

serve as the second printing surface. Allow the glue on both printing surfaces to dry long enough to hold them securely.

5. Put a light color (pink, light brown, yellow) water-soluble ink on an inking slab such as the back of a pie pan, a cookie sheet, or a piece of heavy glass. Roll the brayer across it a number of times until it is evenly distributed and has a tacky or sticky sound.

6. Roll the inked brayer across the surface of the first printing surface that has the head shape on it. When the surface is covered, lay a sheet of tissue paper over the inked surface and carefully rub the paper with a hard smooth surface such as the bowl of a tablespoon. Carefully pull away the tissue and put it aside to dry. Repeat this process for several more prints. Allow these to dry.

7. Prepare a second inking slab, this time with a darker color or black.

8. The second printing surface is now inked and the tissue papers with the first impression are laid, one at a time, over the inked surface and rubbed as before. This time, as the tissue papers are removed, the entire image will be completed. Print the rest of the tissues to complete an edition.

9. Show the children how a graphic artist—a printmaker—numbers and signs an edition.

Useful References

BROMMER, GERALD. *Relief Printmaking.* Worcester, Mass.: Davis Publications, Inc., 1970.

GORBATY, NORMAN. *Printmaking with a Spoon.* New York: Van Nostrand Reinhold Co., 1960.

Linoleum or Wood Block Print

Suggested Topics Holiday greetings, invitations, or announcements. My house is blanketed with snow. Christmas the way it used to be. Holiday decorations in the city.

Primary Objects
- To understand the process of relief printing
- To plan and make a creative non-stereotyped design which can be adapted to linoleum cutting and printing
- To carry out a practical, multi-step process to completion

Materials/Tools
Linoleum blocks, mounted or unmounted
Pieces of soft wood such as white pine
Linoleum cutting tools, both narrow and wide gouges
Cutting board, if available
Water-base printing ink
Inking slab—cookie sheet or heavy glass
Brayers
Tissue paper
Tablespoons

The Lesson

Linoleum block or wood block printing requires careful planning and adequate time. Because the process is fairly complex, we tend to focus attention on the method and we often neglect the design for the block. This may result in an uncreative stereotype of a wreath, Christmas tree, or burning candle.

1. Choose a topic that has potential for individuality, originality, and richness of detail.
2. Have each child make a drawing to serve as the design. Do not permit any cutting until the designs are well conceived and well planned.
3. Demonstrate how to transfer the design by using carbon paper over a wood block or a linoleum block. Explain that any lettering or numbering must be reversed. The print is always a reverse or mirror image.
4. Demonstrate the use of linoleum cutting tools. Stress keeping the free hand in a position so that an accidental slip of the tool doesn't result in a painful injury. If possible, use simple cutting boards which hold the blocks in place (Figure A).

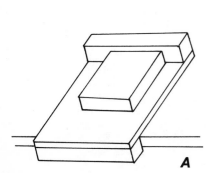

A

5. Have the children trace their designs. Then the teacher may wish to look at them to see if any children are having problems making the transfer.

6. Cutting follows. Use a narrow gouge for thin lines and a wider gouge for thick lines. Remember: what remains, prints; what gets cut away does not print.

7. Put ink on the inking slab and charge the brayer by rolling it through until the ink is sticky or tacky.

8. Roll the inked brayer across the carved surface of the linoleum in several directions until an even coat of ink covers the entire surface.

9. Using tissue or thin paper, cover the surface and rub the reverse side with the bowl of a spoon or a smooth hard surface.

10. Lift one corner and check to see if the paper is taking a good impression. If not, rub harder.

11. Lift the print and let it dry.

12. Mat or mount the prints and display them.

Useful References

ANDREWS, MICHAEL. *Creative Printmaking.* Englewood Cliffs, N.J.: Prentice-Hall, Inc., 1963.

BROMMER, GERALD. *Relief Printmaking.* Worcester, Mass.: Davis Publications, Inc., 1970.

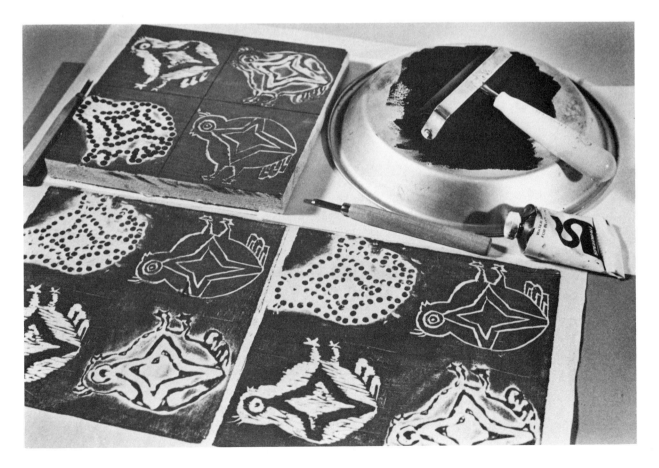

Styrofoam Print

Suggested Topics The oldest house in town. Grazing cattle. A cat and kittens. A classic car.

Primary Objectives

- To plan a design based upon the elements of line and shape
- To produce a small edition of prints
- To understand the process of relief printing

Materials/Tools

Drawing paper

Styrofoam trays from packaged meats (cut away the raised edges so that only a flat, smooth surface remains)

Blunt pencil or ball point pen

Inking slab—cookie sheet, pie pan, or heavy sheet of glass

Brayer

Water-base block-printing ink

Tissue paper

The Lesson

The process used in this project is direct and fast, and results in more detail than most printing processes.

1. Choose a topic with which the children can identify and be imaginative. Talk about printing. Why do artists make prints? (To get multiple copies.) The process we will use is a relief process. Discuss the print—what can be included, how can the space be used, how can interesting detail or texture be achieved, etc.?

2. Have each child make a line drawing on paper, the same size as his Styrofoam tray.

3. When the drawing is completed, copy it onto the Styrofoam with a blunt pencil or ball-point pen, pushing the line well below the surface.

4. Prepare an inking slab by squeezing water-soluble printing ink on a cookie sheet, the back of a pie pan, or a heavy piece of glass. Roll the brayer through it until the ink is evenly distributed and sounds tacky.

5. Have ready some pieces of tissue paper cut somewhat larger than the Styrofoam printing surface.

6. Roll the brayer across the printing surface until it is well covered. Lay a piece of tissue paper over the inked surface. Gently rub the paper with the fingers until the ink impression appears through the tissue.

7. Lift the print. The image will appear in reverse—a white line against a dark background.

8. Allow each child to make about five prints. Then show them how to sign and number their editions.

Useful References

ERICKSON, JANET DOBBS, and SPROUL, ADELAIDE. *Printmaking without a Press.* New York: Van Nostrand Reinhold Co., 1966.

WEISS, HARVEY. *Paper, Ink and Roller.* New York: William R. Scott, 1958.

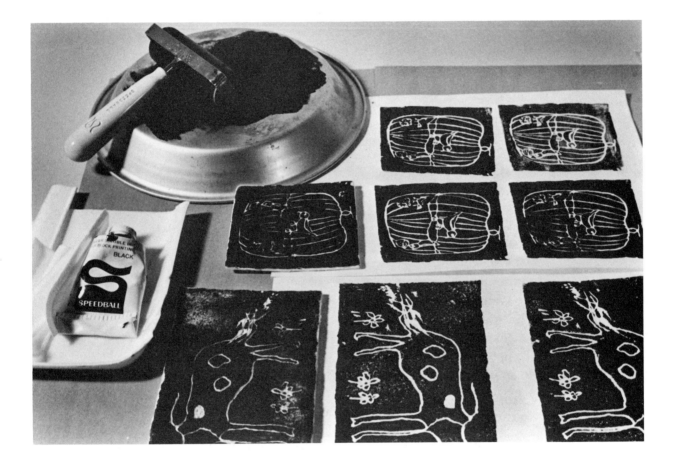

Glue Print

Suggested Topic   Interpreting a photograph.

Primary Objectives
- To make a design for a print based upon a photographic image
- To work freely and spontaneously
- To produce an edition of prints

Materials/Tools

Old magazines with full-page photographs of animals, people, insects, cars, bicycles, etc.

Cardboard

Scissors

White glue

Toothpicks or matchsticks

Water-base printing ink

Paper

Inking slab—cookie sheet, pie pan, or heavy sheet of glass

Brayer

Tablespoons

The Lesson

1. Have each child select a page from a magazine with a photograph that he or she likes. Suggest pictures that have one dominant shape—a large animal, a tree, a head, etc.
2. Paste or glue the page to cardboard (the side of an old box, etc.). Trim the cardboard to about the same size as the photograph.
3. Carefully trail a line of white glue around the dominant shapes. The glue will flow in ways which do not allow precise control, causing a fresh, spontaneous quality to result. Go back over some areas to build up the glue. Use toothpicks or matchsticks to add glue for some details, but the print is unique because of the bold, dynamic quality of the design.
4. Allow the glue to dry completely for several days.
5. Squeeze some printing ink onto the inking slab and roll the brayer through it until the ink sounds sticky or tacky.
6. Roll the brayer across the glue-outlined photograph. The ink will adhere to both the glue and the surrounding areas.

7. Lay a clean paper over the inked surface. Rub the back of the paper with the bowl of a spoon or any other smooth curved surface.

8. Pull the paper free and allow it to dry. Because the glue raises the design, uninked areas appear around the design, creating a "halo" on the otherwise dark surface. The realism of the photograph is lost, and the print emphasizes shape and movement.

9. Repeat the process until each child has pulled about five prints. Mount these on white paper.

10. Explain what an edition is and how artists sign and number an edition. Have the young artists sign and number their editions.

Useful References

ANDREWS, MICHAEL. *Creative Printmaking.* Englewood Cliffs, N.J.: Prentice-Hall, Inc., 1963.

ERICKSON, JANET DOBBS, and SPROUL, ADELAIDE. *Printmaking without a Press.* New York: Van Nostrand Reinhold Co., 1966.

Group Mural of Monoprints

Suggested Topics   A huge bouquet. A garden in bloom. An aquarium.

Primary Objectives
- To experiment with color and shape
- To learn what happens when two colors meet and blend together
- To work cooperatively in producing a group mural

Materials/Tools

A smooth, nonporous surface of glass, enamel, or metal
Liquid tempera paints
Drawing paper
Magazines
Sponge
Scissors

The Lesson

In this project each child will have an opportunity to make a bright, spontaneous monoprint to be used as part of a larger picture or mural combining every child's work. The teacher should first demonstrate steps 1, 2, and 3.

1. Drip bright-colored tempera paint randomly on a smooth nonporous surface such as a cookie tin, a piece of formica, or a sheet of heavy glass.

2. Over the wet paint, lay a sheet of drawing paper or a page from an old magazine (not colored).

3. With the palm of the hand, press the paper into the paint and lift it away. The paint will leave an impression on the paper. Let it dry.

4. Wipe the surface clean with a damp sponge and give each child a turn at making a monoprint.

5. When everyone has a colored print, let them choose the areas of their prints that they like the best and draw a form, such as a flower or fish, over the area and then cut it out with scissors. Other forms are leaves, insects, butterflies, etc.

6. Glue or tape all of the cutouts to a large piece of wrapping paper on the wall to form a group mural. Alternately, display them on the bulletin board.

Useful References

GORBATY, NORMAN. *Printmaking with a Spoon.* New York: Van Nostrand Reinhold Co., 1960.

GREENBERG, PEARL. *Art and Ideas for Young People.* New York: Van Nostrand Reinhold, 1970.

Print and Draw

Suggested Topic   What do you see, and how can you complete it?

Primary Objectives
- To discover in random prints the beginning of images that need completion
- To mix drawing and printing to achieve a pictorial design

Materials/Tools

Drawing paper

Water-base printing ink

Brayers

Inking slab—cookie tin, pie pan, or heavy sheet of glass

Felt-tip markers

Assorted scrap items—weathered wood pieces, bits of tar paper, torn scraps of paper, small pieces of burlap, etc.

The Lesson

Most people can "see" the shapes of animals, people, trees, castles, ships, etc. in clouds, wallpaper motifs, shadows, oil stains, water spots, and the like. This lesson is based upon "seeing something" in a print made with random impressions from unusual materials, and then completing the image. This procedure is sometimes called "closure."

1. Prepare an inking slab by spreading water-base printing ink on a cookie tin or the back of a pie pan. Roll the brayer through the ink until it is evenly distributed and tacky.
2. Have the child select one item from the scrap collection; lay it on the desk or table (protected with newspaper), and roll across it with the brayer. Place a clean sheet of drawing paper over the inked item and rub the paper to pick up an ink impression.
3. Choose a second and third item and print with them in the same way.
4. Now look at each print; turn it upside down and sideways to see if you can discover an image in it.
5. When you see something that suggests an image to you, complete it with a felt-tip marker.

Useful References

Gorbathy, Norman. *Printmaking with a Spoon.* New York: Van Nostrand Reinhold Co., 1960.

Weiss, Harvey. *Paper, Ink and Roller.* New York: William R. Scott, 1958.

Designing with Dots and Drips of Dyes

Suggested Topic   Patterns for animals, fish, birds, flowers.

Primary Objectives

- To experiment with color on a wet surface
- To observe how colors change as one color runs into another
- To use random designs as a basis for creating an image

Materials/Tools

Jars of household liquid dyes
Drawing paper
Small sticks or twigs
Brush or sponge
Scissors
Wrapping paper
Transparent tape

The Lesson

1. Dampen a sheet of drawing paper with a wet sponge.
2. Dip a stick into a jar of dye and allow the color to drip onto the damp paper.
3. Repeat the drips, keeping them far enough apart to avoid fusing into one another.
4. Continue until the entire page becomes a decorative design.
5. Try a second sheet, this time using two colors. Experiment by dragging a stick across the dampened paper leaving a trail of dye. Try straight lines, then wiggly lines. Be sure that the children do not dip the sticks from one color dye into another, because that will soon spoil the colors.
6. When the pages are completely dry, have the children draw the outline of a bird, animal, fish, or flower that might have a patterned surface. For example, leopards, tigers, giraffes, and zebras all have patterned skins.
7. With scissors cut out the animal, bird, fish, or flower.
8. Group the animals together and fasten them on a large sheet of wrapping paper with transparent tape. Group the fish, birds, etc. on separate pieces of paper.

Useful References

BARR, BERYL. *Wonders, Warriors and Beasts Abounding*. New York: Doubleday & Co., 1967.

RÖTTGER, ERNST; KLANTE, DIETER; and SALZMAN, FRIEDRICH. *Surfaces in Creative Drawing*. New York: Van Nostrand Reinhold Co., 1969.

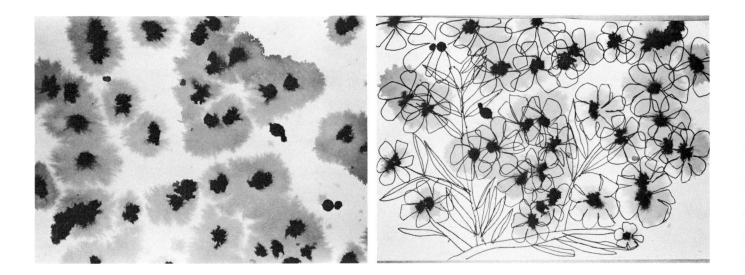

MASKS
AND
PAPIER-MÂCHÉ

8

Background Information about Masks

Masks have been used throughout history in almost all cultures—primitive or sophisticated, ancient or contemporary. They seem to answer an inborn need common to all human beings.

In our society people often associate the word "mask" with the word "falseface," a term originated by the Algonquian Indians to describe the masks worn by members of the Falseface Society. Children think of masks as something worn for a disguise on Halloween or at a masquerade party.

But masks have served many different purposes for thousands of years. Sometimes they were made to represent ancestors, gods, demons, the souls of the dead, spirits of good and evil, spirits of animals, rain, fertility, abundance, and death. In some cultures they played a part in the burial rituals. In Egypt, for example, the faces of dead Pharaohs were covered with masks made of gold, silver, and precious stones.

Some primitive societies today still believe, as did earlier cultures, that the mask can actually transform the wearer into someone or something else. The belief in the magical power of masks accounts for their widespread use in ritual ceremonies and dances. Another purpose is served by war masks, which are made with terrifying faces to frighten the enemy.

Stone Age drawings show men wearing animal skins and the horns of animals as a form of mask. Today Eskimos still wear masks for the same purposes as did the early cave men: to cause a magical-religious transformation which gives to the wearer the spirit represented by the mask. The Zuñi Indians make masks to impersonate gods or spirits called *kachinas*. Worn in dances, the masks are used to re-enact myths about the creation of the world and to show the deeds of ancestral spirits. They are also used in dances performed to bring rain or to enrich the harvest. Kachina masks are usually abstract and geometric, and not terrifying.

An old Slavic custom, especially among the farmers, is for young people to wear masks as they sing and dance in celebration of the Christmas season. These masks may represent goats, foxes, eagles, horses, death heads, or figures from Christian folklore.

Throughout Europe masks have been used for theatrical performances since the time of the Greeks and Romans. Actors always wore masks. In China and Japan masks were in use a thousand years before the birth of Christ in ceremonies that may have been the forerunner of theatre. Today in Japan the Nō dramas and Kyōgen comedies are still performed as they have been for hundreds of years.

Art collectors today treasure the imaginative masks of Africa, New Guinea, Melanesia, pre-Columbian America, and the Indians of North America.

The mask has always been a unifying factor in primitive cultures, since it usually relates the present to the past, the living to the dead, men to gods, and man to nature. It is such a strong, cohesive art form that it can be considered one of man's most important creative and cultural products.

Background Information about Papier-Mâché

The term *papier-mâché* comes from the French words *papier*, meaning paper, and *mâché*, meaning masticated, mashed to a pulp. The art of making articles of papier-mâché, beautifully decorated with oriental motifs and handsomely lacquered, was known in the Far East centuries before it began to be practiced in Europe. Molded paper products were first made in France during the early eighteenth century and later in Germany and England. (In 1765 Frederick the Great established a factory in Berlin just for the manufacture of papier-mâché products.)

Toward the end of the nineteenth century, the peasant art of Europe known as "folk art" or the "art of the land" began to be recognized as a special category of art. The folk artist, usually untrained, tended to preserve the simple traditional forms and methods of workmanship that had been handed down over the years, while relying at the same time on inventiveness and imagination to create new ideas, styles, and articles. While professional sculptors continued to work in wood and stone, folk artists discovered papier-mâché as a material with which to create quick and bold effects. With it they learned to create large and effective carnival and votive figures and delightful smaller toys.

In Victorian England papier-mâché made of paper pulp and glue was used in the manufacture of small tables, chairs, firescreens, clock cases, and other articles of furniture. Today plastic has largely replaced papier-mâché in the manufacture of these items.

In the Far East papier-mâché has been used mainly for decorative work, especially in making masks. Because of its relative strength and lightness, papier-mâché has also been used in Japan to make armor.

Papier-mâché is still used in the cottage industries of Japan and Mexico to create inexpensive traditional masks, dolls, and toys. In Mexico the piñata, a colorful papier-mâché figure of an animal or person built up over a lightweight ceramic or cardboard container, is traditionally used at celebrations and children's parties. The piñata, filled with candy, is hung from the ceiling, and children take turns striking it with a stick until it breaks open and the candy tumbles out. A similar papier-mâché figure, called a Judas, which usually represents an unpopular or disliked person, is blown apart with fireworks during celebrations.

In recent years several Mexican artists have been producing very sophisticated handmade papier-mâché objects for commercial sale. These objects have gained in popularity, because handcrafted items are always sought after.

No doubt papier-mâché products will continue to be made for many years. However, new materials such as plastics and fiberglass will gradually replace papier-mâché in commercial products. Neither plastics nor fiberglass offers the freedom, variety, and spontaneity of papier-mâché; furthermore these materials must be used in carefully controlled environments, while papier-mâché is an any time, any place medium.

Papier-Mâché in the Classroom

Papier-mâché is one of the least expensive yet most versatile mediums for three-dimensional classroom art projects. Lightweight yet strong, it can be used to make animals large enough for children to sit on or objects as small as beads.

The basic materials for papier-mâché are newspapers and wallpaper wheat paste. To mix the paste, use one cup of dry paste and seven cups of water. Add the paste gradually to the water and stir vigorously with a stick or large spoon until the mixture is smooth and lump free. Depending on the project, the mixture may be thickened by sifting in additional dry paste or thinned by the addition of water.

The process involves applying paper that has been saturated with paste over some type of form or framework. The moist paper may be in strips, patches, or pulp. It is applied, layer upon layer, until the object has attained the desired shape and texture. When completely dried the finished product has remarkable strength.

After drying, the object can be covered with a coat of one of the newer fast-drying house paints to seal the surface, before tempera paints are applied. When the surface is sealed, the tempera paints cover better, and this saves paint. Almost any of the regular classroom paints will adhere to the primed surface. After painting with tempera, a final glossy protective coat of shellac, varnish, or polyurethane may be applied.

A point to remember in working with papier-mâché, particularly in mask making, is that these objects are created to obtain special effects and therefore color, shape, size, and textures may have to be exaggerated or heightened. For example, a witch's nose should be extremely long and crooked, the hair stringy and disheveled, the skin sickly green or gray; the mask of a miser might have hollow cheeks, stained and broken teeth, a bluish complexion; and so on. Modeling and painting papier-mâché opens the door to many dramatic and creative possibilities. Explore them.

Paper Plate Masks

Suggested Topics Masks to make everyone laugh. Masks of lions and tigers. Masks of space people.

Primary Objectives

- To learn some of the reasons why various cultures have used masks
- To encourage imaginative play-acting
- To produce masks that simulate other people, animals, etc.

Materials/Tools

Paper plates

Scissors

Transparent tape

Stapler

Colored papers

Crayons

String

The Lesson

Begin this lesson by briefly reviewing the information about masks in the introduction to this chapter. If possible, find some photographs of masks in old *National Geographic* magazine articles on New Guinea, Africa, etc. Use this opportunity to give more meaning to the art activity.

1. Ask the children to suggest ways that they can pretend or seem to be somebody or something else. They might change how they look, the way they talk or make sounds, the posture of their body, and the way they move their body when they walk. For example, if you are going to be a lion you must stalk like a lion, growl like a lion, and have a face like a lion. How does a lion's face look? It has a big mouth with large pointed teeth, two bright eyes, a curly mane (if male), two ears, whiskers, etc.

2. Demonstrate this step. Cut four slits 1½ inches long in the top, bottom, and side edges of a paper plate. Overlap the edges of each slit and staple together. This gives depth or volume to the mask so that it fits over the face. With a scissor point make two small openings to see through. Enlarge them as necessary. Now have the children do this step.

3. The children can now use colored papers, paste, scissors, and crayon to transform the paper plate into something else—the face of a lion or whatever they have decided it should be. Give suggestions from time to time.

Demonstrate how to make paper curls by gently wrapping paper around a pencil. Show how to fold the paper to make an accordion. Encourage richness of detail, color, and texture.

4. Pierce each side of the plate and tie a short length of string through each hole for securing the mask on the head.

5. Use this opportunity for lion (or other) improvisations. For a few minutes let the classroom become lion country.

Useful References

JOHNSON, PAULINE. *Creating with Paper: Basic Forms and Variations.* Seattle: University of Washington Press, 1958.

RILEY, OLIVE. *Masks and Magic.* New York: Studio Publications, 1955.

Paper Bag Masks

Suggested Topics A frightening face. Creature from outer space.

Primary Objectives
• To create large, original characters
• To use masks for play-acting and to improve oral communication

Materials/Tools
Large brown grocery bags
Tempera paints or crayons
Brushes
Colored paper
Paste
Scissors

The Lesson
During this one-session project a simple, original mask is created and used in improvisations.

1. Talk about masks and how man has used them for thousands of years. Discuss how the wearer, like an actor on the stage, becomes someone else when he or she puts on a mask.
2. Open the bag and cut an arch or half-circle at each side to make it rest on the shoulders (Figure A).
3. Have the children slip the bags over their heads and touch the spot where their eyes are. Mark those areas lightly. Remove the bags and have the children cut a small opening for each eye, just large enough to see through.
4. Now have the children paint their masks. If paints are not available, use crayons; or cut features out of colored papers and paste them on.
5. From additional paper make hair, antenna, horns, ears, tongues, ties, etc. Paste them on.
6. In the time remaining, propose a few situations in which the children have an opportunity to wear their masks and act out a role.

Useful References

BECKER, EDITH C. *Adventures with Scissors and Paper.* Scranton, Pa.: International Textbook Co., 1959.

MONTGOMERY, CHANDLER. *Art for Teachers of Children.* Columbus, Ohio: Charles E. Merrill, 1968.

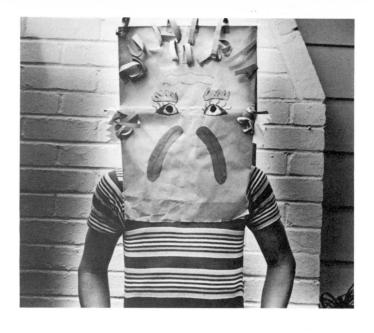

A

Construction Paper Masks

Suggested Topics   Warriors (Norsemen, American Indians, conquistadors, etc.). Comic faces. Frightening faces.

Primary Objectives
- To learn about the use of masks in other cultures
- To create masks which transform the wearers into other roles
- To play-act imaginatively

Materials/Tools
Construction paper, 12" × 18"
Rulers
Scissors
Paste
Stapler
Transparent tape
String

The Lesson
Discuss how Indians and other peoples have used masks. Review the information given in the introduction to this chapter. Select a topic that ties in with recent classroom studies or a recent experience such as a museum visit. Talk about the meaning of masks and about what facial characteristics might best achieve the character of the person to be represented. With a few lines illustrate on the chalkboard how an upturned mouth seems to portray a smile and a downward one a frown; raised eyebrows look surprised and lowered ones look like a scowl.

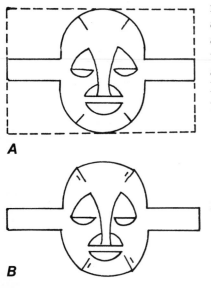

A

B

1. Holding the construction paper horizontally, have the children sketch a large head that touches the top and bottom edges of the paper. At the location for the ears, rule 2-inch wide tabs extending to the sides of the paper (Figure A). These tabs will go around to the back of the head and be joined with tape or staples to keep the finished mask on. Cut away the excess paper (Figure B).
2. Cut four 1½-inch slits: two at the top edge (above eyebrow area) and two at the bottom (below corners of mouth). When the sides of these slits are overlapped and taped or stapled, the mask obtains a rounded contour that will fit the face of the wearer. For still more depth, additional slits may be made and overlapped in the cheek areas.

3. Make slits for the eyes and enlarge them to whatever size and shape seem appropriate. Cut out the lower portion of the nose, leaving it attached to the face so it can extend like a flap; or a separate piece of paper can be folded, cut, and attached with tape to form the nose.

4. On separate pieces of paper plan the remaining facial parts (eyebrows, eyelashes, ears, mouth, hair, moustache, beard, etc.). Encourage the children to use every possible technique—folding, bending, curling, twisting, fraying, tearing, notching, etc.—that can help to transform a flat sheet of paper into a face mask.

5. Wear the masks, have a party, make up a play; then display all the masks on the wall around the chalkboard.

Useful References

BARANSKI, MATTHEW. *Mask Making*. Worcester, Mass.: Davis Publications, Inc., 1954.

BAYLOR, BYRD. *They Put on Masks*. New York: Scribner's, 1974.

Papier-Mâché Half-Mask

Suggested Topics   Theatrical masks. Party masks. Halloween masks.

Primary Objectives
- To increase the understanding of the meaning and use of masks in the theater
- To create masks which only partially cover the face
- To combine facial expressions, the mask, and the voice to create new roles

Materials/Tools

Newspaper

Gummed tape

Aluminum foil

Modeling clay, oil-base

Petroleum jelly

Wallpaper wheat paste

Plastic margarine cups

Paper towels

Fast-drying house paint

Tempera paints

Brushes

Shellac

Assorted scrap items for trimming—feathers, yarn, buttons, bottle caps, rick-rack, fur scraps, etc.

Scissors

The Lesson

The half-mask is a very effective theatrical means because it immediately changes the appearance of the wearer while allowing the uncovered half of the face to move, talk, grimace, and react in various ways. This gives the mask an extraordinary quality of aliveness. Half-masks were used in the Italian improvised comedy known as *commedia dell'arte* to identify stock characters such as Punchinello, Harlequin, and others. These masks are still popular at Mardi Gras and other festivals, but their main function remains theatrical.

1. Have the children take about five full sheets of newspaper and, by folding and crushing, shape them into an oval form about the size and shape of a person's face. (They should be several inches thick if pressed down on the desk.) Attach several pieces of gummed tape across the top of each form

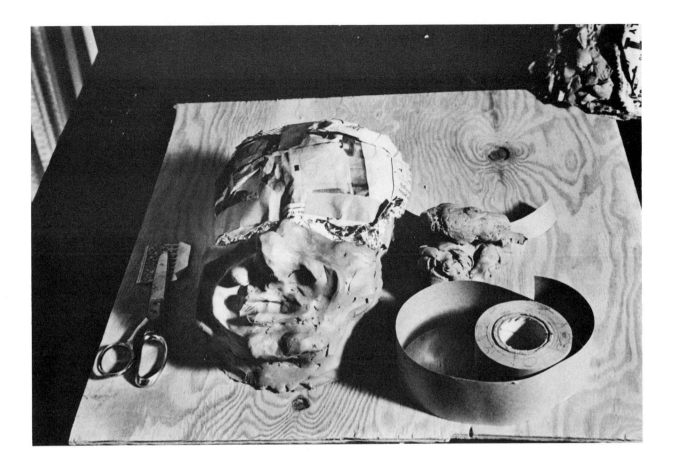

to help it retain its shape, then cover the newspaper with a layer of aluminum foil. These are the forms over which the modeling clay will be applied and modeled.

2. Have the children begin to cover either the upper or lower half of the oval form with small flattened pieces of modeling clay until half the oval is covered. Join these pieces by rubbing them with the finger tips so that it becomes one surface of clay.

3. Now the creation of the character begins as the children fashion noses, foreheads, eyebrows, etc. if they are making an upper half mask, or noses, mouths, and chins if they are making a mask for the lower half of the face. The teacher might at this point remind the children to exaggerate features as is done in theatrical masks.

4. Spread a thin coating of petroleum jelly over the surface of the modeling clay.

5. Mix wallpaper paste and water to a smooth, thick consistency. Give each child a plastic cupful.

6. Tear or cut strips of newspaper about $1'' \times 6''$. Saturate the strips with wallpaper paste and carefully lay them onto the modeling clay. Repeat this process until at least four or five layers cover the mask. Use paper towel strips for the final layer, and instruct the children to make the final layer very smooth, following every detail of the modeling clay.

7. Let the masks dry for a few days. When dry, gently remove the clay from the inside of the mask. Using scissors, trim away any ragged or frayed edges. If the edges are not strong, go around them with another layer of paper, using regular classroom paste instead of wallpaper paste.

8. Apply a sealer coat of fast-drying house paint over the entire mask before painting with colored tempera. Or you may omit the undercoat and paint directly with tempera. Again remind the children to exaggerate in their use of colors so as to make an impact on the audience.

9. Finish the masks with a coating of shellac or varnish to make them shine and to add toughness to their surface.

10. Pierce at the sides and attach strings to tie behind the head.

11. Plan a short play or pantomime using the masks to depict the various roles.

Useful References

KENNY, JOHN B., and KENNY, CARLA. *The Art of Papier-Mâché*. Philadelphia: Chilton Book Co., 1969.

RILEY, OLIVE. *Masks and Magic*. New York: Studio Publications, 1955.

Papier-Mâché Face Mask

Team Project

Suggested Topics   Party masks. Halloween masks. Theatrical masks. Dance masks.

Primary Objectives

- To work in teams to create the first stages of individual masks
- To capture the essential features of an imaginary character
- To experience masks as theatrical means

Materials/Tools

Gummed tape, 1½ to 2 inches wide
Fabric remnants, 15 to 18 inches square
Paper towels (optional)
Newspaper
Plastic containers for water (margarine cups)
Plastic containers for wallpaper paste
Wallpaper wheat paste
Fast-drying house paint, white or buff
Tempera paints
Brushes
Scrap items—yarn, cellophane, buttons, felt, etc.
String

The Lesson

Review the meaning and uses of masks in various cultures, going back to the cave dwellers. Talk about the need to exaggerate or emphasize the size, shape, and color of facial parts so they "carry" to the viewer, just as an actor needs to apply heavy stage make-up in order to "carry" the distance from stage to audience. Have the children decide what types they want to portray in their masks—"good guys" or "bad guys," happy people or sad people, old or young, pretty or ugly, fat or skinny, etc.

1. Divide the class into teams of two. Two children will work together during the first step of the project to help each other make a well-fitting, strong base on which the mask will be formed. Give each team several yard lengths of gummed tape, some newspaper, one square of cloth for each child, and a small container of water.

2. One child of each team sits in a chair with the cloth draped over the face and hair. (It is helpful to lean back and face the ceiling.) The second child moistens a small wad of crumpled newspaper or paper toweling and, using it as a sponge, wets about a one-yard length of gummed tape. The moistened tape is carefully stuck to the fabric under the chin, carried up the cheek, over the top of the head, down the opposite cheek, and back under the chin again.

3. Shorter pieces of gummed tape are moistened and applied over the cloth from side to side until the entire facial area is covered with tape.

4. Slip the tape-fabric form off the child's face, and fill the space in back with crumpled newspaper. This is the form on which layers of papier-mâché will be applied to create the mask.

5. Now the children switch places and repeat the process until everyone has a base form and can begin to work individually on his or her mask.

6. Distribute newspaper and mixed wallpaper paste. Explain the technique. Cut or tear newspaper in strips, saturate the strips with paste, and apply them on the form, layer upon layer, until the mask has at least three layers of papier-mâché over the entire surface.

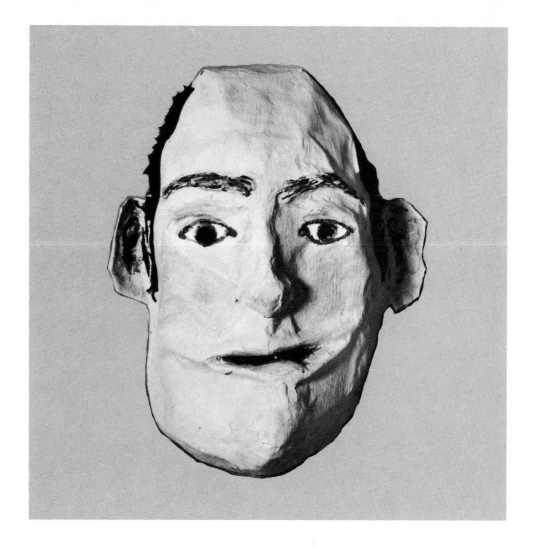

7. To develop features, small wads can be placed on the form and then covered with small strips and paste to make puffy cheeks, a bulbous nose, bulgy eyes, etc. Rolled or folded pieces can be placed on the form and then covered with strips of paper and paste to form eyebrows, wrinkles, furrows, etc. For ears, tongue, lips, etc., shapes can be cut from 8 to 10 thicknesses of newspaper, soaked in paste, and applied in a similar manner.

8. When all the details of the features are in place, apply small bits of paper soaked in paste to make a smooth final layer of papier-mâché. Allow the mask to dry for several days until it is hard and strong.

9. Before painting, the fabric base may be removed or the edges may be trimmed off, as each child chooses.

10. If a fast-drying house paint is available, apply one coat to each mask before painting with tempera. This saves much tempera paint and makes a good surface on which to do the final painting. Urge the children to think about the colors. What color will make someone look fierce, old, mean, shy, young, etc.?

11. Use the assortment of scrap items to create hair, eyebrows, teeth, etc.
12. Pierce at the sides and attach strings for tying on the mask.
13. Use the masks for dramatizing some class-conceived plays. Or do improvizations using appropriate masks to portray various roles in a given situations, for example, the shoplifter apprehended by the security officer and brought before the store owner.

Useful References

BARANSKI, MATTHEW. *Mask Making.* Worcester, Mass.: Davis Publications, Inc., 1954.

RILEY, OLIVE. *Masks and Magic.* New York: Studio Publications, 1955.

The No-mask Mask

Suggested Topics   I am a flower, bird, animal, airplane, Indian Chief, Viking, knight, king, clown, etc.

Primary Objectives

• To construct a mask that shows the wearer's face
• To focus attention on peripheral ornamental details
• To exercise an imaginative way of seeing and appearing

Materials/Tools

Cardboards 12″ × 15″ or larger, one per child
Colored construction paper
Scissors
White glue
Paste
Stapler
Mat knife
Glue gun (useful but not essential)
Sticks of wood, about the size of a ruler
Old magazines

The Lesson

Most masks cover the entire face or a large part of it, thus obscuring the identity of the wearer. This mask uses the face of the wearer as part of the mask, and depends on other details around the face to develop the illusion of being something or someone else.

The lesson will be easier to conduct if you prepare the cardboards in advance. With a mat knife, cut an oval opening for the face about 8 inches long and 5 inches wide in the center of each cardboard. (This eliminates the need to use the mat knife in class.)

1. Begin with a brief discussion of masks in various cultures. Show some examples of the front view of the heads of various animals. Talk about how the mane of a lion gives it a distinctive look, how the horns and head shape of a ram make it easy to identify that animal, and so on. Look at a picture of a knight in armor, examining the helmet, crest, and plume. Show photographs of people wearing unusual headdress or headgear, such as an astronaut, a princess, an African warrior, and others.

2. Let the children search through outdated magazines for photographs of people, animals, or birds, whose heads have unusual or spectacular qualities. Each child is to choose the one she or he wants to represent.

3. Have the children cut hats, ears, beards, hair, crowns, wings, feathers, etc. from colored construction paper or lightweight cardboard. Attach the cut pieces around the oval opening in the cardboard. If a glue gun is available, you can attach heavier pieces such as cardboard, Styrofoam, parts of plastic containers, etc., to give a more three-dimensional structure to the mask.

4. Attach a stick to the back of the mask with white glue or by stapling it securely to the cardboard. (Do not obscure the facial opening.) By means of this stick the mask is held to the wearer's face.

5. Use the masks for some improvisations or for a special party.

Useful References

JOHNSON, PAULINE. *Creating with Paper: Basic Forms and Variations.* Seattle: University of Washington Press, 1958.

RILEY, OLIVE. *Masks and Magic.* New York: Studio Publications, 1955.

Papier-Mâché over Balloon Masks

Suggested Topics Cartoon or comic book characters.
Famous people.

Primary Objectives

- To learn about masks as used in other cultures
- To design a mask that conforms to a pre-determined shape
- To enact new roles based upon the transformation caused by wearing the mask

Materials/Tools

Large balloons (about 14″ in diameter when inflated)
Newspapers
Wallpaper wheat paste
Plastic containers for paste
Fast-drying house paint
Tempera paints
Brushes
Scrap trimmings—felt, yarn, cloth, buttons, cardboard, etc.
White glue
Small rubber bands or string
Mat knife (X-Acto or similar)

The Lesson

1. Talk about masks: their significance in various cultures, their use in drama, their universality since the days of the cavemen.
2. Decide on a topic and discuss what special features of the face and head make these characters unique.
3. Cover the desks with newspapers and provide everyone with a plastic margarine container full of mixed wallpaper paste.
4. Inflate the balloons and tie with small rubber bands or string.
5. Tear newspaper into strips about 1 to 2 inches wide and 6 to 10 inches long. Run strips of paper through the paste and then lay them on the surface of the balloon. Continue this until the balloon is completely covered with several layers. During this process, watch to see that everyone makes several good structural layers.

6. Now have each child decide on what he or she can add at this point to create a special character. It might be paper or plastic cups, smaller balloons, wads of crumpled paper, pieces of cardboard, scraps of Styrofoam, etc. Add these parts one at a time by running strips of paper along the balloon surface up and over the new addition and down again to the original surface.

7. Children who are especially creative may do many variations on the sphere, while those children with less creativity may limit their concepts primarily to the spherical shape. In either case, the project can be successful for every child.

8. Allow the papier-mâché to dry; then coat the entire surface with any fast-drying house paint.

9. With a mat knife, carefully (carefully!) cut a circle large enough for the child to insert his or her head. Cut several small openings for vision. The balloon will, of course, be broken and then pull free from the inner wall of the mask.

10. Paint with tempera. Add yarn for hair, buttons or jar lids for eyes, felt or cloth scraps, etc.

11. Produce some spontaneous drama involving three to four children at a time.

Useful References

BETTS, VICTORIA. *Exploring Papier-Mâché.* Worcester, Mass.: Davis Publications, Inc., 1955.

JOHNSON, LILLIAN. *Papier-Mâché.* New York: David McKay Co., Inc., 1958.

Papier-Mâché Pulp Figures

Suggested Topics   People, vegetables, birds, fruits, animals.

Primary Objectives

- To experience visualizing and working in three dimensions
- To become aware of the main shapes and forms of objects, people, etc.
- To carry a several-step project to completion

Materials/Tools

Newspapers
Wallpaper wheat paste
Sawdust (optional)
Buckets or large containers
Large sieve or collander, or mesh fabric stretched over a bucket
Facial or toilet tissues
Paste
Tempera paints
Brushes
Shellac or acrylic spray

The Lesson

In advance of this project, have the children tear newspaper into small pieces—enough to fill several buckets or large containers. Add water to cover and allow the paper to soak for a day; then strain through a sieve and squeeze out the excess water. In a separate container, mix wallpaper paste with water and stir until the mixture is smooth. Add wallpaper paste mixture to the drained paper pulp and mix thoroughly until the pulp has the consistency of clay. Sawdust may be added to give the mixture more bulk, but it is not essential.

1. Talk with the children about the shapes or forms of things. Who can think of something that is round? Who can think of something square? Who can think of something long, etc.? We recognize objects by their shapes. Who can make the shape of an egg? Let's make that shape with our fingertip in the air. Who can make the shape of a duck, a bird, a rabbit, a tomato, a banana? Today we will each make a shape with papier-mâché.

2. Cover the table or desk tops and give each child a large handful of the paper pulp-paste mixture. This material can be modeled in the manner similar to modeling clay, but of course it is sticky and cannot be rubbed smooth like clay.

3. After the figures have been modeled they must dry for about three days. Drying time depends upon the humidity. When the figures are almost dry, details may be added by using facial or toilet tissue which has been moistened with paste.

4. When completely dry, the figures can be painted with tempera paints. For a final finish, apply a coat of shellac or acrylic spray; this will add a shine to the surface.

Useful References

BETTS, VICTORIA. *Exploring Papier-Mâché.* Worcester, Mass.: Davis Publications, Inc., 1955.

MATTIL, EDWARD L. *Meaning in Crafts,* 3rd ed. Englewood Cliffs, N.J.: Prentice-Hall, Inc., 1971.

Papier-Mâché Roll Figures

Suggested Topics   Jungle or circus animals. Domesticated animals or pets. Walking things: four-legged, six-legged, etc.

Primary Objectives

- To visualize and construct three-dimensional forms
- To capture the essential qualities of a particular animal or person
- To recycle waste material into a creative object

Materials/Tools

Newspaper, at least 32 sheets each
Gummed tape or string
Wallpaper wheat paste
Plastic containers for paste (margarine cups)
Fast-drying house paint (optional)
Tempera paints and brushes
Scrap items—yarn, shavings, buttons, bottle caps, etc.

The Lesson

This project shows children how an ordinary waste material like newspaper can be creatively transformed into a meaningful object. It requires several sessions to complete.

1. Begin with a discussion of how the body structure of various animals is adapted to their eating habits. The giraffe has a long neck with which it can reach fairly high branches. Monkeys and apes have long, flexible arms and legs that enable them to climb to where their favorite fruits are. Elephants use their trunks to bring vegetation to their mouths. Anteaters probe their long snouts into anthills. Focus this discussion on the similarities and differences in animal structure.

2. Let each child decide on one particular animal. How many legs will it have? Are the legs longer or shorter than the body, or about the same length? What other parts will it need?

3. Demonstrate how to make an armature out of newspaper rolls. Use 8 sheets of newspaper to make each roll. Lay the sheets on the desk top and roll them up tight, securing the ends with gummed tape to keep from unrolling. Roll in the shorter direction to make short rolls (about 14 inches long) and in the longer direction to make long rolls (about 22 inches long). Most animals will require two long and two short rolls (see Figure A).

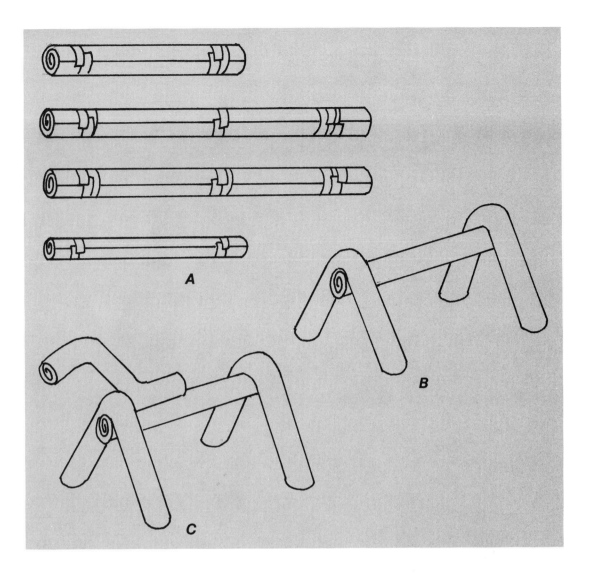

A

B

C

4. Using one short roll for the body, demonstrate how to add a pair of legs by folding a long roll at the middle and placing it over one end of the short roll (Figure B). Tie or tape it in place. Explain that the animal will need a second pair of legs at the other end of the body roll, in order to stand alone.

5. The fourth roll serves as the armature for the neck and head. Bend or curve it, as shown in Figure C, and tie or tape it to the body roll.

6. With the newspaper armature completed, each child may now decide how to adjust the position of the legs, neck, and head. Show them also how to add wads of crumpled paper to "fatten" the body or give more shape to the head. Tape these wads of paper in place.

7. Cover the desk tops with newspaper, and give each child a cupful of wallpaper paste which has been mixed with water to a smooth consistency.

8. Tear or cut strips of newspaper about $1'' \times 6''$ or $1\frac{1}{2}'' \times 9''$. Dip these strips one at a time into the paste and begin to cover the entire animal, one layer at a time. As the layers are added, the children can begin to add any necessary details with papier-mâché, such as eyes, ears, tails, manes, nostrils, etc. The layers of paper and paste will make the figures strong and rigid when they have dried.

9. After the figures have dried for several days, they are ready to paint. If fast-drying house paint is available, cover the entire figure with one coat. This saves on the tempera paints, since the primed layer of paint will absorb less tempera than unpainted newspaper. Otherwise, paint directly with tempera paints.

10. Talk about colors and how they can be mixed to make new colors. Talk about the interesting surfaces that may be achieved with stripes, dots, wavy lines, etc. Discuss the ways that other materials such as yarn, shavings, steel wool, cotton batting, buttons, bottle caps, etc., might be glued on to create even more interesting textural qualities on the hair, manes, tails, eyes, skin, etc.

11. Let the children paint and glue until everyone has completed a unique papier-mâché animal—truly "one of a kind."

Useful References

KENNY, JOHN, and KENNY, CARLA. *The Art of Papier-Mâché.* New York: Chilton Book Company, 1968.

MEILACH, DONA Z. *Papier-Mâché Artistry.* New York: Crown Publishers, Inc., 1971.

Papier-Mâché over Paper Bags

Suggested Topics   Animals and birds.

Primary Objectives
- To create simple three-dimensional forms that represent particular objects
- To do a two-step project requiring a longer work time span

Materials/Tools
Newspaper
Wallpaper wheat paste
Plastic containers for paste (margarine cups)
Tempera paints
Brushes
Paper lunch bags
String, about three 12″ lengths per child

The Lesson
When working with younger children, keep the problem simple and uncomplicated. Select a subject that is relatively easy to shape and does not require small details. Good choices are ducks, rabbits, birds, or mice.

1. Begin with a discussion about the main shape of the subject. Is it round like a ball, or is it shaped like a watermelon? What other parts does it have—a head, tail, wings, legs, etc.?
2. Have each child crumple some newspaper and stuff the bag. Have the children tie the filled bags with a length of string. Begin to squeeze the bag until it takes on the basic shape of the subject.
3. Cover each desk with newspaper and give a container of paste to each child.
4. Have everyone tear narrow strips of newspaper about 6 inches long. Dip strips into the paste, one at a time, and apply them to the surface of the bag. Put on several layers.
5. Now talk about the other parts of the animal, and get the children to think about how they might shape a head, wings, etc., from folded paper or a wad of crumpled paper. After each new part is formed, attach it to the body, using paper strips moistened with paste. Cover the attached parts with several additional layers of paper and paste.
6. Allow the papier-mâché sculptures to dry for several days. When completely dry, they are ready for paint. Tempera paints will give the best coverage and are the easiest to use.

7. Use this opportunity to talk about color and how a new color can be made by mixing two other colors: yellow and blue to make green, red and blue to make purple, and so on. Talk about how the figures may become more interesting by adding stripes, dots, wavy lines, etc.

Useful References

JOHNSON, LILLIAN. *Papier-Mâché.* New York: David McKay Co., Inc., 1958.

MEILACH, DONA Z. *Papier-Mâché Artistry.* New York: Crown Publishers, Inc., 1971.

Papier-Mâché over Plastic or Styrofoam Containers

Suggested Topics   Birds, beasts (including the two-legged kind), bugs, buildings, and cars.

Primary Objectives

- To create imaginative representational objects which adapt to predetermined forms
- To carry out a multi-step project to completion
- To create objects from recycled waste materials

Materials/Tools

Throwaway items of plastic or Styrofoam—bottles, cups, wig forms, fast food containers, etc.

Newspaper

Wallpaper wheat paste

Plastic containers for paste (margarine cups)

Tempera

Brushes

The Lesson

To a large extent this lesson will grow out of the throwaway plastic or Styrofoam items which children can accumulate.

1. Provide each child with at least one container or a piece of Styrofoam. Have them close their eyes, handle the piece, and think of what familiar object the shape suggests. Ask questions: Does it make you think of a house, car, person, animal, bird, etc.? How would you go about changing it to look more like what you have in mind? Would you add something or cut part of it away?

2. When each child has an idea, give out containers of wallpaper paste and newspapers.

3. Demonstrate how a small tight roll of paper taped across a bottle might be arms, or a ball of paper taped onto the neck might become a head.

4. Encourage the children to modify their containers or Styrofoam by adding parts or removing parts.

5. Cover the entire sculpture with small pieces of newspaper dipped in wallpaper paste. Create details as this proceeds, layer upon layer.

6. Allow the papier-mâché sculpture to dry for several days. Then paint it with tempera paints.

Useful References

BETTS, VICTORIA. *Exploring Papier-Mâché*. Worcester, Mass.: Davis Publications, Inc., 1955.

MEILACH, DONA Z. *Papier-Mâché Artistry*. New York: Crown Publishers, Inc., 1971.

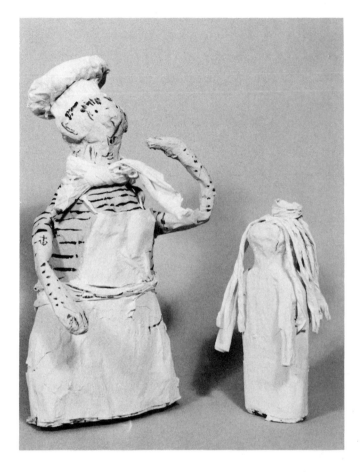

Papier-Mâché Treasure Box or Pencil Holder

Primary Objectives
- To make surface or decorative designs which enhance an object
- To design in a new way using paper and paste
- To increase awareness of design in man-made objects

Materials/Tools
Small gift boxes
Plastic bottles, pint size, cut in half. Use bottom half for pencil holders
Tin cans, washed, tops removed
Newspaper
Wallpaper wheat paste
Plastic containers for paste (margarine cups)
Facial or toilet tissues
White glue
Tempera paint
Shellac, varnish, acrylic spray, or polyurethane spray
Brushes

The Lesson
This project uses processes similar to those used in Mexico and India for construction of simple decorative containers for jewelry, pencils, etc.

1. Let each child choose a container—box, bottle, or can. Cover desk tops with several layers of newspaper. Distribute wallpaper paste and newspapers to each child.
2. Cover the container inside and out with three layers of torn newspaper pieces about 2 inches square saturated with wallpaper paste. Let the containers dry for several days.
3. Plan some simple abstract designs to be made from toilet or facial tissue. Cut 10-inch strips of tissue and twist or roll them into strands or coils.
4. Moisten one strand at a time with white glue and begin to apply a raised design over the exterior surface of the container. The design may be just a decorative repeat pattern or it may evolve into a pattern of flowers, insects, butterflies, etc. When the design is complete, allow it to dry for several days.
5. Paint the container, using small brushes to paint the details of the raised design.

6. When dry, coat the entire container with either clear acrylic, polyurethane, shellac, or varnish to give it a glossy, protective finish.

Useful References

BETTS, VICTORIA. *Exploring Papier-Mâché.* Worcester, Mass., Davis Publications, Inc., 1955.

KENNY, JOHN, and KENNY, CARLA. *The Art of Papier-Mâché.* Philadelphia: Chilton Book Co., 1968.

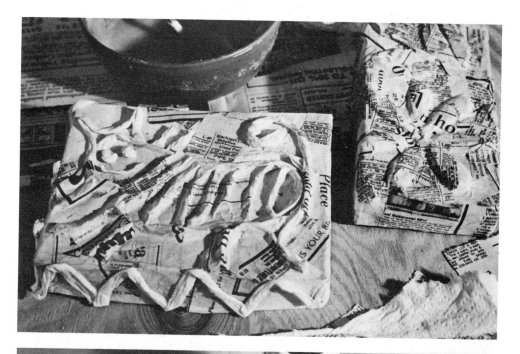

Stand-up Papier-Mâché Figure

Suggested Topic Ethnic roots—the peoples of the world.

Primary Objectives
- To increase interest and pride in one's heritage
- To do simple research for purposes of information, authenticity, and inspiration
- To increase the range of individual appreciation of historical and folk costumes

Materials/Tools

Wire dress hangers, 2 each

Wood squares for bases, 8″ × 8″, about ½″ to 1″ thick

Fencing staples (¾″ long) or 1″ finishing nails

Pliers and hammers

Newspaper

Gummed tape

Wallpaper wheat paste

Plastic containers for paste (margarine cups)

Scissors

Straight pins

Tempera paint and brushes

Varnish, shellac, or clear polyurethane

The Lesson

This project might be the culmination of a study of our ancestors (Africans, Asians, Europeans, Native Americans, etc.). How did our ancestors dress? Did they have special costumes for special occasions? Encourage the children to search for examples of costumes in the school library or at home.

1. Have a helpful parent cut open the wire hangers (discard the hooks), straighten the wires somewhat, and bend one end of each wire into a U-shape about two inches long (Figures A and B). This U-shaped end will be the means of attaching the figure to the wood base.

2. Give each child about ten double-page sheets of newspaper, two dress hanger wires, one wood square, and eight pieces of gummed tape, each about six inches long. After distributing the supplies, the teacher should demonstrate steps 3–8.

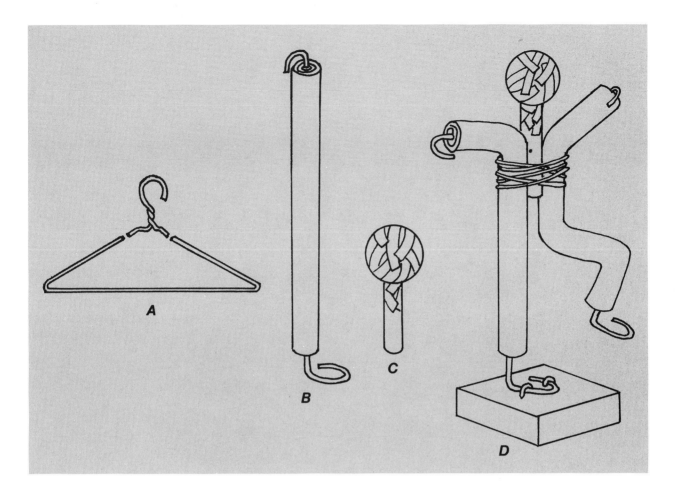

3. Show how to make a tight newspaper roll about 22 inches long. Tape the roll at the ends and at the middle so it doesn't unroll. Make another roll of the same length. Insert a wire into the center of each roll and bend over any excess wire that protrudes (Figure B).

4. Bend each roll at right angles about one-fourth of the way from one end. Each right angle will become an arm. Below the bends that form the arms, tie or tape the two rolls together for a distance of about five or six inches. This portion will represent the body.

5. Somewhere below the middle, separate the two rolls and bend them to create the effect of walking, running, sitting, or whatever posture is desired.

6. To make the figure stand, separate the "feet" (i.e., the U-bends) and bend the wire at these ends to create the soles of the feet. These are attached to the wood base either by small fencing staples or by 1" nails bent over the foot. Try to suggest action in the figures before attaching the feet to the base.

7. For the head and neck, make a short roll of newspaper, about eight inches long, and tape it securely. Around one end of the roll (neck) crumple a sheet of newspaper into the shape of a ball and fasten it securely to the roll with gummed tape (Figure C).

8. Attach the neck roll with tape to the body portion of the two longer rolls. Then tie or tape the three parts together (Figure D). Now the figure has two arms, two legs, a neck, and a head, and is standing on a wood base.

9. After demonstrating steps 3–8, have the students construct their basic figures in a similar way. Then distribute containers of wallpaper paste and let them begin to work on their figures with papier-mâché.

10. With small pieces of newspaper dipped in wallpaper paste, cover the entire figure. Add wads of paper to fill out the chest or stomach. Smaller wads will make hands and facial features.

11. Using scissors, cut a pattern out of newspaper for each item of clothing—skirt, shirt, trousers, hat, etc. When they seem to fit, use the pattern to cut three or four thicknesses of newspaper. Moisten these layers with wallpaper paste and pin the clothing in place. Use additional paste and paper to attach the costume firmly.

12. Allow the entire figure to dry. Additional parts or details can now be added. When dry, paint the figure and the costume. Urge the children to use or mix colors appropriate to the skin and costume of their figure.

13. For a glossy finish, coat with varnish, shellac, or clear polyurethane.

14. Have an exhibit of the "Peoples of the World."

Useful References

KENNY, JOHN B., and KENNY, CARLA. *The Art of Papier-Mâché.* Philadelphia: Chilton Book Co., 1969.

MEILACH, DONA Z. *Papier-Mâché Artistry.* New York: Crown Publishers, Inc., 1971.

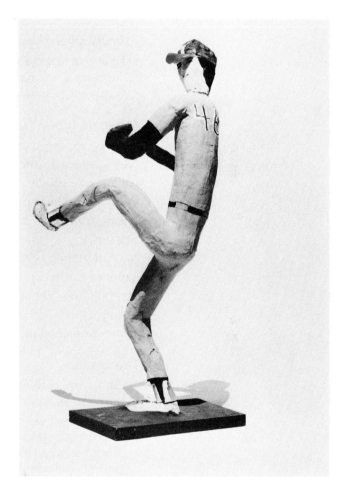

Dress-up Hats

Primary Objectives

- To create three-dimensional forms from flat paper
- To learn about hat styles through the ages
- To invent new uses for discarded materials

Materials/Tools

Kraft wrapping paper, cut in sheets about 24″ square

Newspaper cut into 22″ squares

Gallon size plastic bottles or round half-gallon ice cream containers

Wallpaper wheat paste

Plastic containers for wallpaper paste

Scissors

Masking tape

Colored construction paper

Scrap items—ribbon, yarn, fabric, buttons, etc.

String

Tempera paints and brushes

The Lesson

1. Show the class illustrations of men's and women's hats of the past and pictures of elaborate Easter bonnets. Call attention to crown shapes, brims, and decorations.

2. Have each child cut a hat crown shape from a gallon size plastic bottle or a round half-gallon size ice cream container. If neither is available, crumple sheets of newspaper into a ball about the size of a child's head. Then wrap it several times with masking tape or string so it holds it's shape.

3. Saturate the surface of two sheets of wrapping paper with wallpaper paste and place the two pasted sides together. If kraft paper is not available, use newspapers, but moisten at least four sheets and lay them on top of one another. The paper, now damp, will be limp.

4. Drape the moistened square over the plastic crown or crumpled ball of paper and form it with the hands until it takes the shape desired. Tie a string around the base of the crown to help retain the shape, and flatten or rumple the paper to form the desired brim. Cut away any excess to shape the brim—probably round or oval, narrow or wide. (This can be done now or later, after the paper dries.)

5. Allow the hat to dry completely. As it dries, the wallpaper paste will harden, and the hat will retain its shape.

6. When completely dry, paint the hat with tempera or spray it out-of-doors with spray paint. Add decorations such as stripes and dots, paper flowers, ribbons, buttons, fabric, etc. to make it something special.

Useful References

JOHNSON, PAULINE. *Creating with Paper: Basic Forms and Variations.* Seattle: University of Washington Press, 1958.

LALIBERTÉ NORMAN, and MOGELON, ALEX. *Masks, Face Coverings and Headgear.* New York: Van Nostrand Reinhold, 1973.

Papier-Mâché Fruits and Vegetables

Suggested Topic   The fruits and vegetables we grow and eat.

Primary Objectives
- To see the beauty in nature's designs
- To make careful observations of shapes, colors, and textures
- To recycle waste material into an art object

Materials/Tools
Newspaper
Gummed tape
Wallpaper wheat paste
Containers for paste
Scissors
Tempera paints
Brushes
Shellac

The Lesson
The day before the lesson, discuss the various fresh fruits and vegetables we find at this time of year. Have as many children as possible bring at least one to school the next day to be used as a model. Try to get a variety such as apple, orange, pear, banana, pineapple, tomato, squash, avocado, cucumber, pepper, radish, beet, cabbage, celery, etc. Tell the children to leave attached any stems, leaves, or tops. Plan to bring in a few additional items for those who do not bring anything. Using the specimens brought in as examples, talk about the variety of designs in nature. Point out the shapes, colors, textures, patterns, etc.

1. Have the children crumple or shape newspaper to match the overall shape and size of the fruit or vegetable they are making. Put a strip or two of gummed tape around it to retain the shape.
2. Cover the table tops and distribute containers of wallpaper paste.
3. Tear newspaper strips, dip them into the wallpaper paste, and begin to cover the form.
4. After several layers have been put on, cut, fold, or roll any additional shapes which may be needed to complete the fruit or vegetable. Attach these, piece by piece, using paper strips saturated with paste.

5. Continue covering the object, adding on, developing texture, etc. This may require more than one session. As the object dries, it becomes hard and strong and is easier to work on.

6. When the papier-mâché fruit or vegetable is completed, let it dry thoroughly before painting.

7. Use tempera paints. Experiment in mixing color. Paint the objects in their natural colors, mixing colors to obtain different hues. Call attention to any patterns such as subtle stripes, flecks, spots, etc. that are part of nature's design.

8. Shellac the entire group and exhibit them before the children take them home.

Useful References

Lavoos, Janice. *Design Is a Dandelion.* San Carlos, Calif.: Golden State Junior Books, 1966.

Meilach, Dona Z. *Papier-Mâché Artistry.* New York: Crown Publishers, Inc., 1971.

Papier-Mâché Power Object

Suggested Topics A cave man's club; a king's scepter; a knight's mace; a shepherd's crook; a magician's or fairy's wand; a shaman's rattle or cane; a conductor's baton; a policeman's night stick; a spaceman's ray gun; a bishop's crosier

Primary Objectives

- To learn some of the symbols of power used throughout history
- To use discarded materials in innovative ways
- To assemble parts into an organized design

Materials/Tools

Newspaper

Wallpaper wheat paste

Containers for wallpaper paste

White glue

Kraft gummed or masking tape

String

Tempera paints and brushes

Scrap materials—wood scraps, bottle caps, buttons, yarn, feathers, Styrofoam cups and containers, plastic bottles, etc.

The Lesson

1. Begin this lesson with a discussion of objects as symbols of power. Have some examples in mind and several illustrations or photographs from sources such as the *National Geographic*, encyclopedias, or books on the Indians of North America. For example, the Haida and Tlingit Indians of the northwest coast of Canada or the Hopi Indians of the southwestern United States carried remarkable power objects. Illustrations of kings with scepters, bishops with crosiers, shamans or witch doctors with rattles would be good examples. Following the discussion, suggest the use of the dictionary and encyclopedia for definitions and illustrations of these words: *mace, crosier, scepter, shaman,* and *baton.*

2. Demonstrate the general idea of these objects with a few examples. Roll about six sheets of newspaper into a long roll and wrap tape around the roll near the ends to keep it tightly rolled. Make a shorter roll of several sheets of folded newspaper and tape it securely. Form a cross from the two rolls and temporarily tie them together. This now represents a religious power symbol. Remove the shorter roll, then insert the longer roll into the neck of

a pint-size plastic bottle. When held upright, it has the appearance of a scepter, mace, or baton. Remove the bottle, drop a few pebbles or beans into it and then insert the shorter roll. Shake it to simulate a shaman's rattle.

3. Distribute newspaper, wallpaper paste, and tape. Have the children make one or two rolls of newspaper and tape the ends.

4. Encourage the children to search through the scrap materials to find objects to add on to their roll of newspaper. Show them how to "fatten" the roll with crumpled newspaper covered with strips of newspaper saturated with wallpaper paste. When the rolls have been modified by adding Styrofoam cups, inserting the ends in plastic bottles, attaching cardboard rolls from paper towels, making wings of cardboard, etc., the entire power object must be covered with pieces of cut or torn newspaper saturated with wallpaper paste.

5. Allow the power objects to dry completely. The wallpaper paste will make them strong and will securely hold the added parts. Paint the papier-mâché objects with tempera paints.

6. Have the children make a second search now for smaller objects that can be added over the painted surface. Attach items such as buttons, bottle caps, feathers, fur scraps, yarn, etc. with white glue.

7. Have everyone show their power objects and talk imaginatively about what the objects represent and how they might be used.

Useful References

Andrews, Michael. *Sculpture and Ideas.* Englewood Cliffs, N.J.: Prentice-Hall, Inc., 1965.

D'Amico, Victor, and Buchman, Arlette. *Assemblage.* New York: Museum of Modern Art, 1972.

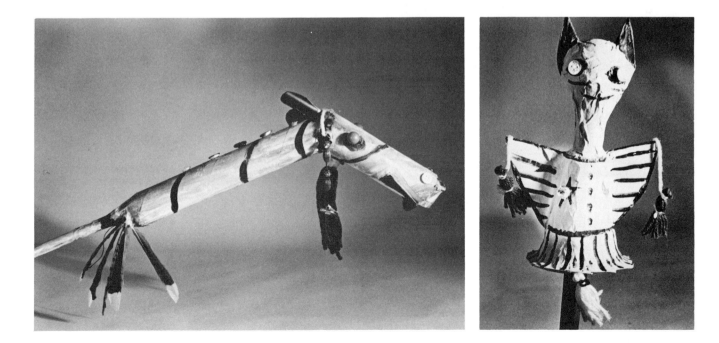

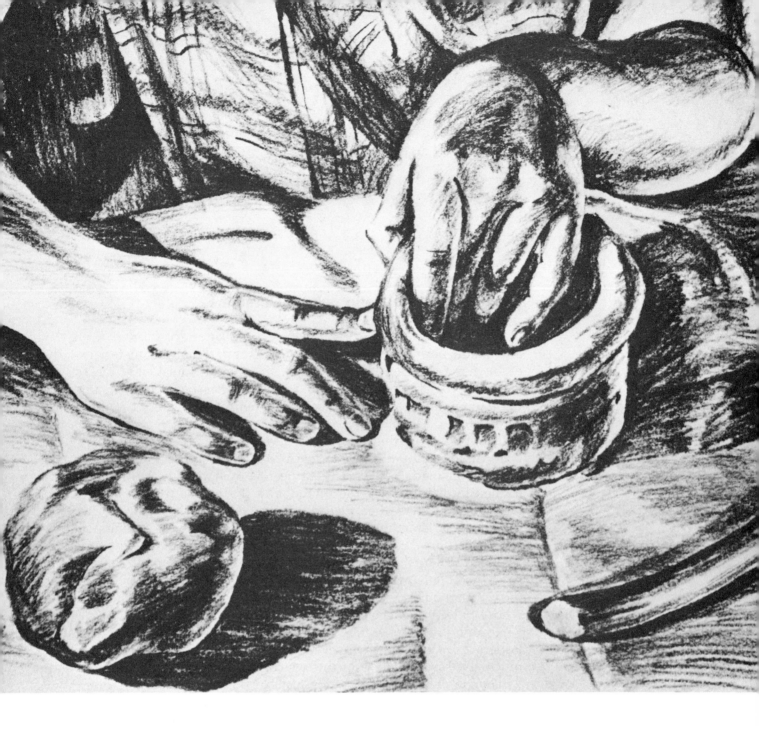

CERAMICS 9

*Nature is so much richer than anything
you can imagine.*

GEORGE TOOKER

Background Information about Ceramics

In the broadest sense, ceramics includes all pottery formed from clay and made permanently hard by heat. Clay, a natural material of the earth, has two main characteristics: first, when moist, it is plastic and can easily be shaped; and second, when it has been fired (heated to a high temperature), it becomes permanently hard and cannot be returned to a plastic state.

Examples of earthenware, which was the first type of pottery, have been discovered dating to about 7000 B.C. This very same type of pottery is still made today. The earliest known ceramic containers were formed by hand, using the fingers and thumbs as the basic tools. The Japanese still use this method to make some tea bowls. Another method was later invented in which coils resembling strands of rope were piled up, coil upon coil, until the shape of a container was achieved. Then the coils were pressed together, scraped, shaped, and smoothed. This method is still employed by many ceramics craftsmen today, particularly the Indians of the southwestern United States, whose pottery has become famous.

No one is certain where or when the potter's wheel was invented. Potters have used the wheel in many different parts of the world in much the same way. One difference is that Western potters turn the wheel counter-clockwise, while Eastern potters turn it clockwise. With the potter's wheel, a lump of clay is placed upon a flat disk, usually rotated by the foot. As it spins, the potter first forces the lump into a solid cylindrical mass, then slowly forces one thumb into the center of it. Using both hands, the potter then uniformly squeezes the clay from both the outside and the inside as it rotates, so that the walls become thinner and are raised up into the shape of a bowl, cylinder, or bottle. This requires much practice and considerable skill.

As ceramics came to be used for many utilitarian purposes, potters found easier and quicker ways to make pottery. During the eighteenth century they adapted a process to wheel throwing called ''jollying'' or ''jiggering.'' This consisted simply of using patterns or templates of plaster and metal which shaped the object rather than shaping it entirely by hand. Potters discovered the process of shaping clay in molds thousands of years ago. The Mayans of Mexico and the ancient Greeks were masters of molded pottery.

Even the earliest pottery shows a universal desire to decorate. Some examples show finger and fingernail marks; others show that fiber or straw was pressed into the damp clay for decoration. At a later time, designs were pressed in by seals, or carved into the hardened clay before it was fired. Sometimes a thin layer of colored clay was brushed over a contrasting color. Sometimes a design was scratched through the top layer to expose the lower layer. The Pennsylvania potters of German origin were famous for their *sgraffito* (scratched) ware. Sometimes liquid clay, called *slip*, was brushed or "trailed" onto another colored clay to produce a design. *Trailing* might be likened to squeezing a thin decorative icing onto a cake, or squeezing toothpaste from a tube. Four thousand years ago potters in Mesopotamia and Manchuria learned to mix metallic oxides with their clay. These mixtures were then used like paint to create beautiful designs on pottery.

After the potter shapes a ceramic object and sets it aside to dry, the moisture in the clay begins to evaporate and the clay begins to harden. The surface can then be rubbed and polished with a smooth object such as a piece of glass, the bowl of a spoon, a marble, or a pebble. This is called *burnishing*. If the clay is particularly fine, it can be burnished until it shines. Much of the famous pottery of the Incas of Peru has been burnished to a high sheen.

When perfectly dry, the finished pieces are fired. Today's potters use gas, electric, and wood-fired kilns, depending on available fuel sources. In primitive cultures, the dried pottery was simply stacked in a shallow hole in the ground and a wood fire was built over it. Intense heat causes a physical change to take place. When the temperature reaches about 1000° F., the clay hardens and can never return to a plastic state. As a simple rule, the higher the temperature, the harder the finished pottery. If pottery is heated to a high enough temperature, its porosity is sufficiently reduced so that a container will not seep liquids.

Glazing is the final step in pottery making. After being made permanently hard by firing, the piece of pottery is coated with a finely-ground glass powder mixed with water. Glazes may be applied by brushing, dipping, or spraying. The pottery is then returned to the kiln and reheated. During the glaze firing, the glaze fuses into a glass-like layer which seals the surface of the pottery. A vast assortment of glazes is available which produce many colors, transparent or opaque surfaces, and smooth or textured surfaces.

Ceramics in the Classroom

Tactile experiences, that is, experiences of touching, feeling, and manipulating, are as important in art education as the visual experience of viewing, recording, and selecting. Through the use of plastic materials such as oil-based modeling clay and natural earth clay, the child has the opportunity to become more sensitive and more skillful in manipulative processes.

Modeling is just as natural to children as drawing, and we can observe many parallels between them. At the scribbling and uncontrolled stages, the child's modeling also appears as an uncontrolled mass. Later, during the stages when the child is making horizontal marks, vertical marks, and circles, the child is likely to construct numerous

balls or coils of clay which repeat the same shapes over and over. Later these shapes may be grouped or joined together to form an object, an animal, or a person in a manner similar to the way children combine circles and lines when they first begin to name their scribbles.

The first type of clay that children usually get to work with is an oil-base product such as Plasticene, Plastilene, Modello, etc. Unlike natural clay, in which the particles are held together with water, commercial clays are held together with oil and glycerine. Because these substances do not evaporate, the clay does not dry out or lose its plasticity. It can be reused indefinitely (however, as it becomes old it becomes tough), but it is not intended to be fired or made permanently hard. Since younger children are less likely to form strong attachments to their creative products and are much more involved in the process of creating, the oil-base modeling clay is a satisfactory material in the early grades, but becomes less desirable as a medium as children grow older and form stronger attachments to their creations.

For the true ceramics experience you need natural clay. It may be obtained in either moist or dry form. The dry form, which is less expensive, is easily mixed by placing about three cups of dry clay in a plastic freezer bag, adding one cup of water, squeezing out all the air before closing the bag, and kneading the exterior of the bag until thoroughly mixed. If the mixture seems sticky or sloppy, open the bag and add more dry clay; if too dry, add water. Experiment with measured amounts of dry clay and water until you obtain a satisfactory consistency. There is no precise water/clay ratio that can be applied to all clays.

If your community has a brick manufacturing plant, you may be able to obtain various mixtures of natural clay at minimal costs. Provide for about two pounds of moist clay per child for a typical project.

Moist clay for classroom use should be mixed at least a week in advance in order to develop a consistent quality throughout. If too moist, it can be dried somewhat by kneading it on a plaster bat, that is, a large slab of perfectly dry plaster.

When the clay is quite plastic and does not stick excessively to the hands, it can be stored in plastic bags. Always gently squeeze out excess air and tightly seal the bags. If bags are airtight, clay will keep for long periods in this condition.

When clay is modeled or made into ceramic containers, any parts to be joined must be moist, must fit together without air bubbles or gaps, and should be scored. By adding more water to clay and mixing it until smooth and creamy, slip can be made for joining pieces together. Scoring in this case is the process in which two contiguous clay pieces are partially joined by using a pointed tool such as a nail to drag clay from one piece to the other piece.

After pieces have been constructed, they must dry thoroughly in the air before firing. If they are heated in a kiln with excessive water still in them, the moisture will turn into steam, expand, and break the piece. To avoid this, when the pieces are placed in a kiln, they should be warmed slowly for several hours at very low heat.

As the temperature rises above 1000°F. and gets to about 1800°F., the clay continues to harden. Potters usually refer to clay that is fired once as "bisque" or "bisquit." At this stage the clay has permanently hardened. Bisque ware is porous and is capable of holding a glaze applied on its surface.

Before removing the pieces the kiln must be allowed to cool slowly. Refrain from trying to "take a peek" until the temperature is down to about 100°F. A sudden temperature change might cause your ceramics to shrink, and cracking can result.

Glazes that have silica formulas similar to glass may be applied as soon as the pieces have cooled. Most commercial classroom glazes are labeled as cone 05 or 06. That simply indicates that they will melt, cover bisque, and attain their color at 1825° to 1850°F. Various colors and textures are available in the temperature ranges of the school kilns. In most instances the glazes may be applied easily with large brushes, sometimes going over the piece with several coats to avoid too thin a coating. Avoid handling the pieces to which the glaze has been applied as the dry glaze will easily brush off before it has been fired again.

Do not glaze the bottom of the ceramic piece, or it will stick to the "kiln furniture" during the second firing process. When heated, the glaze becomes molten and will flow.

Stand each piece on a special ceramic stilt or triangle especially made for this purpose. Do not allow pieces to touch one another, or they will be permanently joined at the end of the second firing.

As in the first firing, increase the heat slowly until it reaches the temperature prescribed for the glazes you are using. Let the kiln cool until it is almost room temperature. Too rapid cooling will cause the glazes and clay to shrink rapidly and crack or craze.

The final results of a good firing are worth waiting for. No two firings ever produce exactly the same results, so part of the joy of opening the kiln is in the pleasure of new effects.

Pinch Pot

Primary Objectives

- To become familiar with ceramics as a universal craft throughout history
- To experience the process of simple modeling and forming of natural clay
- To create a simple clay container

Materials/Tools

Moist natural clay
Newspaper to cover desks
Cloth pieces, approximately 12″ × 16″, to use as a work surface
Kiln

The Lesson

Begin with a discussion of how people have used clay in all parts of the world for thousands of years. Mention some of the familiar everyday objects that are made from clay such as dishes, bowls, flower pots, and vases.

1. Demonstrate the process. Take a lump of clay a little smaller than a tennis ball and shape it into a sphere. Press a thumb into the clay and begin to rotate and press the clay in a pinching action. The deeper the thumb goes and the more the thumb and fingers press the wall, the thinner the wall becomes, and the higher it rises. This should proceed slowly and carefully to avoid stretching the clay too rapidly and causing breaks or fissures. As the wall rises, the hands and fingers continuously shape the pinch pot into a simple container. All we want is a simple, honest shape.

2. Give the children a lump of clay and have them begin to shape it as in the demonstration. Walk among the children, assisting them individually and recommending when to stop if a good shape is achieved. Urge the children to try to keep the wall an even thickness and to keep it thick. Walls that are too thin will collapse.

3. Place the pinch pot on the piece of cloth and begin to refine it with the fingertips until it is smooth and finished.

4. A decorative pattern can be made by pressing objects such as screw heads, bolts, plastic forks, paper clips, etc. into the outside of the wall in a regular repeat. Or, when the pinch pot is partially dry, a design can be carved into the exterior wall with any small tool, such as a linoleum cutter.

5. Still another finish can be obtained by carefully rubbing or burnishing the exterior wall with a very smooth object such as the bowl of a teaspoon, a marble, or a smooth stone. Repeated burnishing will bring the surface to a higher polish which, when fired, appears shiny and nonporous.

6. Fire the pinch pots in a kiln at cone 05 or 1886°F. if the kiln has a pyrometer.

Useful References

BALL, F. CARLTON, and LOVOOS, JANICE. *Making Pottery without a Wheel.* New York: Van Nostrand Reinhold Co., 1965.

BARFORD, GEORGE. *Clay in the Classroom.* Worcester, Mass.: Davis Publications, Inc., 1964.

Coil Bowl

Primary Objectives

- To experience one of the processes used in the construction of ceramic containers
- To increase the understanding and appreciation of ceramics as a universal art and craft form
- To complete a small, simple, well-designed bowl

Materials/Tools

Moist natural clay, 2 to 3 pounds per child

Fabric squares, about 15" × 15"

Water pans or jar lids, 3- to 4-inch diameter

Plastic storage bags

Paring knives

Newspaper to cover desks

Kiln

The Lesson

Plan this project so that the coil bowl can be completed in two sessions, one for creating the basic form and the second for giving it a finish. Keep the bowls small enough so that everyone finishes and the pieces all succeed. Demonstrate the first five steps of this process.

1. Place a lump of clay on the fabric and press it into a flat pad approximately one-half inch thick. Using a jar lid or water pan, mark a circle on the pad of clay. With the point of a knife, cut around the circle and remove the excess clay. The circle of clay is the base of the bowl.

2. Demonstrate making a coil. Take a lump of clay and squeeze it into the shape of an oversized wiener. Place it on the fabric and roll it with the palms of both hands. As it gets thinner, it becomes longer.

3. When the coil is about one-half inch in diameter; lay it on the round base, forming a ring. Cut the coil so that the ends meet.

4. Carefully press the coil so that it sticks to the base. Make a second coil and repeat the process.

5. Join the coils by dragging the index finger down across both coils to the base. Repeat that process around the entire inside of the bowl. Then, holding one hand against the outside wall, smooth the inside with the fingertips of the free hand. Now repeat the process of downward dragging on the exterior of the bowl.

6. Have the children do the first five steps and then continue to enlarge their bowl with additional coils. Encourage them to keep the first bowl simple in shape without allowing it to get too wide or too thin through stretching. To widen the top use slightly longer coils, rather than stretching shorter ones.

7. If the bowl cannot be completed in one session, dampen a cloth, wring it to remove excess water, and gently drape it over the bowl. Place the bowl with damp cloth in a plastic bag. Gently squeeze out excess air and tie the opening.

8. When work resumes, be certain that the clay of the bowl is still plastic and damp. Otherwise new coils cannot be added. Some moisture can be added to the top coils with a dampened sponge. As the clay dries it shrinks, so it is important to try to keep the clay uniformly moist.

9. When the bowl has its desired shape, the exterior surface can be scraped with the flat edge of a piece of sheet metal, or it can be textured with a plastic comb, fork tines, or a similar tool.

10. After bowls have dried completely, fire them in the school kiln at cone 05 or 1886°F. if the kiln has a pyrometer.

11. If glazes are available, glaze the pieces and refire.

Note: When coil pots are made again, greater liberty may be taken with the size, shape, and texture. The process is essentially the same, however, very large pots requiring proportionately thicker and longer coils.

Useful References

KAMPMAN, LOTHAR. *Creating with Clay.* New York: Van Nostrand Reinhold Co., 1971.

SEIDELMAN, JAMES E. and MINTOUYE, G. *Creating with Clay.* New York: The Macmillan Co., 1967.

Decorative Tile

Primary Objectives

• To increase knowledge of the ceramics process
• To learn another process of decorative design for ceramics
• To complete a tile with a decorative design applied to the surface

Materials/Tools

Moist clay
Rolling pin
Two strips of wood, 3/8" to 1/2" thick and 15" long
Fabric, preferably cotton or cotton blend
Cardboard
Scissors
Paring knives
Assorted found objects for pressing designs
Engobes (commercial colored slip)
Kiln
Glaze

The Lesson

The procedure in this lesson must be followed carefully. A good demonstration and clear directions are essential for success.

1. Place a baseball size lump of well-kneaded clay on a smooth surface which is covered with fabric.

2. On either side of the clay, place the two strips of wood in a parallel position about eight inches apart.

3. With the hands, pat the clay into a thick pancake-like slab about one inch thick. Then begin to roll it, keeping the rolling pin on the parallel wood strips, until the clay is smooth and uniform in thickness.

4. With scissors, cut a cardboard template (pattern) about five inches square. Lay the template on top of the clay. With a sharp knife, cut around the template and remove the excess clay. For shape variation, use a circular shape such as a plastic margarine container lid as the template.

5. The tile is ready for decoration, either by pressing in a design with found objects or by brushing on a design with colored engobes.

6. If engobes are used, they may be brushed directly into the damp tile much like thick tempera to create the design, or the entire surface of the tile can be covered with a coating of engobe of a contrasting color. After the tile has

dried to a leather-like hardness, a design can be created using linoleum tools by cutting through the top layer and exposing the contrasting clay of the tile. This process is called "sgraffito," which means "scratched" in Italian.

7. Warping can result from irregular drying: the top, which is exposed to the air, dries more rapidly than the bottom. To prevent warping, turn the tiles over frequently during the drying period, or let them dry on wire racks from ovens or on old window screens.

8. After the piece is entirely dry, fire it once for bisque at cone 05 or 1886°F. if the kiln has a pyrometer. Then glaze and fire again. The engobes will appear much brighter or more colorful after application of the glaze.

Useful References

BIRKS, TONY. *The Potter's Companion.* New York: E. P. Dutton & Co., Inc., 1977.

KRUM, JOSEPHINE R. *Hand-Built Pottery.* Scranton, Pa.: International Textbook Company, 1960.

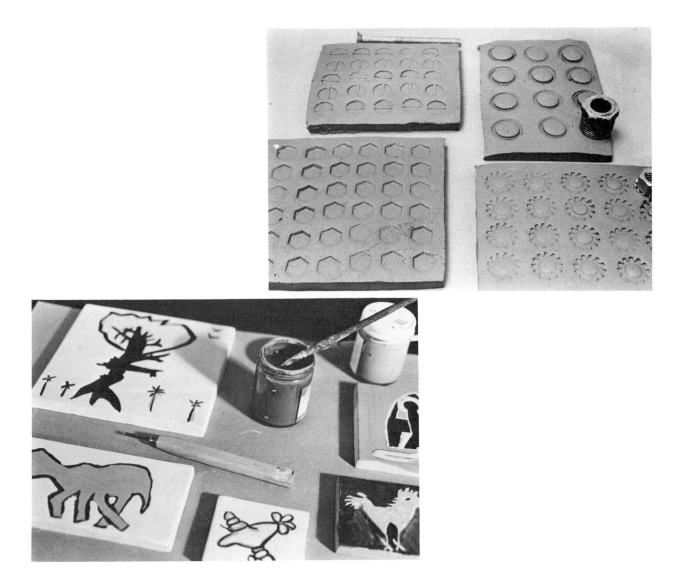

Hollow Ceramic Figure

Suggested Topics   Bulky figures—animal, bird, or fish.

Primary Objectives

- To design and construct a hollow figure
- To learn the process of making hollow figures and the reason for making them hollow
- To be able to follow directions regarding methods of modeling and joining

Materials/Tools

Newspapers

Moist clay

Plywood pieces, about 6" × 8", to serve as work surfaces

Modeling tool made from a sharpened Popsicle stick or tongue depressor

The Lesson

To be successful, the figure will have to be compact. It cannot have any long, thin legs, arms, necks, wings, etc., which are easily broken off from the main body of the clay. Examples of good subjects are a hippopotamus, a pig, a bear, a nesting chicken, or a whale. Discuss how fragile clay is during the drying stage and before it becomes hard by firing.

1. Crumple some newspapers into the shape of an egg or a wiener.

2. Make a slab of clay about ⅜ to ½ inch thick, large enough to wrap around the newspaper wad. Wrap the clay around the crumpled newspaper. This will serve as the body portion of the figure. (In the firing process the paper will turn to ash, leaving this portion hollow.)

3. Add more clay for other body parts, making certain the clay is always carefully joined. If short legs are added, it may be necessary to make them extra heavy at first and then carve away the excess before the clay has dried completely. Clay is somewhat stronger and easier to carve when it is not entirely dry.

4. Discuss with each student the characteristics of his or her animal. What makes it a bear or a mouse? Talk about details. Talk about the texture of the surface. What can we invent to treat the surface interestingly?

5. Open a passageway somewhere on the bottom so that the newspaper receives outside air. This is the escape hole for the air and moisture in the center of the figure. It is absolutely necessary!

6. If additional work sessions are needed, cover each piece with a dampened cloth, place in a plastic bag, and seal the bag to retain moisture.

7. When the figure is completed, let it dry in the air as slowly as possible. When it seems completely dry, place in a warm kiln and continue drying for several hours before slowly increasing the temperature for firing. Care at this step may get even poorly constructed pieces safely through the firing process. Haste can cause even the best constructed pieces to expand too rapidly and break during firing.

8. At the bisque stage, the pieces can be glazed and refired. They can also be left in natural fired clay condition or they may be painted with acrylic paints.

Useful References

PETTERSON, HENRY. *Creating Form in Clay.* New York: Van Nostrand Reinhold Co., 1968.

RÖTTGER, ERNST. *Creative Clay Design.* New York: Van Nostrand Reinhold Co., 1962.

Tiles with Nature Designs

Primary Objectives

- To develop an awareness of and sensitivity to the interesting forms in natural materials
- To develop a sense of organization or composition through selecting and combining different elements
- To learn the processes of firing and glazing

Materials/Tools

Moist clay

Fabric, preferably cotton or cotton blend

Rolling pin

Two strips of wood, ⅜" to ½" thick and about 18" long

Cardboard

Scissors

Paring knife

Salt shaker filled with powdered clay

Assorted leaves, weeds, seed pods, sea shells, nutshells, tree bark, twigs, etc.

Kiln

The Lesson

1. Cover a table top or drawing board with a piece of fabric.
2. Take a piece of well-kneaded clay about the size of a large orange and "patty cake" or press it until it is about three-quarters of an inch thick.
3. Place the two strips of wood on either side of the clay. With the rolling pin roll out the clay until it is smooth, of even thickness, and level with the two strips of wood.
4. Cut a cardboard template approximately 5" × 5" to serve as the guide around which to cut the tile from the larger piece of clay.
5. Lay the template over the clay, and with the tip of a paring knife, cut through the clay and remove the excess.
6. Put some dry clay in a salt or flour shaker and dust the top of the clay with a light coating.
7. Select a variety of natural items: weeds, seed pods, leaves, etc., and lay them on the surface in an interesting arrangement.
8. Gently press these items into the clay, causing them to leave an impression on the surface. When the impression is clear and deep enough, care-

fully lift off the nature materials. This must be done while the clay is still damp, because clay shrinks as it dries and is likely to crack if solid objects are left embedded.

9. Before the clay is completely dry, trim the edges of the tile with the paring knife to give it a clean, finished edge.

10. Have each child inscribe his or her name and the date on the reverse side of the tile, using a sharp pencil or the point of a compass.

11. To prevent excessive warping, turn the tiles over frequently during the drying period, or let them stand on wire racks.

12. When completely dry, fire in the kiln to cone 05 or 1886°F. if the kiln is equipped with a pyrometer.

Useful References

SEIDELMAN, JAMES E. and MINTOUYE, G. *Creating with Clay.* New York: The Macmillan Co., 1967.

RÖTTGER, ERNST. *Creative Clay Design.* New York: Van Nostrand Reinhold Co., 1962.

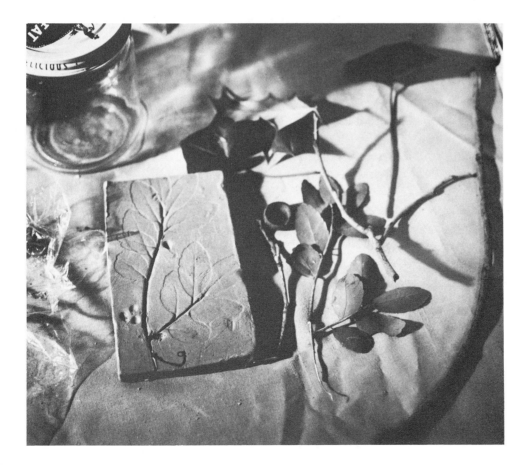

Free-Form Burnished Ceramic Bowl

Primary Objectives

- To learn to mold clay over existing forms
- To recognize forms that have natural beauty and are appropriate for ceramic containers

Materials/Tools

Moist clay

Fabric, cotton or cotton blend

Large smooth stones, 4- to 8-inch diameter

Rolling pin

Two strips of wood, ⅜" thick and about 18" long

Cheesecloth, gauze, or other lightweight cloth

Paring knife

Pebbles, marbles, spoons, for burnishing

The Lesson

1. Cover a smooth work surface with a piece of fabric.
2. Knead the clay until it is smooth and plastic.
3. Take a piece of clay almost the size of a large orange and pat it with the hand until it is about three-fourths of an inch thick.
4. Lay the slab of clay on the fabric and place the two wood strips on either side of it.
5. Roll out with the rolling pin until the clay slab is level with the wood strips.
6. Select a smooth stone. Using the point of the paring knife, cut a circular or oblong shape from the flat clay large enough to cover about half of the stone. (A plastic bowl makes a good circular pattern.)
7. Place a piece of cheesecloth or gauze over the stone.
8. Carefully lift the clay and gently form it over the stone until it conforms to the stone's shape.
9. Leave it on the stone just long enough for it to begin to get stiff due to drying. As soon as it will retain its shape, slip it off the stone and let it begin to dry. Trim the edges while still damp.
10. Begin burnishing when the clay is firm and not completely dry. Rub the exterior surface gently with a pebble, marble, the bowl of a spoon, or a smooth piece of wood. The more the piece is rubbed, the more polished it will be after firing. Handle it with care.

11. Allow to air dry until all moisture is gone from the clay. It is now ready to fire in a kiln to make it permanently hard. Fire at cone 05 or 1886°F. if the kiln is equipped with a pyrometer.

12. After one firing, the interior may be glazed if glazes are available.

Useful References

MAVROS, DONALD O. *Getting Started in Ceramics.* New York: Bruce Publishing Co., 1971.

BALL, CARLTON F., and LOVOOS, JANICE. *Making Pottery without a Wheel.* New York: Van Nostrand Reinhold Co., 1965.

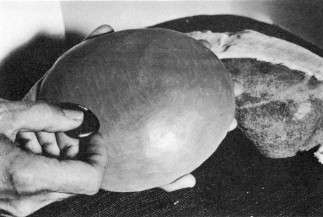

FOLK ART AND MISCELLANY 10

All the good ideas I ever had came to me while I was milking a cow.
                                    GRANT WOOD

Background Information about Folk Art

Folk art is generally considered to be the art of people who are not trained as artists and who create their art often while producing the necessities of life. As a result, folk art is often functional or utilitarian, for example, a cup and spoon with decorative carving, a blanket chest with brightly painted designs, or fancy breads for festival days.

Obviously such things are not created for museums, even though many fine examples are now preserved in museums. In fact, for many folk art pieces permanence is never a consideration: papier-mâché objects are made to be blown apart with firecrackers; marriage bowls are made to be broken; carnival figures are used once and then discarded; festival breads are eaten; flower designs on roads are trampled by religious processions.

Characteristic of some folk art is that it grows out of tradition and relies largely upon local natural materials, such as straw or wood, which are easy to come by and require few sophisticated tools. A Mexican folk artist might use tin snips and a soldering iron to fashion an elaborate picture frame. An Ashanti might model small figures of wax and develop a process for casting them in brass.

Folk art appears in many different forms. In architecture we find carved woodwork, spires, painted doors, and the wonderful doors of granaries. Painting and drawing examples include portraits, scrimshaw, painting on glass or on velvet, *fraktur* (Pennsylvania German illustrated manuscripts), decorative work on walls or beams, on blanket chests, etc. In sculptural forms there are carved and modeled toys, papier-mâché objects, toy soldiers, Christmas crèches, and many more.

Printmaking examples include carved wooden designs pressed into cookies or clay, small ink prints of saints on paper, and announcements of events like carnivals and circuses.

Folk arts are practiced the world over. From the beautiful masks and costumes of Africa to the carved walrus tusks of the Arctic; from the carved and painted chairs in Poland to the scarification designs on the shoulders of African warriors; from Ukrainian decorated Easter eggs to New England hickory nut dolls—the folk art tradition knows no bounds.

Very few generalizations can be made about folk art. Some examples are "child-like" or naive; others are sophisticated in design. The colors may be bright or they may be somber and restrained. Some works are freely executed while others are meticulously rendered. Realistic or abstract, useful or ornamental—folk art as a whole defies categorizing.

Perhaps the single most important source of motivation and inspiration for folk art comes from religion. The variety of religious-related folk art seems almost endless: Easter eggs, breads, candlesticks, ivory carvings, retables, papier-mâché figures, costumes, altar cloths, and many, many more.

Other sources of inspiration for folk artists are parades, festivals, carnivals, and celebrations of all kinds.

Within this diversity, folk art does have one common denominator. In all its manifestations folk art grows out of the universal need for self-expression and the need to embellish our surroundings. Folk artists make objects to use, to enjoy, and to give pleasure to the maker. Their work is not intended for museums—although many museums now place high value on it. In their sincere, unpretentious approach to art, folk artists are similar to children. Both are responding to the need to express one's self and to enrich one's environment.

Seasonal Decorations of Baker's Clay

Suggested Topics Tree hangings; gift package ornaments.

Primary Objectives
- To design and model imaginative, non-stereotyped decorations
- To develop decorative surfaces through color and texture

Materials/Tools

Baker's clay (see below)

Wax paper

Acrylic or tempera paints

Brushes

Cookie sheets

White glue

The Lesson

Baker's clay is an inedible dough made by combining 4 cups of all-purpose flour with 1 cup of table salt and 1½ cups of water. Mix the ingredients in a bowl, and knead until the mixture is about the consistency of bread dough. The batch should be used immediately so it does not dry out and lose its plasticity.

1. Give each child a portion of baker's clay, and have them model on wax paper a flat gingerbread-type animal, angel, bird, or person. Parts may be joined by pressing or pinching them together. The surface can be textured by pressing or pushing small objects into it, leaving indentations.

2. Lay the finished pieces on cookie sheets. Bake at home in a 350° oven until the dough begins to brown. Smaller pieces take about an hour; thicker pieces may require two hours.

3. After the pieces have been removed from the oven and allowed to cool, they may be decorated with tempera or acrylic paints, or they may be sprayed with a clear fixative such as polyurethane, varnish, or shellac.

4. For hanging the ornaments, attach a short length of string with white glue and allow it to dry for one day.

Useful References

JOHNSON, ILSE, and HAZELTON, NIKA STANDEN. *Cookies and Breads: The Baker's Art.* New York: Van Nostrand Reinhold Co., 1967.

WILLIAMSON, ETHIE. *Baker's Clay.* New York: Van Nostrand Reinhold Co., 1976.

Diamond Kite

Primary Objectives
- To design and construct a kite that can fly
- To follow instructions and complete a multi-step process
- To create a surface design to enhance the kite's appearance

Materials/Tools
Pine or spruce wood strips (from kite supply store) ⅛" thick and ⅜" wide;
   each kite requires one 34-inch length and one 28-inch length
Kite string, several balls
Kite paper or mylar, 30" × 36", one sheet per child
Pencils
White glue
Rulers
Scissors
Coping saw
Mat knife (X-Acto or similar)
Spray paints or tempera paints
Cloth remnants

The Lesson
Kite making originated in China approximately two thousand years ago and
spread throughout Asia. Kites were flown for pleasure and sometimes to
frighten enemies who thought them to be gods flying in the sky. Today kites
are still flown for pleasure and for the challenge to those who fly them. This
lesson could relate to the study of Ben Franklin and his experiments with
electricity.

1. After a short discussion, demonstrate sawing a shallow cut with a coping
   saw in the ends of the wood strips (Figure A). If your school has a wood-
   shop you can save time by completing this step in advance with the help
   of the Industrial Arts teacher.

2. Continue the demonstration by making a pencil mark 12 inches from one
   end of the 34-inch stick and another at the mid-point of the 28-inch stick.
   Lay the two sticks so they form a cross at the marks. Put a dab of white
   glue between the sticks and tie them together with kite string.

3. Cut a piece of kite string 9 feet long. Tie one end to the end of one of the
   crossed sticks; then insert it into the shallow saw cut on the end of the
   stick and continue it through each of the three other cuts, returning

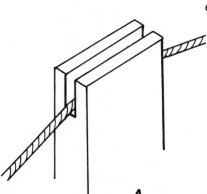

A

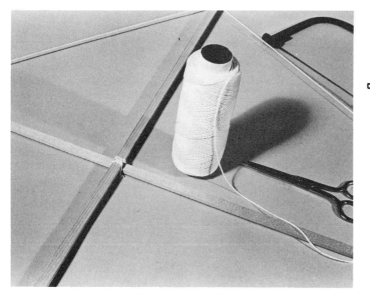

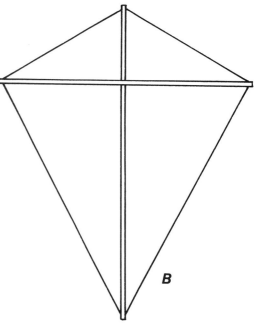

B

the string to the starting point. Tighten the string and tie it. The frame will begin to feel rigid and strong (Figure B).

4. Give each child two sticks, one of each size, and 9 feet of kite string. Have the class do each of the steps that have been demonstrated.

5. When the frames are completed and the string tied in place, give each child a sheet of kite paper. Lay the kite frame on the paper and lightly trace the exact outline of the diamond shape made by the string. Lift away the frame. Measure an additional ¾" out from the penciled outline and draw another line that runs parallel to the first diamond shape. Cut out the larger diamond shape from the piece of kite paper (save the trimmed-off paper). Crease the ¾" area on each of the four sides. Now the creased edges of the paper will conform to the kite frame and string.

6. The paper is now ready for a design. Stencils may be cut from drawing paper and laid on the kite paper, then sprayed with color from a spray paint can. Always do this in a well-ventilated area or out-of-doors. Designs can also be painted with tempera paints.

7. At each of the corners on the paper where the folds intersect, measure 1" from the intersection and cut off each of the four corners (Figure C).

8. Lay the paper painted side down and place the frame over it. Put white glue on one of the folded areas. Fold it over the string and glue it to the main part of the kite paper. Do this with each of the other three folded areas. Now the kite paper will be securely attached to the frame (Figure D).

9. In order to fly, the kite requires a "bridle" on which to attach the string for flying. Cut two 3-inch squares of kite paper from the excess paper that was trimmed off in step 5. On the unpainted side of the kite paper, glue each of the squares under the longer of the cross sticks, one piece about 6 inches above the point of intersection and the other about 8 inches below the point of intersection. With a sharp pencil point, punch a small hole through the center of each of the squares. Tie a 20-inch piece of kite string to the long stick directly beneath one of the holes. Carefully push the string through the hole and back into the other hole. Leaving the string loose or slack, tie the loose end of the string to the stick at the point of the

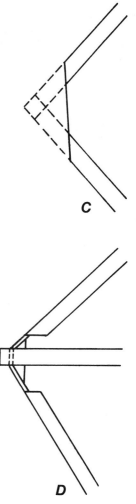

C

D

second square. This now provides a bridle on the painted side of the kite to which the ball of kite string, used for flying the kite, is attached.

10. The crosspiece, or shorter stick of wood, needs to be bowed. Tie a piece of string to one end and draw it across the back side of the kite to the other end of the crosspiece. Pull the string slowly until the wood has a slight bow; then tie the string securely.

11. Finally, to keep the kite from spinning and diving while airborne, it needs a tail. Use a long strip of cloth about 1½ inches wide and 3 feet long. Tie the cloth strip to the wood stick at the bottom point of the kite and let it dangle behind the kite as it flies.

Useful References

NEWMAN, LEE SCOTT, and NEWMAN, JAY HARTLEY. *Kite Craft.* New York: Crown Publishers, Inc., 1974.

HUNT, LESLIE. *Twenty-five Kites that Fly.* New York: Dover Publications, Inc., 1971.

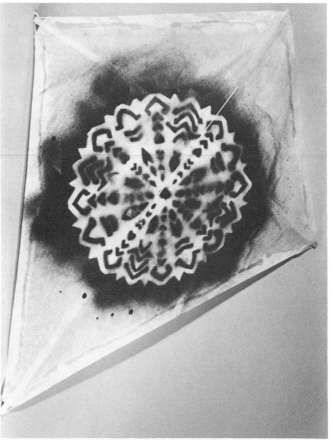

Banners, Pennants, and Flags

Suggested Topic   Holidays or special events.

Primary Objectives

- To learn about the use of banners and flags as symbolic devices
- To design symbols based upon special events
- To create original, unstereotyped designs

Materials/Tools

Kraft wrapping paper
Tempera paints
Large brushes
Colored papers
Scissors
Paste
Thin sticks about 36" long

The Lesson

Banners, flags, and pennants are used universally to identify organizations and groups in parades and assemblies marking special events and holidays. They add color and excitement to festivals, rallies, and sports events.

1. Begin with a discussion of the holiday or special event. What are the symbols of that day? What ideas can children invent that will symbolize it? Point out the fact that banners and flags are also colorful decorative designs.
2. Give each child a piece of kraft paper about 18"×36". On this they can either paint a banner with large brushes and tempera paints or make the design using colored construction paper, paste, and scissors.
3. When the banners are completed, staple one end to a thin strip of wood.
4. Hang the banners around the room, or use them in a parade.
5. Older children can make banners out of fabric with felt appliqués.

Useful References

LALIBERTÉ NORMAN, and MCILHANY, STERLING. *Banners and Hangings.* New York: Van Nostrand Reinhold Co., 1966.

MEILACH, DONA Z. *Creating from Fibers and Fabrics.* Chicago: Henry Regnery Co., 1973.

Cut Paper Designs

Suggested Topic A geometric repeat

Primary Objectives
- To create designs based upon symmetry
- To improve manual skill in cutting with scissors or knives

Materials/Tools
Thin paper
Scissors
Mat knives (X-Acto or similar)
Paper for mounting the design
White glue or school paste

The Lesson
Paper cutting is a popular folk art in many parts of the world. Each culture has its own style but there are many similarities. The primary differences are in the type of paper and the subject of the designs. If a paper is folded once and then cut, two identical designs will appear. If it is folded twice, four designs will result. With thin, strong paper that can take several folds, it is possible to get even more repeats.

1. Start with a square or a rectangle of paper. Fold it in half either straight or on the diagonal.
2. Sketch a design on the folded paper. Part of the design can reach the folded edge, but remember that some of the folded edge must be retained uncut or the paper will separate into two parts.
3. Cut the design out with scissors, or with a mat knife on a cardboard surface to avoid cutting the table tops. Open the design and lay it on a contrasting colored paper. Does it need to have more cut away? Do the outside edges need to be cut to give them more interest?
4. Now that the children understand the process, can they think of a more interesting design?
5. Now try a design with two folds. Proceed in the same way.
6. When the designs are completed, open them out and press them between magazines overnight.
7. Use school paste or white glue to mount the designs on papers of contrasting color.
8. For more elaborate effects, try cutting various designs from different colored papers and then combining designs before mounting them.

Useful References

JABLONSKI, RAMONA. *The Paper Cut-Out Design Book.* Owings Mills, Md.: Stemmer House Publishers, Inc., 1976.

NEWMAN, THELMA R., and others. *Papers as Art and Craft.* New York: Crown Publishers, Inc., 1973.

Calligraphic Illustration

Suggested Topic ''Spelled out'' pictures.

Primary Objectives
- To discover ways of communicating through visual symbols
- To recognize graphic symbols as design and begin to appreciate their particular beauty
- To invent new personal graphic symbols

Materials/Tools

Drawing paper

Pencils

Felt-tip pens

Crayons

The Lesson

Talk with the children about different ways people use to communicate: sounds, signs, symbols, pictures, etc. If possible, show examples of illuminated medieval or Persian manuscripts, in which pictures were used in combination with letters and words to convey a meaning. In this project the children will create a full-page design which combines a picture with a pattern of words that relate to the picture.

1. Choose a letter of the alphabet, let us say ''D,'' and list on the chalkboard as many objects beginning with that letter as the children can think of: *doll, dog, dish, donut, daddy, donkey,* etc.
2. Have each child choose one of the words and, on a piece of paper, write a short jingle pertaining to their word, for example: ''The dog jumps over the log''; ''The donkey sees a monkey''; ''There's a fish in my dish''; and so on.
3. On a 12″ × 18″ sheet of paper have the children make a contour drawing in pencil of the object represented by the word.
4. Within the contour drawing have each child begin to write or paint his or her jingle, either following the main contours or simply in lines, until the entire drawing is filled and the form recognizable.
5. If, at this stage, individual children want to do something in the empty spaces outside of the drawing, encourage them to fill the entire page.

Useful References

CATALDO, JOHN W. *Words and Calligraphy for Children.* New York: Van Nostrand Reinhold Co., 1969.

KLAGER, MAX. *Letters, Type and Pictures: Teaching Alphabets through Art.* New York: Van Nostrand Reinhold Co., 1975.

Models
Group Project

Suggested Topics   Boats, houses, cars, planes, castles, etc.

Primary Objectives
- To combine group planning, group decisions, and group work with individual interpretation
- To design and construct a scale model of an object

Materials/Tools
Paper, drawing and construction
Scissors
Plastic bottles, quart size and smaller
Cardboard boxes, shoe box size and smaller
Styrofoam fast-food packaging
Balsa wood
Rulers, tape measures
White glue
Model airplane glue
Mat knives (X-Acto or similar)
Modeling clay
Tempera paints
Brushes

The Lesson

Man has made models for thousands of years. The tombs of Egypt have disclosed models of ships, looms, and other objects. People of all ages enjoy making miniature replicas of houses, airplanes, sailboats, etc. For children especially it is a very rewarding experience. This lesson is a good opportunity to use some mathematics through a discussion of scale and to find practical applications in the use of measuring tools such as rulers or tape measures. The project will require several work sessions.

1. Have the class choose a topic that involves many separate objects—a farm, an airport, a city. Ask for suggestions and list on the chalkboard various items that might be part of, say, a model farm: barn, house, silo, tractor, horses, cows, pick-up truck, etc.

2. Talk about scale. For example, suggest that 1 inch on the model might represent 1 foot for the full-sized object. On that scale, if a pickup truck is actually 15 feet long, the model would be 15 inches long. Would that be too

big for a classroom? If so, let someone suggest another scale. When the scale is determined, let each child select one object from the list.

3. At this point each child must pick out from among the assortment of boxes, plastic containers, Styrofoam, paper, wood scraps, etc. items that suggest the shape or part of the shape of their chosen object.

4. Each child must calculate the size of the model based on the scale. This will involve questions of size such as how long is a tractor or the front of a farmhouse? How high is a two-story house or a silo? To find the answers to these questions the children learn to inquire, measure, calculate, and do simple research.

5. Since this project requires several sessions to complete, it gives the children an opportunity to find other materials for completing their models.

6. When all the models are completed, assemble them into a group exhibition so everyone can share in the accomplished work.

Useful References

ASPDEN, GEORGE. *Model Making.* New York: Van Nostrand Reinhold Co., 1964.

LIDSTONE, JOHN. *Building with Balsa Wood.* New York: Van Nostrand Reinhold Co., 1965.

Pysanky Egg Decoration

Primary Objectives

- To appreciate an old Ukrainian folk art form
- To create decorative designs appropriate to the egg shape
- To work with precision in creating a pleasing design

Materials/Tools

Pysanky dyes and kistka (sold at Russian or Greek Orthodox church sales-
   rooms or at crafts supply shops)

Beeswax

White vinegar

Pencils

Candles

Large-mouthed pint-size glass jars, for holding dye baths

Tablespoons

Paper towels

Clear acrylic or varnish spray

Liquid spot remover, small can

The Lesson

Pysanky (PEE-sahn-key) egg decoration is a centuries old Ukrainian tradition.
In the springtime the egg, symbol of renewed life, is transformed with dyes
into a thing of beauty. Decorated eggs are given as special gifts to friends, to
be cherished forever. The designs are applied to the eggs by means of a special
tool called a *kistka*, which consists of a stylus and a funnel part for holding a
small quantity of beeswax. The wax is kept liquid by the flame of a candle.

1. Begin by arranging the work space. Place the candle in a holder so it won't
   topple and position it near the hand that will hold the kistka. Near the
   candle, place a small lump of beeswax that will be used to continually re-
   plenish the wax in the kistka.

2. Wash an egg in a small bowl of water. Blot it dry with paper towels. With
   a pencil, draw a line completely around the egg, dividing it into two equal
   parts. Make a second line, going around the egg in the other direction, dividing the surface into four parts. Make some additional divisions with
   lines, repeating the same lines in each of the parts of the egg to keep the
   design symmetrical.

3. Heat the funnel part of the kistka in the candle flame and scoop a small
   amount of beeswax into the larger end of the funnel. Reheat and practice

a few lines on a piece of paper until you have the knack of making a nice line. With the burning candle close to the hand using the kistka and the beeswax lump near its base, alternate dipping the metal tip of the kistka into the beeswax and then warming it over the candle's flame. The beeswax must be kept warm so that it remains liquid and flows easily. Overheating causes the wax to flow too rapidly, causing blots, so a little practice is required to learn the right consistency. Try to keep the funnel part of the kistka at right angles to the egg's surface. As soon as the wax stops flowing from the funnel, reheat it in the candle flame.

4. Begin to cover the lines made with the pencil. The black lines left by the warm beeswax will be white or the color of the egg shell in the finished pysanky.

5. When the lines are covered with wax, dip the egg into the first color, usually yellow, using a tablespoon or a looped wire made from a dress hanger. Remove the egg and pat dry with paper toweling.

6. Draw the lines to enclose any areas in the design that are to be yellow. Cover these lines or areas with beeswax as in step 3. Dip the egg into another dye, such as orange, and leave it until the entire egg is well colored. Remove and pat it dry.

7. With a pencil, mark any lines or areas in the design that are to remain orange. Cover those lines or areas with wax and dip the egg into a dark color, or black. Let the dye color the egg, then remove and pat it dry.

8. Hold the egg over the flame of the candle to let the beeswax melt in the flame; remove the egg and wipe away the melted wax with paper towels or tissue. Repeat this until the wax has all been removed. The egg may now look dirty and covered with soot from the candle. Put out the candle's flame.

9. Moisten some facial tissue with liquid spot remover and carefully wipe away the soot from the egg's surface. A bright, colorful egg is now ready for spraying with a clear acrylic spray or varnish.

10. It is not necessary to remove the liquid contents from the egg because it will eventually evaporate. But if you wish, the insides can be evacuated by drilling a small hole in each end of the egg shell and blowing out the liquid.

Useful References

JORDAN ROBERT PAUL. "Easter Greetings from the Ukrainians." *National Geographic*, 141, no. 4 (April 1972), pp. 557–63.

Rag Dolls

Primary Objectives
- To create three-dimensional dolls of fabric
- To learn some simple procedures for making patterns and sewing

Materials/Tools
Fabric remnants, plain and patterned

Needles

Thread

Needle threader

Scissors

Polyester or cotton batting

Yarn

Paper

Pencils

The Lesson
Dolls have been a part of childhood for thousands of years. In many graves from pre-Columbian Peru, small fabric dolls have been found much like the simple ones that American pioneer mothers made for their children. This similarity is repeated in many diverse cultures, demonstrating the universality of dolls.

1. On a piece of 9″ × 12″ paper, draw a figure whose head touches the top of the page and whose feet touch the bottom.
2. Because the figures are to be stuffed, make sure to draw the arms and legs "fat" enough to hold some stuffing when they are sewn.
3. Cut out the paper figure and use it as a pattern. Lay the pattern on a piece of plain fabric and trace around it with a soft pencil.
4. Demonstrate on the chalkboard how to make a seam allowance. Have the class add a one-half inch seam allowance around the contour of their figures.
5. Cut out the figure and, using it as a pattern, cut out a second one from the plain fabric.
6. Demonstrate how to thread a needle and how to make simple running stitches.
7. Put the two figures together with the "wrong sides" of the fabric on the outside. Sew around the head, turn it right-side out, and stuff the head with cotton batting.

8. Demonstrate how to turn under the seam allowances on an arm and how to sew the edges on the "right side."

9. When an arm is completed, stuff it and go to the other arm.

10. Continue with the body, legs, and feet, sewing and stuffing one part at a time.

11. Now, what features can we add—hair, a mouth, eyes, etc.? Put them in with yarn stitches or small fabric appliqués.

12. Use the patterned fabrics to make clothes for the doll: a dress, coat, scarf, etc.

Useful References

ENTHOVEN, JACQUELINE. *Stitchery for Children: A Manual for Teachers, Parents and Children.* New York: Van Nostrand Reinhold Co., 1964.

HARTUNG, ROLF. *Creative Textile Design: Thread and Fabric.* New York: Van Nostrand Reinhold, Co., 1963.

Baker's Clay Self-Portrait

Primary Objectives

• To create small, humorous self-portraits
• To attempt uninhibited self-characterization

Materials/Tools

Flour and salt for baker's clay (see below)
Mixing bowls, one for every two children
Wax paper
Modeling tools
Cookie sheet or pie tin (each child to bring one)

The Lesson

Tell the class that everyone, including the teacher, is going to make a self-portrait for exhibiting during parents visiting day. Write the formula for baker's clay on the chalkboard. Explain that two children will work together to mix one batch of clay, which they will divide equally.

1. Demonstrate how to make a batch of baker's clay. Mix 4 cups of flour, 1 cup of salt, and 1½ cups of water in a mixing bowl. Knead this mixture with the hands until smooth and uniform in consistency. If it seems too stiff, add a few drops of water at a time until it is smooth and plastic. If it gets too moist, dust in a few tablespoons of flour.

2. Cover the desk tops with newspaper and give each child a piece of wax paper about 12 inches square on which to model the portrait.

3. Have the children take about two-thirds of their portion of clay and form it into an oval face shape on the wax paper. From the remaining clay, form and add on a nose, eyes, ears, mouth, eyebrows, etc., pressing each facial part firmly to secure it to the oval shape. Stress that the features should be modeled in such a way as to emphasize the special identifying characteristics of the subject.

4. When the modeling is completed, carefully slip the portrait from the wax paper onto the cookie sheet or pie tin.

5. Take the portraits home and bake them at 350°F. for about an hour. Longer baking time is required if the clay is thicker than an inch at any spot. They can over-bake without any serious harm to them.

6. These portraits are charming in their natural baked color, but they can also be painted successfully if the children want to add the element of color.

7. For permanence, they can be preserved indefinitely by applying a coat of shellac or a clear acrylic spray.

8. Attach a 6-inch loop of strong string to the back of the portraits with a dab of white glue as a means of hanging them on the wall.

Useful Reference

JOHNSON, ILSE, and HAZELTON, NIKA STANDEN. *Cookies and Breads: The Baker's Art.* New York: Van Nostrand Reinhold Co., 1967.

Baker's Clay Jewelry

Suggested Items   Beads, necklaces, bracelets, pendants.

Primary Objectives
- To note the universal desire to create ornaments for the body
- To make an object using repetition as a main element of design

Materials/Tools
Flour and salt for baker's clay (see below)
Wax paper
Wood kitchen matches (used) or soda straws
Cookie sheets or pie tins
Tempera or acrylic paints
Brushes
Shellac
Yarn
Darning needles, for stringing the beads

The Lesson
The baker's clay for this lesson can either be mixed in advance or as a demonstration. The following formula will make enough clay for four children. Combine 4 cups of flour, 1 cup of salt, and 1½ cups of water in a mixing bowl and mix thoroughly with a fork. Knead with the hands for several minutes until the mixture is uniform and plastic. Model or shape it on a lightly floured surface such as a cookie sheet or a piece of wax paper. Use soon after mixing to avoid drying out.

Focus this lesson on a necklace made from baker's clay beads, but explain that other jewelry forms such as pendants, bracelets, earrings, etc. can also be made with this material. Many issues of the _National Geographic_ magazine contain excellent pictures of the jewelry and body ornaments of other cultures. Show some of these for enriching the understanding of jewelry as a universal art form.

1. Cover the desks with newspaper. Give the children some baker's clay and have them roll a bead. Try making different shapes: round, egg-shaped, cylinders, button shapes, etc.
2. Have each child decide on one, two, or three shapes and begin to produce them. As each bead is formed, push a match stick through its center, turn the stick gently, then withdraw it. That will form the hole needed for stringing.

3. When each child has formed enough beads for a necklace, place the clay beads on a pie tin or cookie sheet and bake in an oven at 350° F. until the clay begins to brown. Beads should bake in less than one hour.

4. After pieces have cooled, paint them with acrylic or tempera paints. If tempera is used, shellac them the following day. Encourage children to experiment in painting the beads; some might be enhanced with dots, stripes, etc.

5. String the beads on yarn. Experiment with repeat patterns: alternate, two at a time, one then two, etc.

Useful References

DOCKSTADER, FREDERICK J. *Indian Art of the Americas.* New York: Museum of Indian Art, Heye Foundation, 1973.

JOHNSON, ILSE, and HAZELTON, NIKA STANDEN. *Cookies and Breads: The Baker's Art.* New York: Van Nostrand Reinhold Co., 1967.

Hobby Horse

Suggested Topics Race horse, ranch horse, spotted pony, wild mustang, etc.

Primary Objectives

- To develop a three-dimensional soft sculptural form derived from two-dimensional photographs
- To utilize common materials to create a new form
- To learn some cutting and sewing skills

Materials/Tools

Men's cotton or cotton/polyester socks

Dowel sticks, broom handles, or branches about ½" to ¾" diameter, about 30" long

Buttons, fabric, scraps, yarn scraps

Scissors, needles, thread

Stuffing: old nylon stockings, panty hose, cotton or polyester batting

The Lesson

1. Look at photographs of horses or horse's heads. Talk about the head shape, the location of eyes, ears, nostrils, and mouth.
2. Demonstrate cutting off the toe from one sock which has been turned inside out. Save the toe portion for step 6.
3. Thread a needle and sew the sock together where the toe portion was removed. This will form the mouth.
4. Turn the sock right side out. Stuff the foot portion; then insert a dowel stick or a branch into the leg portion.
5. Continue to stuff the leg of the sock until it is firm. Then securely wrap and tie the top of the sock to the dowel or branch.
6. Take the toe portion which was removed earlier and cut it into two parts to form the ears. Each portion is folded to form a triangular shape and the open edges are sewn together. Sew the two triangles to the top of the horse's head.
7. Now let each child decide how to achieve the eyes, nostrils, mane, markings, and so on, using buttons, felt, fabric, yarns, and other scraps. This might include stitches or appliqué for special effects.
8. When the horses are finished, give them names and then put them in the "corral." This would be an ideal time to sit around the campfire and read a good story about a horse.

Useful References

MATTIL, EDWARD L. *Meaning in Crafts,* 3rd ed. Englewood Cliffs, N.J.: Prentice-Hall, Inc., 1971.

MEILACH, DONA Z. *Soft Sculpture and Other Soft Forms.* New York: Crown Publishers, 1974.

Kachina Dolls

Primary Objectives
- To learn about the history, customs, and art forms of American Indians
- To recycle scrap materials into a sculpture object
- To make adaptations of American Indian designs for a contemporary toy

Materials/Tools
Cardboard mailing tubes
Small cardboard boxes
Plastic bottles, pint-size or quart-size
White glue
Styrofoam, from fast-food packaging
Scissors
Mat knives (X-Acto or similar)
Colored construction paper
Scrap items: feathers, fur, buttons, fabric remnants, wood shavings, etc.
Tempera paints
Brushes

The Lesson
The word *kachina* is used by the Pueblo Indians (Zuñi and Hopi) to refer to a variety of supernatural beings such as the spirits of the dead, rain and cloud spirits, and spirits that inhabit springs of water. When the Pueblo Indians wear kachina masks in their dances they feel they are actually transformed into the supernatural spirits represented by the masks. They also carve and paint cottonwood kachina dolls, fashioned after the dancers, as playthings for children.

1. Talk about the Pueblo kachinas. Ask the children to think of things that might be "inhabited" by special spirits.
2. Examine the designs of American Indians. What did they represent? (The sun, the moon, birds, animals, trees, etc.)
3. Let each child plan and construct his own interpretation of a kachina, using a plastic bottle and small cardboard box or tube.
4. Add parts made from pieces of cardboard, construction paper, or Styrofoam, so that the doll has a head and arms.
5. With paper, fabric, yarn, feathers, etc., decorate the figure so that it becomes a kachina doll. Paint the parts that seem appropriate.
6. Make an exhibit of all the dolls.

Useful References

DOUGLAS, FREDERICK H. and D'HARNONCOURT, RENÉ. *Indian Art of the United States*, New York: Museum of Modern Art, 1941.

LIDSTONE, JOHN. *Building with Cardboard*. New York: Van Nostrand Reinhold Co., 1968.

Accordion Book

Primary Objectives
- To construct a book using traditional methods of China and Japan
- To work through a multi-step process requiring several work sessions
- To create designs suitable for a book cover

Materials/Tools
Drawing paper, white, 12" × 18", cut 6" × 18", two pieces per child
Drawing paper, white, cut 8" × 8", four pieces per child
Cardboard, chip board, or poster board, 6" × 6", two pieces per child
Scissors
Paste or white glue
Rulers
Pencils
Felt-tip pens
Watercolors
Brushes
Water containers
Newspaper

The Lesson
The first books that people used were all made by hand. Machines have largely replaced the handmade process except for the few craftsmen who cling to the older traditional methods of bookmaking. Among the oldest and simplest forms is the accordion book. Oriental in origin, it is still used in China and Japan.

This project should be done in three sessions, the first to make decorative cover papers, the second to construct the accordion book, and the third to illustrate the book.

Session one
1. Give each child four sheets of white drawing paper cut into 8" × 8" squares.
2. Have the children cover their desk tops with newspaper. Distribute watercolor paints, brushes, and small plastic containers for water.
3. Have each child select two colors and moisten each in the watercolor pan with a few drops of water.

4. Dampen the surface of one piece of paper at a time by sprinkling some water on it and spreading it evenly over the surface with the hand.

5. When the paper is uniformly damp and free from puddles of water, pick up some of the moist watercolor with a brush, and randomly touch the damp paper surface. The color will run, making an interesting area. Do it again on another part of the paper. Clean the brush and change to the second color. Let the colors run, fuse, or remain as isolated spots.

6. Put this design aside and do a second one, a third, and a fourth. The best two of these designs, when dry, will be used as the cover papers for the book.

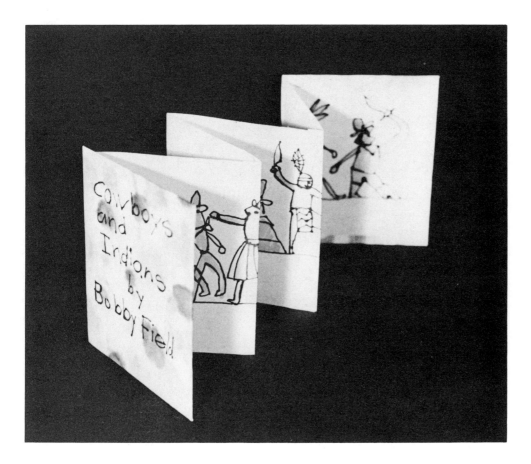

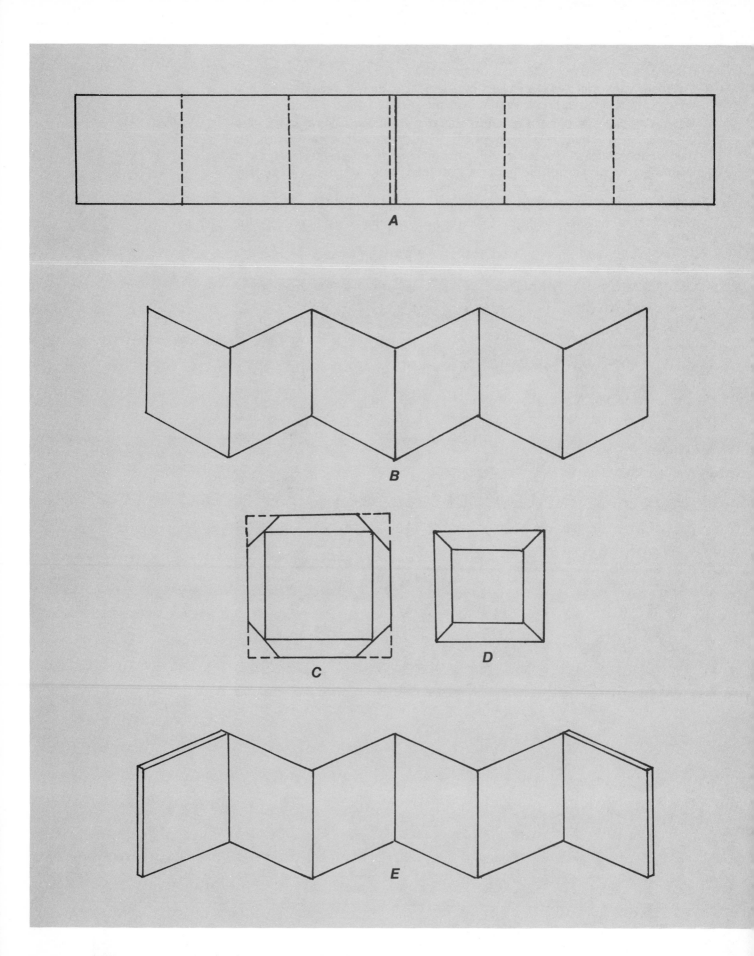

A

B

C

D

E

Session two

1. Cut white 12″×18″ drawing paper in half the long way, making sheets 6″×18″. Give each child two sheets and two 6″×6″ squares of light-weight cardboard or poster board.

2. Using paste or white glue, have the children join the two sheets of drawing paper with a one-half inch overlap to form one long continuous strip (Figure A). Using a ruler, measure 6 inches from one end and carefully make a fold. Measure 6 inches from that fold and make another fold in the opposite direction. Continue measuring and folding at 6-inch intervals, alternating the folds so that the paper is pleated like an accordion (Figure B). It does not matter that the last section will be about a half-inch shorter than the other pages.

3. The covers are made from two squares of cardboard for binders or stiffeners and two of the watercolor designs made in the first session. Lay one of the decorated papers face down and place a cardboard on top. Center the board, then fold over the edges of the paper, creasing them carefully. For a neat finish, cut off the corners of the paper exactly where the creases intersect (Figure C). Now apply paste along the four folded margins and press the cardboard carefully in place (Figure D). Make the second cover in the same manner.

4. Using paste or white glue, attach the first page of the accordion-pleated paper to the inside of one cardboard cover. Attach the last page to the inside of the other cardboard cover (Figure E).

Session three

Relate this session to a lesson in English composition.

1. Write a short story that will be enhanced with some illustrations.

2. Carefully copy the story on the pages of the accordion book and draw the illustrations with pencil, using only one side of the paper.

3. Go over the marks with a felt-tip pen, then color the illustrations with watercolors or crayon.

Useful References

NEWMAN, THELMA R., and others. *Paper as Art and Craft.* New York: Crown Publishers, Inc., 1973.

RÖTTGER, ERNST. *Creative Paper Design.* New York: Van Nostrand Reinhold Co., 1962.

Plaster Scrimshaw

Primary Objectives
- To learn about one of the art forms of Eskimos and sailors
- To learn to work with fine lines, creating small detailed designs

Materials/Tools
Plaster of Paris (see below)

Paper cups, muffin tins, or small pie tins

Dark tempera paint and brushes

Sharpened pencils

Darning needles or small wire nails sharpened on a metal file

Thin cardboard

White glue

Clear acrylic or shellac

The Lesson
Scrimshaw is an ancient art practiced by Eskimos and sailors. Intricate carvings or line drawings are scratched into ivory, bone, and shells, and the scratched lines are darkened with lamp black or carbon. This lesson is a variation on true scrimshaw.

1. Take this opportunity to relate the lesson to the study of Eskimo cultures or readings about whalers and whaling ships. The library is a good source for materials illustrating the kinds of sailing vessels that provided the sea homes for "scrim shanders," the makers of scrimshaw.

2. Mix plaster of Paris according to directions on the bag. Fill a #10 can from the cafeteria about one-third full of water. Add plaster of Paris by the handful until an "island" of plaster stands about one inch above the water level. Begin to mix with your hand until the plaster has the consistency of heavy cream and begins to feel a little warmer.

3. Pour plaster into paper cups or muffin tins to a depth of one-fourth to three-eights of an inch. Pour a few extras to allow for breakage.

4. Set the plaster aside to dry for several days until it is strong enough to handle. When it seems perfectly dry, tear away the paper cups or lift the pieces out of the tins.

5. Make a smooth mixture of a dark tempera and brush the top surface of the plaster disks.

6. While paint is drying, plan a design to fit the round shape. Redraw the design in pencil directly on the painted plaster disk.

7. With a finely sharpened nail or the point of a large needle, begin to scratch the design through the tempera surface, exposing the white plaster below. Continue until the design is complete.

8. Cut a circle of thin cardboard a bit smaller than the plaster disk and glue this to the back with white glue to give added strength to the ornament.

9. Brush the entire piece with a clear acrylic or with shellac.

Useful References

BURLAND, COTTIE. *Eskimo Art.* New York: Hamlyn Publishing Group Limited, 1973.

GARCIA, M. *The Ship and the Sea in Art.* Minneapolis: Lerner Publications, 1965.

Soft Jewelry

Primary Objectives
- To learn to use discarded scraps and found objects
- To innovate designs with unusual materials

Materials/Tools
Felt scraps
Scraps of fabric, leather, lace, vinyl, etc.
For stringing: heavy cord, shoe laces, yarn, etc.
Beads, buttons, old costume jewelry, sequins, feathers, etc.
Scissors
Needles and thread
White glue

The Lesson
Jewelry has played an important part in almost every culture from the simplest to the most sophisticated. It has been worn to ward off evil spirits, to appease the gods, or to embellish the wearer. Both men and women wear jewelry.

1. Show examples or photographs of jewelry worn by natives of New Guinea and Africa or by ancient Egyptians and American Indians. Their jewelry will suggest new ideas.
2. From the collection of materials, let each child choose enough felt scraps to sew into a geometric shape. This will serve as the main element of the necklace. Then choose an additional item or two such as a feather, bead, shell, piece of worn wood, or other found item.
3. Suggest ways to cut, sew, and stuff pieces of felt and how to sew or glue on sequins, beads, etc. Take the time to demonstrate when demonstration will help.
4. Plan the assembly and the stringing of the necklace. Materials for stringing might include fishing line, yarn, shoe laces, cord, plastic tubing, dental tape, or whatever will serve the purpose.

Useful References

MEILACH, DONA Z. *Creating Art from Fibers and Fabrics.* Chicago: Henry Regnery Co., 1973.

SAUNDERS, ROBERT J. *Relating Art and Humanities to the Classroom.* Dubuque, Iowa: Wm. C. Brown Company Publishers, 1977.

Peep Shows or Dioramas

Suggested Topics   Landscapes, room interiors, stage sets.

Primary Objectives
- To utilize common, everyday materials in a new context
- To work in a new scale (small objects to represent large things)
- To stimulate imaginative ideas through a choice of topics and solutions

Materials/Tools

Shoe boxes with lids

Scrap items: yarn, string, bottle caps, jar lids, wood, weeds, nuts, seeds, twigs, hardware, stones, cotton batting, thread, etc.

White glue

Colored construction paper

Scissors

Paste

Mat knife (X-Acto or similar)

Modeling clay (in which to plant trees, bushes, telephone poles, etc.)

The Lesson

This lesson can be done as a group project in which each child contributes to one big scene set up in a large cardboard carton with a side (or side and top) removed. Or it can be done as individual projects, using shoe boxes, as described below.

1. Cut a hole the size of a quarter in one end of a shoe box.
2. Have each child peak through the hole into the empty box. Then begin to stimulate their imaginations by asking questions. What would you see if you were peeking into a room in a palace, or a prison cell, or an airplane hangar, or a space ship, or a pioneer's cabin? What if you peeked through a hole and saw a ranch, a garden, a jungle, a battle, or a ??? What would the ground be like: rough, smooth, dark, light? What would the walls be like? And so on.
3. Have the children search the scrap collection for objects appropriate to their scene, and begin placing them in their boxes. As each item is positioned, the child should look through the hole to see what it looks like now. What else does it need to go with it?
4. Use modeling clay or white glue to attach items to the interior of the box.

5. When everything is in place, put the lid on the box. Cut a few square openings in the lid and sides to allow light to enter the box. This works like stage lighting.
6. Exhibit the dioramas on the window ledges.

Useful References

HERBERHOLZ, DONALD, and HERBERHOLZ, BARBARA. *A Child's Pursuit of Art: 110 Motivations for Drawing, Painting and Modeling.* Dubuque, Iowa: Wm. C. Brown Company Publishers, 1967.

LINDERMAN, EARL W. *Invitation to Vision: Ideas and Imaginations for Art.* Dubuque, Iowa: Wm. C. Brown Company Publishers, 1967.

Model Room Interior

Suggested Topics   Ranch house, ski lodge, city apartment, pioneer's cabin, etc.

Primary Objectives
- To observe proportion, scale, and relationships among objects
- To examine style in furniture and furnishings
- To create an illusion of a larger space through minature objects

Materials/Tools
Cardboard boxes
Scissors
Mat knives (X-Acto or similar)
Balsa wood
Masking or transparent tape
White glue
Paste
Colored construction paper
Scrap materials: fabric, felt, etc.

The Lesson
Coordinate this lesson to the study of family environments, either contemporary or historical. Each child will create a model of his ideal environment—a room in which he or she would enjoy spending time. Encourage the children to look through magazines and books for examples of the kinds of interior furnishings that would appeal to them or be appropriate in the way of furniture, pictures, floor coverings, window styles, etc.

1. Cut away the top and one side of a box; what's left will serve as the room space.
2. The first thing to decide is whether you want a closet, shelves, etc. and where to locate your door and windows. Cut them out or add them on.
3. Now paper or paint the walls. For the floor covering you might use scraps of linoleum tiles; or perhaps a piece of fabric will do for a rug.
4. Plan and make tables, chairs, couches, and other furniture, using folded cardboard, balsa wood, fabric, etc. and glue or tape.
5. As parts are added, scrap materials suddenly "become" something else: a bottle cap turns into a lamp shade, a piece of fabric becomes drapery, a spool becomes a stool.

6. The problem of proportion is encountered as objects seem "too big" or "too small" to go together. All we want is to develop an awareness of relative proportion, so there is no need to take measurements and seek mathtmatical accuracy. That could take the fun out of creating.

7. When everyone is finished, ask the children to add that one more thing which will personalize their room: a school pennant, a picture of their favorite star or athlete, a musical instrument, a pet, etc.

Useful References

PATTEMORE, ARNEL W. *Art and Environment: An Art Resource for Teachers.* New York: Van Nostrand Reinhold Co., 1974.

TROGLER, GEORGE E. *Beginning Experiences in Architecture: A Guide for the Elementary School Teacher.* New York: Van Nostrand Reinhold Co., 1972.

Heraldry

Suggested Topic   A coat of arms for my family.

Primary Objectives
- To learn something about heraldry
- To create personal insignia designs based upon family occupation or history
- To develop an organized, harmonious design

Materials/Tools

Cardboards 10″ × 12″ or larger
Colored construction paper
Felt-tip markers
Scissors
Paste

The Lesson

Begin this lesson with a discussion based on family names and histories. Ask the children to tell some of the things they know about their own family histories. Talk about genealogy and how family histories are charted and recorded. This may require a bit of research in the school encyclopedia. Show pictures of royal and state coats of arms and insignia on banners, shields, etc. Inquire if there are any names within the class that indicate an occupation, such as Miller, Weaver, Baker, Smith, etc.

1. Stimulate the children to think of what emblems might be appropriate for their personal family coat of arms—perhaps the country of their ancestors; or a symbol of their occupation; or the family automobile, pet, favorite sport, hobby, etc. If someone has won an award or medal, that might be shown on a crest or a shield.

2. Let each child sketch three or four symbols that are suitable, and then cut them from construction paper.

3. Let each child decide on a shape for his shield, and then cut it from a contrasting colored paper. Mount the shield on a cardboard and paste it down.

4. Arrange the symbols on the shield and paste them down.

5. Does the shield need more colors? If so, add them. Does it need decorative areas—stripes, dots, etc.? If so, add them.

6. Print the family name with a marking pen. Or cut out the letters from colored paper, assemble them where desired on the coat of arms, and paste them in.

7. Hang them all above the chalkboard.

Useful References

BECKER, EDITH C. *Adventures with Scissors and Paper*. Scranton, Pa.: International Textbook Co., 1959.

LALIBERTÉ NORMAN, and MCILHANY, STERLING. *Banners and Hangings*. New York: Van Nostrand Reinhold Co., 1966.

Papier-Mâché over Balloon Piñata

Suggested Topic   A party piñata representing a bird or an animal.

Primary Objectives

- To create imaginative designs adaptable to the globular forms of balloons
- To learn about how Mexicans use piñatas at parties and festivals
- To complete a multi-step process that requires a longer interest span than the typical art lesson

Materials/Tools

Balloons, various sizes and shapes
Rubber bands
Newspaper
Styrofoam cups and fast-food containers
Plastic containers for paste (margarine cups)
Tempera paints
Brushes

The Lesson

Begin with a discussion of piñatas as a Mexican folk art. Describe how they are used at parties and celebrations. Filled with candies and small gifts the piñata is hung by a heavy cord from a tree branch or rafter. The children at the party are blindfolded in turn and given a chance to strike at the piñata with a stick. When it finally breaks open, the candy tumbles out and everyone scrambles in search of a piece. (If possible, bring a piñata to show in class. Tourists often bring them home from Mexico as souvenirs.)

1. Cover the desk tops with paper. Distribute newspaper and cups of wallpaper paste. Give everyone a balloon and a rubber band. Inflate the balloons and close the opening with the rubber band.

2. Examine the various balloon shapes. What do they suggest? A long balloon might resemble a dachshund; an oval one might resemble the body of a goose or a racoon. Discuss ways to change the shape by adding parts. A small balloon might become a head; four Styrofoam cups might be used as legs; two Styrofoam meat trays could be wings; and so on.

3. Have the children cover the entire balloon with several layers of torn newspaper strips saturated in the wallpaper paste.

4. Begin to add other parts to form the bird or animal. Use long strips of newspaper covered with paste for attaching Styrofoam parts. Cover all appendages with a second coat of papier-mâché.

5. When all the major parts are in place, allow the figures to dry for several days. Additional parts or details may be added at any time.

6. Talk about color and other decorative effects. What colors would best characterize each child's creation? What can color add? What happens if stripes, dots, or texturing with a sponge are added to the surface?

7. Paint the figures. Encourage the children to think of ways to make the painting more interesting: a pattern of wavy lines, squiggly lines, concentric circles, triangles, squares, etc. A cellulose sponge cube or small wad of newspaper dipped in moist paint and then repeatedly dabbed on a surface can also create pleasing designs.

Note: At some point the children will undoubtedly wonder about what happens to the air inside the balloon. You can explain that as the papier-mâché dries it becomes strong and retains its shape. Meanwhile the air slowly escapes and the balloon pulls away from the walls, eventually returning to its original, uninflated form.

Useful References

BETTS, VICTORIA. *Exploring Papier-Mâché.* Worcester, Mass.: Davis Publications, Inc., 1955.

MEILACH, DONA Z. *Papier-Mâché Artistry.* New York: Crown Publishers, Inc., 1971.

APPENDIX: A VISUAL ALPHABET FROM A TO Z

Subject matter for artists and child artists can be anything from the real world or the imagination. Sometimes lessons with good potential fail for lack of a good idea—a topic, a subject which can capture the imagination and interest of children. If a lesson starts with nothing, it might end with nothing. An abundance of good subject matter is available right in our own environments. Famous artists like Baskin, Oldenberg, Dürer, and Picasso used fleas, typewriter erasers, rabbits, and goats. Artists find inspiration in stones, trees, rocks, foliage—anything in their real or imaginary environments.

Before giving in to the temptation to say "draw whatever you want to draw," skim through these pages of old images to see if they might be a springboard for a good topic for your lesson. Think of something that can be talked about, looked at, and researched by the children so that whatever is drawn, painted, modeled, etc. will have a richness resulting from a deeper understanding and feeling for the subject. Once an idea "hits the air" in a class discussion it is likely to change and something even more interesting will emerge. Remember, neither artists nor children can create from a vacuum.

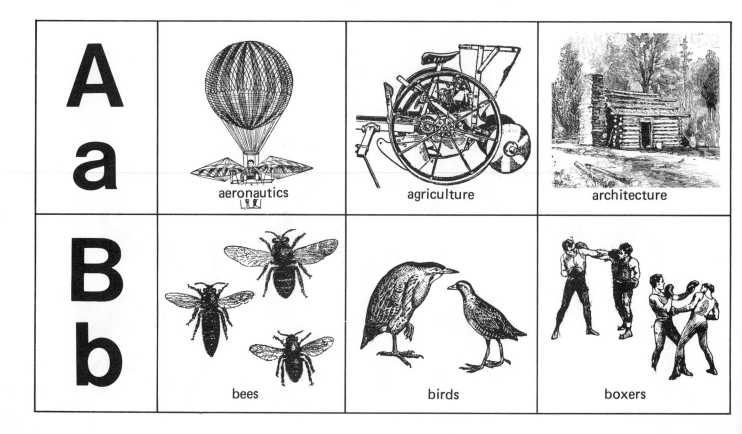

A a — aeronautics — agriculture — architecture

B b — bees — birds — boxers

C c	chimpanzee	cones	cowboy
D d	daisy	dinosaur	dogs
E e	eagle	elephant	eye
F f	flies	football	fowls

G g	galleon	grapes	gymnasts
H h	hand	helmets	horse
I i	ibis	insignia	iris
J j	jaguar	jonquil	judo
K k	kangaroo	katydid	koala

L l	lanterns	lion	lobster
M m	machines	masks	musical instrument
N n	nautilus	nests	noses
O o	octopus	oil rig	oranges
P p	parachute	pig	python

Q q	quail	Quaker	quince
R r	rabbits	railroads	roofs
S s	scout	sharks	swimmers
T t	tarantula	teepee	telephone
U u	umbrella	umbrette	urial

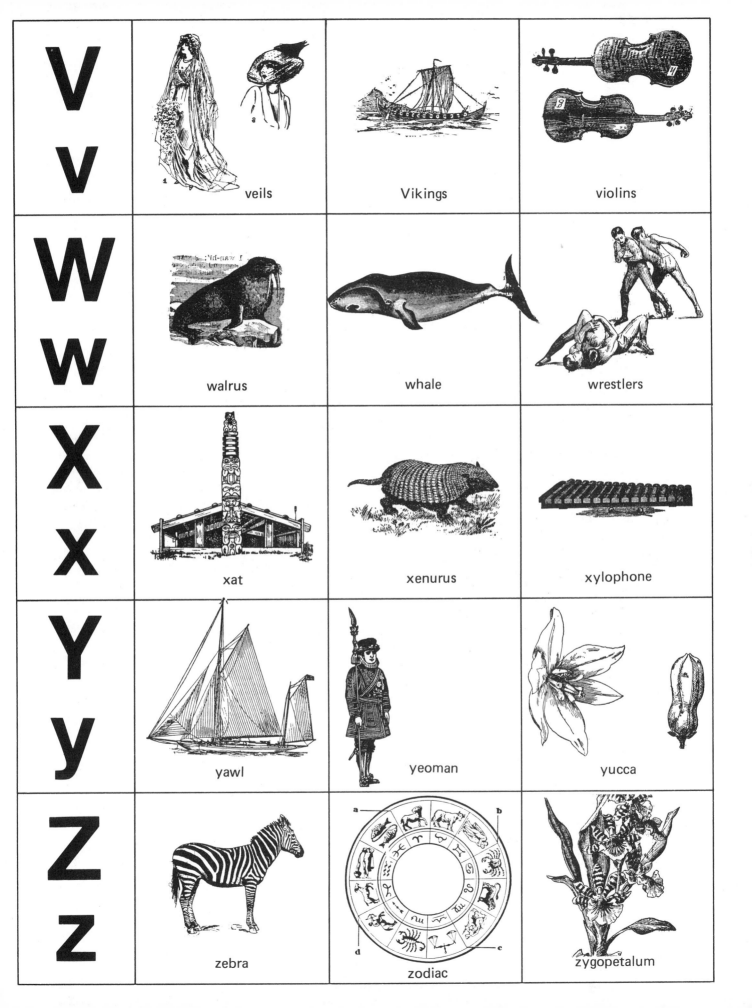

V	veils	Vikings	violins
W	walrus	whale	wrestlers
X	xat	xenurus	xylophone
Y	yawl	yeoman	yucca
Z	zebra	zodiac	zygopetalum

GLOSSARY

abstract Designating art that originated with a recognizable form which has been distorted or simplified in some way.

acrylic A moist paint having plastic as a binder for the pigments.

additive process A method of making sculpture in which a form is created by building up or adding on material.

analogous colors Colors that are adjacent on a color wheel.

annealed wire Iron wire that has been made flexible by heating and cooling.

appliqué A decorative craft in which smaller pieces of fabric, cut into shapes and designs, are sewn (or sometimes glued) to the surface of a larger piece.

armature A framework or skeleton, usually made of wire, on which the artist builds up a sculpture in clay, plaster, or other substances.

assemblage The process of creating a three-dimensional art work by combining various *found objects*. The art work is also called an assemblage.

balance A means of maintaining visual equilibrium.

balsa An extremely light, strong wood.

banner A piece of fabric attached by one edge to a staff; used by monarchs, lords, or commanders as a standard for displaying a distinctive symbolic device.

batik A resist method of dyeing designs on fabric by coating with wax the parts that are to resist, i.e., not take, the color when fabric is submerged in the dye.

beeswax A dull yellow plastic wax secreted by bees to form honeycombs.

binder A substance in paints that causes the particles of pigment to cling together.

bisque (biscuit) Ceramic ware that has been fired but not glazed.

brayer A hand roller, usually made of rubber, used for applying ink to a printing surface.

bridle On a kite, the leader string to which the flying string is attached; used to distribute the stress evenly.

burnish To smooth by rubbing repeatedly with a hard smooth surface.

calligraphy The art of beautiful handwriting.

caricature A comic or grotesque representation made by exaggerating or distorting features.

casting The process of reproducing an object, such as sculpture or jewelry, by means of a mold into which liquid plaster, concrete, or molten metal is poured; also the object produced by this process.

chasing A metalwork process in which the design or pattern is indented into the finished surface by means of metal tools that are struck with a hammer. (See *repoussé*)

ceramics The art of making objects from clay, glass, or other nonmetallic minerals by firing at high temperatures; also the products so produced.

chip board A cardboard made from waste paper.

clay A natural material from the earth, composed mainly of fine particles of hydrous aluminum silicates and other minerals such as feldspar and kaolin. When moist, it is plastic; when fired at a high temperature, it becomes permanently hard.

closure The act or means of completing an image.

coat of arms The particular heraldic symbols depicted on an ornamental shield or banner.

coil method In pottery, the process of building up the walls of a vessel by applying a series of coils of clay, one upon another.

collage A combination of two-dimensional materials such as pieces of paper, photographs, fabrics, cardboard, etc. on a flat surface.

318

collagraph A print made from a surface that has been constructed in the manner of a collage.

color wheel A circular arrangement of colors that indicates their relationships according to a particular color theory.

compass A device for determining direction by a magnetic needle.

complementary colors Colors opposite one another on a color wheel which, when mixed together neutralize each other.

composition An ordered relationship among design elements.

concentric pattern A design in which all the parts have a common center.

content The subject matter of an art work, including any emotional, symbolic, intellectual, or narrative connotations.

contour A line representing the edge of a form.

contour drawing A drawing that outlines the shape of an object with a line usually made by following the shape of the object with the eyes while simultaneously drawing with the hand.

contrast The difference between the lightest and the darkest parts of a picture; also the juxtaposition of various elements such as color and shape.

crayon A stick of pigment used for drawing, usually consisting of wax and pigment or a clay base and pigment.

crèche A display representing the Christmas nativity scene.

crewelwork A type of embroidery that is done with a special twisted yarn called *crewel*.

decorative design The enrichment of the surface of an object or a material. The design may be part of the structure of the material (as in weaving) or it may be applied to the surface (as in appliqué).

degree A 360th part of the circumference of a circle.

diorama A scenic representation, usually done in miniature, in which three-dimensional figures or objects are combined with a painted background.

dry-point A method of intaglio printing in which the image is scratched into the surface of the printing plate with a steel needle. The print is also called a dry-point.

earthenware A coarse, porous pottery, usually buff or reddish, that has been fired at a low temperature.

edition The total number of impressions made at one time from the same block or plate and printed in the same way.

embroidery The process of making decorative designs with hand needlework.

engobe A commercial form of *slip* (liquid clay) used for decorating pottery.

engraving An intaglio printmaking process in which the image is made by scratching directly into a metal or wood surface to create lines or depressions capable of holding ink during the printing process.

etching An intaglio printmaking process in which the image is made by coating the surface of a metal plate, scratching through the coating, then submerging the plate in acid. The acid burns away the plate through the scratched lines, providing depressions to hold the ink during printing.

exaggerate To distort or make something out of proportion to its usual size and shape, generally for emphasis and attention.

fiber A natural or synthetic material capable of being used as a thread or a warp.

fire (firing) In ceramics, the process of exposing a clay object to high heat, usually in a kiln, to harden it permanently.

fixative A preparation, such as clear acrylic spray, that is applied to a surface to prevent flaking, fading, etc., or to impart a permanent finish.

flexible Capable of being bent repeatedly.

folk art The art originating with the common people of a country or region, generally reflecting their life style.

form The shape or outline of an object.

found object Any discarded item that is used for a new purpose in art.

frame In photography and cartooning, one picture in a series.

genealogy The record of the descent of a person, family, or group from an ancestor.

glaze A thin glass-like coating that is fused to the surface of a ceramic object by heating to a high temperature in a kiln.

graphic Descriptive of those activities which include calligraphy, drawing, and printing.

graphic design Usually refers to design for printed material such as advertisements, books, labels, etc.

heraldry The art of designing insignia.

heritage Something transmitted or acquired from a predecessor.

hue The name by which a color is called.

impression In printmaking, a print resulting from an inked surface making contact with a paper surface.

intaglio A printmaking process in which the image is recessed below the surface through carving, cutting, or etching.

intensity The relative purity of a color.

kiln A special oven or furnace that can reach very high temperatures; used for firing and glazing ceramic objects.

kraft paper A strong, brown-toned paper made from wood chips; used for bags and heavy wrapping paper.

line A continuous mark made by a pencil, pen, chalk, or other instrument drawn across a surface.

lithography A process of printing from a flat stone or metal surface. The method is based on the principle that grease and water repel each other.

loom A frame or device for holding the warp through which the weft is woven to make a fabric.

mace A heavy, spiked club used as a weapon in the Middle Ages. Also a ceremonial staff borne as a symbol of authority.

margin An edge or border.

marionette A type of puppet with movable parts that is operated from above by strings.

mask A covering worn over the face to disguise the appearance or identity of the wearer.

mat A border, usually of cardboard or paper, that is put around a picture.

mezzotint An intaglio process in which the surface of a metal printing plate is textured by means of a tool called a *rocker*. The ink remains deposited in the small depressions cut by the rocker. The print is also called a mezzotint.

mobile A construction or sculpture of wire with suspended balanced shapes that can be set in motion by air currents.

modeling The process of manipulating plastic material such as clay, including adding on or building up the form.

modeling clay A plastic material used for modeling, usually containing natural clay, oil, glycerine, and color. It is not used for firing or for permanent objects.

mold The shaped form or hollowed pattern around or in which an object is formed.

monoprint A one-of-a-kind print usually made by pressing a clean paper surface into the moist paint or ink of an image made on another surface.

motif A single or repeated design or color.

mural A work of art that is either a wall or ceiling surface.

neutral color A color not associated with a hue—such as black, white, or a gray value.

nonobjective Having no resemblance to objects or natural forms.

oxidation The change in the surface of metal when a substance such as sulphur combines with the oxygen from the air.

palette The group of colors an artist chooses for a picture; also refers to the board or table on which the artist arranges colors for painting.

papier-mâché A lightweight, strong material made of paper and paste.

pastel Chalk-like crayon made of finely ground color; a picture made with pastel crayons. The tints of colors are also referred to as pastels.

pattern A model used as a guide in making things; also refers to an artistic design.

pigment Coloring matter usually in the form of a fine powder, that is mixed with oil, water, etc. to make paints and dyes.

piñata A decorated papier-mâché container filled with candies and gifts that is hung up at Mexican parties and celebrations, to be broken open by children in a game.

plaster of Paris A white, powdery, slightly hydrated calcium sulfate used chiefly for casts and molds as a quick-setting liquid or paste.

Plasticine Trademark of an oil-base modeling clay, not intended for firing.

polychrome Made with or decorated with several colors.

pottery Objects made from clay; also refers to the potter's workshop or place where clay objects are made. (See *earthenware*)

primary color One of three basic colors (red, yellow, or blue) which cannot be produced by mixing colors and which serve as the basis for mixing other colors.

print The picture or design, usually on paper, imprinted from an artist's etching plate, linoleum or wood block, etc., and repeated to obtain multiple images that are identical.

profile A representation of something as seen from a side view.

proscenium arch The opening of a stage through which the spectators see the performance.

puppet A small-scale figure that fits over the hand and arm and is manipulated with the hand and fingers.

relief print The print resulting from the process in which portions of the printing block or plate are carved away, etched away, or otherwise removed. Ink is applied to the raised surface and transferred to a paper on contact.

relief sculpture Any sculpture in which the subject figures or objects project from a background.

repetition The regular, orderly recurrence of a shape, color, or pattern.

replica A close reproduction or facsimile.

repoussé A metalwork process in which the

design is made by pressing or tapping the metal from the reverse side. (See *chasing*)

resist Any substance used to block out a surface to prevent dyes or acids from acting upon the blocked-out area.

retable A raised ledge or shelf behind an altar, used for holding ornaments, lights, etc.

rhythm A predictable pattern of strong and weak accents that results in a movement with a natural recurrence or flow.

rubbing A replica of a recessed surface made by holding a piece of paper on the surface and rubbing the paper with a marking material such as graphite.

scale The proportion between two sets of dimensions.

scepter An ornamental staff held by a sovereign on ceremonial occasions as a symbol of authority.

scoring Marking scratches or grooves on a clay surface, with a pencil point or other tool, to facilitate the tight joining of parts.

scrimshaw Carefully carved and decorated articles made of ivory, bone, shells, etc.; an art form that originated with sailors.

secondary color A color created by mixing any two primary colors.

sgraffito A method of scratching a design on pottery.

shade A darker variation of a color, achieved by adding black. Also the darker value of a color.

shaman A priest or medicine man of certain religions based on a belief in good and evil spirits. The shaman uses magic for curing the sick and controlling events.

shape The area created by the boundaries formed by lines, colors, or values.

shuttle A device used in weaving for passing the threads of the weft through the threads of the warp.

silk screen (serigraphy) A stencil method of printing a design through a piece of silk or fine fabric on which the areas that are not to print have been blocked by an impermeable film.

slip Liquid clay mainly used in making pottery with plaster molds.

stable Describing something that resists motion or change, that is firmly in place.

stencil A pattern made from an impervious material (such as a sheet of heavy waxed paper), with openings through which color is applied to another surface held under the stencil.

stenciling The process of creating a design or pattern on another surface, using a stencil and colors.

stitchery Work done with a needle and threads or yarns, other than plain sewing.

structural design A design of the basic form of an object rather than the enrichment of its surface.

Styrofoam Trademark of a lightweight, rigid, polystyrene plastic.

subtractive method A method of making sculpture in which a form is created by cutting, carving away, or otherwise removing material.

symmetrical design A design in which parts equal in size, shape, and position fall on opposite sides of an imaginary dividing line.

symmetry The correspondence in size, shape, and position of parts on opposite sides of a dividing line.

tactile Perceptible to the sense of touch.

tempera An opaque, water-soluble paint, available in liquid or powder form.

template A pattern, usually in the form of a thin plate or board, used as a guide for forming the shape of an object.

textile markers Commercial felt-tip marker colors of considerable permanency, made especially to go on fabrics.

texture The visual or tactile surface characteristics and appearances of an object.

tint A lighter variation of a color, achieved by diluting or adding white. Also a lighter value of a color.

trapunto A quilted design in high relief, made by working with two layers of fabric. The design is outlined in a running stitch, and padding is then inserted through a cut on the underside, after which the cut is sewn closed.

value The lightness or darkness of a color.

ventriloquist A person who entertains by appearing to carry on a conversation with a puppet-like figure. The ventriloquist provides both voices and manipulates the figure with the hand.

warp A series of threads extending lengthwise on a loom, through which the weft is woven.

watercolor A paint in which the liquid is a water dispersion of the binding materials (gum arabic, glue, etc.) and the pigments.

watercolor wash Diluted watercolor applied to a paper surface. This is usually done quickly over a large area.

weaving The process of interlocking two sets of parallel threads, usually held at right angles to one another on a loom, to create a fabric.

weft The yarns or threads woven across the warp to create a fabric.

INDEX

Shahn, Ben, 16
Shape, 19, 21, 23, 24
Shuttle, 122, 124, 128, 129
Silk screen, 171
Slip, 78, 251
Soft jewelry, 302
Spain, 35
Spray print, 178
Squeegee, 171
Stage, puppetry, 164–65
Stamp print, 182
Stencil, 142, 143, 176, 178
Stenciling, 142, 176
Stencil print, 176
Stitchery, 121, 126, 130, 132–35
Stocking puppet, 156
Stone Age, 120, 204
Story illustration, 68
Style, 5, 9, 20, 21, 36
Styrofoam, 114, 115, 182, 188, 192
Styrofoam print, 188, 192
Styrofoam sculpture, 100
Subtractive method, 84, 234, 235
Surface printing method, 171
Symbolic stage, 5
Symbols, 18, 36, 246
Symmetrical design, 184

T

Tactile experience, 76–77, 251
Tempera painting, 42, 44, 55–59
Textile markers, 138
Textiles, 120–21
Texture, 19, 24, 25, 35
Thailand, 146
Tie-dye, 140
Tiles, 258–59, 262–63
Tillstrom, Burr, 147
Tint, 25
Tooker, George, 250
Toothpicks, 106
Toulouse-Lautrec, Henri, 6
Trailing, of clay, 251
Trapunto, 130–31

U

Ukrainian folk art, 268, 282

V

Value, 24, 25, 27
Van Gogh, Vincent, 6
Vegetables, papier-mâché, 244

Venus of Willendorf, 75
Visualization stage, 6, 33

W

Wachowiak, Frank, 4
Wall hanging, 140–41
Wallpaper paste, 206
Warp, 123, 124, 128
Watercolor, 46, 47, 50, 52
Watercolor painting, 50
Wax crayon, 52, 60, 136
Wax crayon batik, 136
Weaving, 120, 121, 122–25, 128–29
Weft, 124, 125, 128, 129
Wire sculpture, 104
Wood, Grant, 268
Wood block, 171, 190

X

Xipe Totec, 22

Z

Zuñi Indians, 204, 296